Also by Jane Grigson

The Mushroom Feast

THE ART OF MAKING
SAUSAGES, PÂTÉS,
AND OTHER CHARCUTERIE

The Art of Making SAUSAGES, PÂTÉS, and Other CHARCUTERIE

by Jane Grigson

Illustrated with drawings by
M. J. Mott

(Formerly Published in Hardcover as
The Art of Charcuterie)

Alfred A. Knopf   New York   1985

CONTENTS

ILLUSTRATIONS

·∘⟨ INTRODUCTION ⟩∘·

It could be said that European civilization—and Chinese civilization too—has been founded on the pig. Easily domesticated, omnivorous household and village scavenger, clearer of scrub and undergrowth, devourer of forest acorns, yet content with a sty—and delightful when cooked or cured, from his snout to his tail. There has been prejudice against him, but those peoples—certainly *not* including the French—who have disliked the pig and insist that he is unclean eating are rationalizing their own descent and past history: they were once nomads, and the one thing you can't do with a pig is to drive him in herds over vast distances.

The pig as we know him is of mixed descent. An art of *charcuterie*—the *chair cuit,* cooked meat, of the pig—could hardly have been developed very far, however much people relied on pig meat, fresh or cured, as the staff of life, with the medieval pig carved on misericords, or painted in the Labors of the Months (pig-killing in November, or pig-fattening with the acorn harvest). He was a lean, ridgy, and rangy beast, with bristles down his back. Two thousand years ago the Gauls in France were excellent at curing pork, and Gallic hams were sent to Rome. But what made the pig of the European sty—rather than the pig of the autumn oak forests—really succulent was a crossing of the European and Chinese pigs in England round about 1760, by the great Leicestershire stockbreeder Robert Bakewell.

The Chinese porker was small, plump, and short-legged. The European pig was skinny and long-legged like a wild boar. The cross between the two resulted in the huge pink beast of prints by James Ward of 160 years ago. Cobbett wrote that the cottager's pig should be too fat to walk more than a hundred yards. Spreading through Europe, this was the creature on which French cooks got to work when the Revolution turned them out of their princely, aristocratic kitchens along the Loire and in the Île-de-France.

The trade of *charcutier* goes back at least as far as the time of classical Rome, where a variety of sausages could be bought, as well as the famous hams from Gaul. In such a large town slaughterhouses, butchers' and cooked-meat shops were necessarily well organized to safeguard public health. This system was still being followed—after a fashion—in medieval Paris, although in the later Middle Ages a great increase in cooked-meat purveyors put an intolerable strain on such control as there was. From this insalubrious chaos the *charcutiers* emerged and banded together, by edict of the king in 1476, for the sale of cooked pork only, and raw pork fat. But they did not have the right to slaughter the pigs they needed, which put them at the mercy of the general butchers until the next century. At the beginning of the seventeenth century *charcutiers* gained the right to sell all cuts of uncooked pork, not just the fat. Now the trade could develop in a logical manner. Incidentally, in Lent, when meat sales declined, the *charcutier* was allowed to sell salted herrings and fish from the sea.

In the larger cities of the eighteenth century the *charcutier* developed a closer connection with two other cooked-meat sellers —the *tripier*, who bought the insides of all animals from both butcher and *charcutier* and sold cooked tripe, and the *traiteur*, who bought raw meat of all kinds and sold it cooked in sauces as *ragoûts*, either to be eaten at home or on his ever-increasing premises. Remember that for many people at all income levels the private kitchen was a poor affair, often nonexistent; everyone sent out to the cooked-food shops for ready-made dishes. It was a big trade, jealously guarded, so that the *traiteurs* considered that their functions as *ragoût*-makers had been usurped when a soup-maker, Boulanger, who described his dishes as *restaurant* or restorative, began to sell sheep's feet in sauce, to be consumed on his premises. He was taken to court in 1765 by the *traiteurs*, but he won, thereby gaining enormous publicity and a fashionable trade. More important still, he had broken through the closed-shop organization by which the cooked-food purveyors worked.

By the end of the century the guillotine had put many great cooks out of work. They soon saw the opportunities offered by the growing restaurant trade and the old cooked-food trades *vis-à-vis* the more widely distributed prosperity of a new social order. The *traiteur* began to specialize in grand set pieces which he supplied on a catering basis to nineteenth-century bourgeois homes. The *charcutier* increased the range and quality of his pork products, and began to sell cooked tripe to his middle-class clients as well. Only the *tripier* seems to have lost in prestige, supplying poor families and shabby hotels with what Henry James described as "a horrible mixture known as *gras-double*, a light gray, glutinous nauseating mess."

In the twentieth century all these categories have become blurred at the edges and interdependent. They have also benefited from most stringent food laws. French small-town hoteliers and restaurateurs now delight their clients with delicious preliminaries to the main course, supplied usually from the *charcuterie* nearby rather than their own kitchens. This is where English hotels outside London are at such a disadvantage. There are no high-class cooked-meat and bakery trades in England. The chef with a small staff cannot send out for *saucisses en brioche*, *quiches Lorraines*, or a good pâté, leaving himself free to concentrate on his meat, fish, and sauces.

Toward the end of the nineteenth century, France, like every other European country, benefited from the development of refrigeration. Nobody needed the huge pig any more. With cold storage mild, round-the-year ham and bacon curing became possible, which meant that less fat was needed to mitigate harsh-tasting lean meat. At the same time there was a big increase in machine and sedentary occupations, which lessened people's need for a high-fat diet. So the pig grew smaller. Now his weight is watched as carefully as any film star's.

Probably the English pig—which is called a "bacon-type" pig in the United States—is now being taken too far toward leanness, at any rate for the finer points of *charcuterie*. He has become too much a factory animal: we neglect his ears, his tail, his trotters, his insides, his beautiful fat, and his flavor (pig's ears by the hundred thousand are fed to mink, from one of the Wiltshire bacon factories, which is a bit like feeding caviar to canaries). But with a little care and persistence the English housewife can bully out of her butcher what is known as "overweight pig," and for very little money she can obtain the fat parts, as well as the extremities and the offal—the basis of many of the most delicate and delightful dishes it is possible to make. The American housewife, on the other hand, I am told, has it easier, because the pork sold in the United States comes from "butcher-type" pigs, which have much more fat than our English ones. The skillful and economical housewife can buy a pig's head for $2.00 to $2.50; this is what she can make from it—pig's ears with a piquant sauce (page 257), brains in puff pastry (page 261), Bath chap (page 255), 1½ lbs. of sausage meat for making pâté (page 71) or *crépinettes* (page 117), and some excellent *rillons* (page 333) which are more usually made from belly of pork. There is on average 4½ lbs. of boneless meat on a pig's head. And an excellent clear soup (page 276) or aspic jelly (page 40) is to be made from the bones.

So I hope that this book, in some degree, will contribute to reinstating the pig in its variety in English and American kitchens, as well as help the holiday maker traveling in the country where the pig is most valued.

I have naturally taken much information from French textbooks of *charcuterie* and the *cuisine bourgeoise*. Nobody can produce a cookery book these days without a deep appreciation of

Elizabeth David's work. I am indebted to her for suggestions, encouragement, and advice most generously given; also to many French friends, particularly Madame Potier of Paris and Les Deux Sèvres, the very best of cooks; Adey Horton, of Paris, the Master of the Sunday Lunch; Maurice and the late Fernande Beaubrun of St. Jacques des Guerets; Madame Champy of Trôo; Monsieur and Madame Berlu of the *boucherie* at Trôo; Monsieur and Madame Cureau of Montoire, whose *charcuterie* cannot easily be surpassed. Two Wiltshire butchers, Mr. W. W. Nichols of Swindon, and Mr. R. Sawyer of Wootton Bassett, have patiently supplied information and unexpected cuts of pork. Messrs. Harris Ltd., of Calne, kindly allowed me to visit their factory. I should like as well to thank my family and many English friends who have been made to eat an unconscionable quantity of the diverse parts of the pig in the last four years.

JANE GRIGSON

Broad Town and Trôo, 1966

THE ART OF MAKING
SAUSAGES, PÂTÉS,
AND OTHER CHARCUTERIE

 PICNIC GUIDE TO THE CHARCUTIER'S SHOP

Every small town in France, at any rate in the more prosperous districts such as Touraine, Burgundy, or the Île-de-France, is likely to have more than one *charcuterie*. Probably one, and one only, will be worth going to, on the *place* or in the main shopping street, its windows crowded with a variety of good things, its marble slabs and its tiled floors clean and inviting, with a brisk white-coated wife in attendance (the *charcutier* himself leads a pale, mainly nocturnal existence, at the back, transforming pork into his delicacies).

The other *charcuteries* will be mediocre, even a little gray, with fewer lines, tucked away in a side street. Only the master in each town can afford the good position, and match up to the standard which many of the townspeople demand. He is likely to have as neighbors, more or less, the one good *pâtisserie* (pastry cook) and the best *boulangerie* (baker), with its many varieties of bread. The *charcutier* will sell olives, anchovies, condiments, and a few proprietary goods (e.g., *saucissons secs*, salami of one kind and another). He will sell various salads of his own making, and a few confections of rabbit (e.g., *pâté de lapin*), chicken, or beef. But transmutations of the pig are his mainstay.

Occasionally the butcher (*boucher*) is *charcutier* as well, particularly in smaller places, and, as you would expect, his range of *charcuterie* is fairly restricted—sausages, black puddings, a simple pâté or two, and some *rillettes*.

Many of the *charcutier's* products can be eaten cold, with salads (which are sold in cartons by weight) or bread. Following is a list of his standard items, for quick use in the day's picnic shopping (with page references to the recipes). It must be understood that items vary according to season and province.

—————•◆•—————

READY TO EAT

Rillettes. Potted belly of pork, sowbelly (page 289), sometimes with the addition of goose or rabbit. A major delicacy of Touraine and Anjou; but not infrequently made in factories (tinned *rillettes* may be bought in some grocer's shops), as well as by the *charcutier* himself.

Rillons. Small pieces of browned sowbelly (page 289). These sometimes have an unappetizing look, altogether belied by their taste. They are among the finest products of *charcuterie.*

Petit Salé. Sowbelly of pork and spareribs salted and boiled (page 181), sold in larger pieces than *rillons,* delicately pink and white.

Galantine de Porc (page 251). Nearer to brawn—or what Americans call headcheese—than to galantine, made of the head meat of the pig.

Fromage de Tête (page 248). Brawn, or headcheese, often bread-crumbed on the outside.

Hure (page 251). Brawn, once again, but often presented with a half-inch layer of jelly on the outside.

Pâté de Campagne (page 71). Pâté made from the lean and fat meat of the pig, veal, ham, etc. Ingredients vary locally and according to season and taste.

Pâté de Foie de Porc (page 75). Pâté made from the lean and fat meat of the pig, with the addition of pig's liver.

Pâté de Lapin (page 80). Pâté made from rabbit and pork.

Pâté de Gibier (page 98). Pâté made from pork and game, which may be specified, e.g., *pâté de lièvre*—hare pâté. (Other pâtés are given on pages 84 to 100.)

Jambon (ham), including mild cures such as *jambon de Paris, jambon de York* (i.e., ham cured in the mild York style, see page 197, but often a canned and insipid travesty), and the delicious smoked hams, many of which are eaten raw, in very thin slices, like the famous *jambon de Bayonne*. Many regions make their own not so famous *jambons crus;* always inquire.

Jambonneau (page 198). Picnic ham, or shoulder, mildly cured, from the hock. Charmingly presented as small bread-crumbed cones, with a neat piece of bone sticking out of the top, like a stem. Sold by the half, or quarter, if you do not want a whole one.

Porc Rôti (page 229). Roast pork, most usually the loin, boned and rolled, and very lightly salted.

Saucissons Secs (page 134). Salami of various kinds, regional, national, and international, and other dried or smoked sausages including *saucisson à l'ail* (garlic sausage), *andouille* (large black-skinned tripe sausage), the slightly smaller *chorizos* or *saucisses d'Espagne* (red-pepper sausage). The *charcuterie* will usually stock frankfurters, and the very similar *saucisses de Strasbourg*, of good quality.

Museau de Boeuf en Salade. Boiled ox muzzle, sliced thinly and dressed with plenty of parsley and chives, and vinaigrette.

CHARCUTERIE THAT REQUIRES WARMING OR COOKING

Quiche Lorraine. Bacon, egg, and cream flan—many variations, and sizes, according to region (page 187).

Oreilles de Porc (page 256). Pig's ears, cooked, in jelly. Tasty, though seldom eaten in England or the United States. In France the crisp cartilage is eaten as well as the meat, and they are usually served grilled, with a coating of egg and bread crumbs, though you need do no more than warm them through.

Pieds de Porc (page 267). Pig's trotters, which you in America call pig's feet, often split in half and bread-crumbed. Sold by the piece. Fry in butter, or brush with melted butter and grill.

Queues de Porc (page 274). Pig's tails, cooked, and finished with a coating of bread crumbs. Fry in butter, or brush with melted butter and grill.

SAUCISSES (*page 114*). SAUSAGES FOR COOKING DIVIDE INTO:

Saucisses de Porc. Small pork sausages, sold, as in England and the United States, in chipolata and larger sizes. By French law they are 100 per cent meat and do *not* contain preservatives.

Andouillettes. Small tripe sausages, or chitterlings (page 278), of bland and mild flavor, making an excellent picnic lunch. They may be contained in very knobbly lengths of gut, for which they are none the less delicious. Sometimes wrapped in stiff white paper, sometimes pressed into four-sided shapes and neatly glazed with a mixture of pork and veal lard. As they are expensive, buy one or two according to the size of the family, break them up in the pan when they are cooked, and add beaten eggs, one to two per person, to make an omelette.

Boudins Blancs (page 147). White puddings, though more sausage-like and less puddingy than their counterparts in England. Of delicate flavor, containing (from the best *charcuteries*) a proportion of chicken with the pork. The most expensive of all the sausages.

Boudins Noirs (page 338). Black or blood puddings. Spicier and tastier and with more character than the factory-made black puddings of England and America. Whether presented sausage-style, or in an immense coil, the cheapest of all the sausages. Delicious with fried apples.

Saucisson-cervelas (page 146). Saveloy or larger sausage for poaching in nearly boiling water. Eat with potato salad, improved with some chopped raw onion and mustard.

Saucisses de Francfort (page 134). Usually a proprietary brand, often sold in plastic wrappings. Five minutes in nearly boiling water. Eat with potato salad, etc., like the *cervelas* sausage above.

Saucisses de Strasbourg (page 134). See the preceding entry.

Crépinettes (page 117). Small flattish cakes of sausage meat, encased in veiny, white caul fat (*crépine*). Fry or grill.

Chair à Saucisse (page 115). All-pork sausage meat, on a tray, in a mound. Sold, as in England and the United States, by weight, and used for stuffings and homemade pâtés.

Saucisse en Brioche (page 164). A large pork sausage, up to a pound in weight, encased in *brioche,* and sold by the slice. It has been described as an extra-fine toad-in-the-hole; an extra-fine sausage roll would be a better description. Eat warm.

Friandises (page 157). Small sausages enveloped in puff pastry, in other words a sausage roll. Best eaten warm.

Pâtés Chauds. Mixtures of meat cooked in short-crust pastry, pasty, or turnover style. Best eaten warm. Occasionally hot pies are baked on a large shallow plate, and sold by the slice, which will be weighed to determine the price; see *gâteau à la Berrichonne,* page 103.

Tripes (page 280). Tripe is sold in various forms apart from tripe sausages (*andouillettes and audouilles,* above). Often it is sold in hunks from a jellied slab, starred with carrot circles; sometimes in pots and cartons. Needs warming through, and is intended to be improved, according to taste, by the addition of wine, hard liquor, tomatoes, and parsley.

Lard is, confusingly, the French for bacon (*tranche de lard* is a slice of bacon). *Saindoux* is the name given to what we call lard. Bacon is not much sold in France, though it is always available; housewives there use fresh pork fat cut in strips or pork belly in cooking, where we might use fat bacon, called fat back in America—see pâtés (page 71) and the casserole of shin of beef on page 239. Fresh pork fat is sometimes difficult to come by in England and America. Bacon provides a substitute, and many grocers are pleased to get rid of a fat end for a very low price. Remove the rind and put the piece into a pan of cold water, so that it is well submerged. Bring to the boil slowly, simmer for 5 to 10 minutes according to size. This draws out the excess salt, and removes the smoky flavor that would otherwise be too dominant. Cool, then chill the bacon until it is easily cut into thin slices.

CUTS OF FRESH PORK AND OFFAL

The *charcutier* also sells uncooked fresh pork and offal, including:

Échine. British spareribs (shoulder or blade end in U.S.)

Palette. Bladebone (shoulder butt or Boston butt in U.S.)

Gorge. Neck, and part of hand (no U.S. cut for this)

Épaule. Shoulder

} Hand of pork, shoulder (U.S. picnic shoulder)

Plat de côtes. Part of spareribs in U.S.

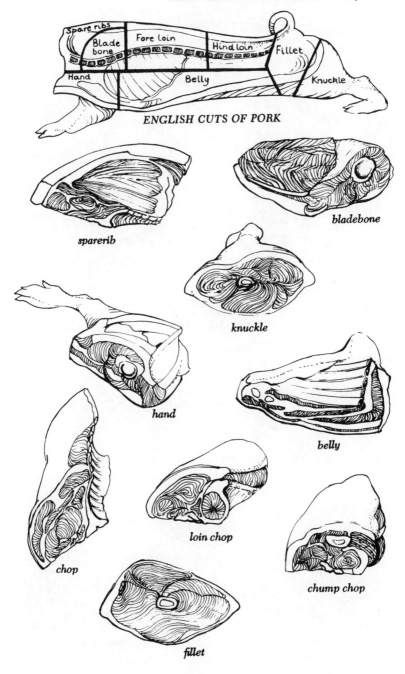

ENGLISH CUTS OF PORK

sparerib

bladebone

knuckle

hand

belly

chop

loin chop

chump chop

fillet

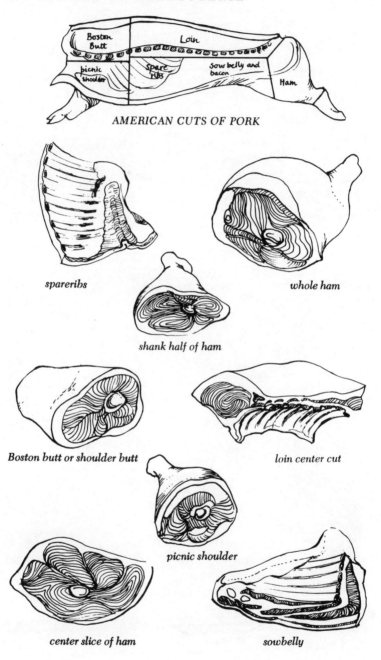

AMERICAN CUTS OF PORK

spareribs

whole ham

shank half of ham

Boston butt or shoulder butt

loin center cut

picnic shoulder

center slice of ham

sowbelly

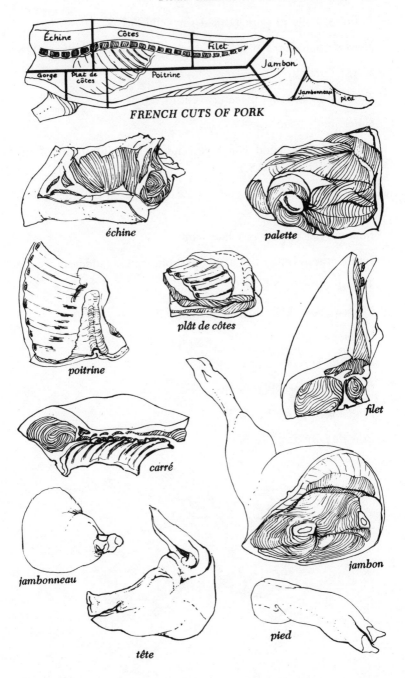

FRENCH CUTS OF PORK

échine

palette

plât de côtes

poitrine

filet

carré

jambonneau

jambon

tête

pied

Poitrine. Belly of pork (called sowbelly in U.S.)

Lard de poitrine. Fat belly of pork (called fat sowbelly in U.S.)

Côtes. Foreloin

Carré. Foreloin in a piece (rib cut in U.S.)

Côte. Single chop

Longe or *filet.* Hind loin (loin end in U.S.) and part of fillet (center cut in U.S.)

Noisettes. Small round cuts, or escalopes, from the fillet (center cut in U.S.)

Jambon. Leg of pork or whole ham

Jambonneau. Hock; and hand (part of picnic shoulder in U.S.)

Tête de porc. Pig's head

Pieds de porc. Pig's trotters (feet in U.S.)

Queues de porc. Pig's tails

Abats de porc. Pig's offal

Cervelle de porc. Pig's brain

Rognons de porc. Pig's kidneys

Foie de porc. Pig's liver

BREADS AND WINE

Since *charcuterie* and bread go together in picnic meals, here are some of the types of bread to ask for (all sold by weight, and priced by weight). The *boulanger* will always divide anything larger than a *ficelle*.

DAILY BREAD

Ficelles (meaning "string"). Thin sticks of bread.

Baguettes (meaning "rod, wand"). Longer, thicker sticks of bread.

Pains (meaning "bread"). The commonest of the long loaves.

Pain gruau (meaning "fine-wheat bread"). Bread of the finest flour.

Pain au lait (meaning "milk bread"). Large and small rolls.

Pain de mie (meaning "crumb loaf"). Shaped like small English tin-baked loaves (American "sandwich" bread loaves), but much lighter in texture. Used for *Croque-Monsieur* (page 219), stuffings, toast, etc.

FANCY BREAD

Croissants (meaning "crescent"). Made from high-fat dough.

Brioches. Large and small fluted buns, made from high-fat dough, mixed with eggs.

Pain brioché. *Brioche* dough baked in a loaf pan.

Pain mousseline (meaning "muslin bread"). *Brioche* loaf, shaped like a chef's hat.

KEEPING BREAD

Gros pain (meaning "large bread"). Often enormous ovals of coarser, but delicious, bread. Improves with keeping a day or two.

Pain complet (meaning "whole bread"). Wholemeal loaf.
Pain de seigle. Rye bread.
Couronnes. Circles ("crowns") of bread.

WINE

Wine, *vin ordinaire rouge, rosé,* or *blanc,* is sold (like special waters, which should, incidentally, be varied every four or five days for children) by the liter. A charge above the price of wine (*ordinaire* and château-bottled) or water is made for the bottle, unless you are exchanging an empty one. Ask if there is a *bouchon plastique* (plastic cork or, rather, stopper) beneath the foil cap. If there isn't, the grocer can usually provide you with one.

PICNIC STOVES

Small portable *butagaz, camping-gaz,* stoves are obviously ideal. The cylinders are much more easily exchanged in France than in our country or the United States.

Less expensively you can use small stoves (about $2.00 and up from camping and hardware stores), filled with solid fuel or methylated spirits (*alcool à bruler;* not colored in France, so mark the bottle), or a primus (the French for paraffin is, confusingly, *pétrole*—not always obtainable, particularly in summertime). *The shop for paraffin and methylated spirits is the droguerie, not the ironmonger's* (*quincaillerie*); the *droguerie* is usually recognizable by displays of paint and plastic household goods.

COMPARATIVE WEIGHTS AND MEASURES

DRY WEIGHTS

Un kilo (gramme) = 1000 grams = 2 lbs. 3 oz. = 35 oz.

Une livre
un demi-kilo } = 500 grams = 1 lb. 1½ oz. = 17½ oz.

Une demi-livre = 250 grams = 8¾ oz.

Cent grammes = 100 grams = 3½ oz.

30 grams = 1 oz.

LIQUID WEIGHTS

Un litre = 1000 grams = 1¾ English pints = 35 Imperial fluid oz. = 33½ American fluid oz.

Un demi-litre = 500 grams = 17½ Imperial fluid oz. = 17 American fluid oz.

Un quartlitre = 250 grams = 8¾ Imperial fluid oz. = 8¼ American fluid oz.

Un décilitre = 100 grams = 3½ Imperial fluid oz. = 3⅓ American fluid oz.

or

Cent grammes = 100 grams = 3½ Imperial fluid oz. = 3⅓ American fluid oz.

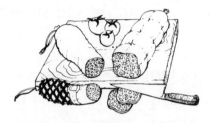

·◦❦ CHARCUTERIE ❦◦· EQUIPMENT

There are in fact very few *charcuterie* and pork recipes that can't be carried out with normal kitchen equipment—apart from sausages. To stuff your own sausages you need to have a sausage-making attachment for your electric mixer, or at least a hand-stuffer consisting of a metal cylinder, a detachable horn, and a wooden plunger. Or you might be lucky enough to find a butcher willing to put your own mixture into skins for you.

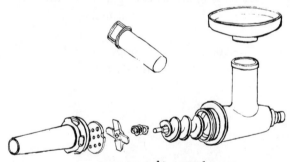

sausage-making attachment

I find that the joy of any trade is in part due to the constant use of loved and tried tools and equipment. I wonder if I would make *rillettes* or pâté so often, if I hadn't collected an assortment of the appropriate pots in France to store them in. *Rillettes* in a jam jar, or pâté in a glass oven dish, are perfectly feasible propositions, but not nearly such appetizing ones. Junk shops in England can usually provide old Strasbourg pâté pots, of cream to gold earthenware and a lion's head each side as lugs. For 2/– in a Newport Street market I once bought a huge oval French *gratin* dish in yellow and brown ware. At Abergavenny on the same journey, a deep loaf-tin-shaped pot, in cream earthenware, for 6*d*, has gone into the oven a thousand times with pâté, or held brawn (or headcheese) as it sets in the cool larder. But for brawn I really prefer pint mugs from an old pub sale; they are evenly cylindrical so that a tin of soup wrapped in aluminum foil acts as a weight, fitting beautifully

mug-shaped rillette pots

into the mug. The brawn unmolds in a firm roll, ready to be pushed over the warm toasted crumbs before being sliced and served.

Even without sale bargains, you will not find it expensive to buy traditional French dishes and terrines at Elizabeth David's shop at 46 Bourne Street, London S.W.1,* provided you stick to stoneware. Cheaper and softer earthenware is not economical as it chips easily. If you are considering a lifetime's wear, invest in vitrified cast-iron pans produced in splendid colors by Le

* Americans might try The Bridge Company, 212 East 52nd Street, New York City.

gratin dishes

Creuset; they are available at Elizabeth David's shop too, and
throughout the country at good kitchenware suppliers.*

But *charcuterie* does not require expensive equipment—
though an electric mixer is undeniably a great help, particularly

pressing brawn (headcheese)

if it has a sausage-making attachment. Here is a list of other
things I would hate to be without in my dealings with the pig.
Most of them, but not all, are strictly practical.

---

* You will find Le Creuset ware in America at The Bridge Company,
212 East 52nd Street, New York City; and many other fine kitchen suppliers across the country.

Sharp knives, in several sizes, the first requirement of any kitchen. Do not be tempted by stainless steel, which is more difficult to keep properly sharpened. Nowadays French carbon-steel knives are cheaply available from better household stores in England and the U.S.—one famous make is Sabatier. Protect the points with corks every time you put them away, and use Scotchbrite to keep the blades clean.

cook's knife

Larding needle, with its delicately graduated point is better for testing meat as it cooks than a metal skewer. Larding is a satisfactory by-occupation of *charcuterie* (see page 325).

larding needle

Iron frying pan. Unless the frying process is to be concluded with the addition of wine, use a heavy, inexpensive French wrought-iron pan; they are cheaper than English ones even in our country. Catering supply stores often stock them, and at Elizabeth David Ltd., you will find them in many sizes (46 Bourne Street, S.W.1).* I use the lid of a black iron Dutch oven, which lives permanently in the warmth above a solid-fuel stove, and has the additional safeguard of an inside coating of tasteless vegetable oil. This averts rusting. As iron turns a wine sauce black (harmless but unappetizing), enameled cast-iron frying pans or French *Equipinox* pans are a useful, though far costlier, addition to the kitchen.

iron frying pan

Fish kettle (or *fish boiler*) may sound illogical, but its strainer tray enables large quantities of *boudins blancs* and black puddings to be poached with the minimum risk of their bursting. A good, if smaller, substitute is a cheap collapsible metal chip ("French fries") basket or salad shaker, and a large saucepan into which it fits easily.

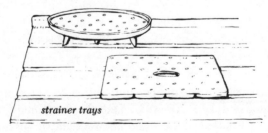

strainer trays

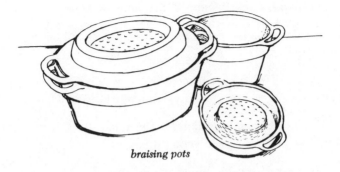

braising pots

Strainer trays and *Bowls*. The old-fashioned kind of meat dish provides a good flat straining surface, particularly if a galantine is to cool under a weight. Wide, shallow French bowls, really for draining cheese, are practical for small things like *rillons*.

Casseroles and *Baking dishes* need no suggestions from me. I prefer stoneware, or vitrified cast-iron produced by Le Creuset and many other European firms (see page 17), but glass ovenware and earthenware are quite suitable for *charcuterie* even if they are not so tough.

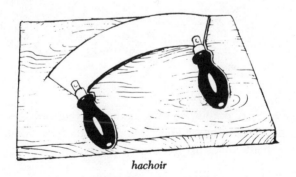

hachoir

Chopping block, of reliable flatness and generous size.

Hachoir or *Mezzaluna* for chopping meat, better than grinding. The Cuisinart Food Processor, if you are fortunate enough to own one, does a fine job of mincing meat.

Parsmint, a tiny "Moulinex" for chopping herbs.

Garlic crusher—also called a garlic press—not necessary, but a great time-saver.

Bowls of all sizes, particularly larger ones; nothing is worse than managing a large quantity of mixture in a small bowl.

Kitchen tongs, essential for the removal of trotters (pig's feet), ears, etc., from simmering liquid.

Perforated spoons, Wooden spoons, and a *Ladle.*

Large sieve and *Colander.*

a bain-marie

Bain-marie, or old roasting pan that you can use instead; there's no need to buy a special one, but do have some way of standing small saucepans and baking dishes in hot water.

Pepper mill and *Salt mill.* Absolutely essential—see pages 31 and 34.

Aluminum foil, String, Butter muslin, and *Cheesecloth.* *"Heavy-duty" white thread* and a thick *Needle* should always be to hand in the kitchen, as well.

spoon-shaped kitchen scale

---◆◆◆---

MEASURING EQUIPMENT

Scales. Buy the new metric and pound scale made by Salters. European recipes can then be used without preliminary (and sometimes inaccurate) mathematical calculations (in the U.S. you might buy the above-illustrated kitchen scale, which is a handy gadget whereby you can weigh small amounts and translate metric weight into the American equivalent in ounces). But here is a table of equivalents for those, who like me, have English-only scales.

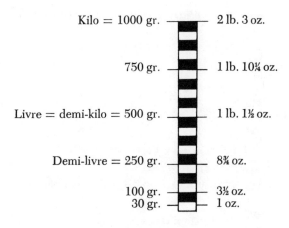

Kilo = 1000 gr.	2 lb. 3 oz.
750 gr.	1 lb. 10¼ oz.
Livre = demi-kilo = 500 gr.	1 lb. 1½ oz.
Demi-livre = 250 gr.	8¾ oz.
100 gr.	3½ oz.
30 gr.	1 oz.

Spoons. The main point of disaster is the tablespoon. In the United States it is equivalent to the French *cuillère à soupe,* or *à bouche,* and the English dessertspoon, measuring about 15 grams, or ½ ounce. The English tablespoon is almost twice the

American tablespoon, measuring, heaped, 1 ounce. The French *cuillère à café* equals the American and English teaspoon, measuring about 5 grams or 1/6 ounce. But be careful, the sizes of "teaspoons" and "coffee spoons" on the market vary a great deal, so invest in a set of plastic or metal measuring spoons made specifically for kitchen use.

Luckily most recipes give more detailed measurements for large quantities than spoonfuls, and when you are down to the small quantities given in spoons there is bound to be a little give and take, particularly in flexible meat recipes. But cakes and puddings can turn out very badly indeed if there is some confusion in the cook's mind between American and English tablespoons. In this American edition of *The Art of Charcuterie* United States measurements are used.

Liquid measures. As cups vary in American and English systems, for this edition I have changed the measurements to American cups and pints for liquid measures. Here is a table of these equivalents.

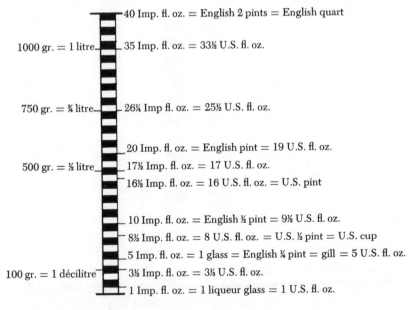

40 Imp. fl. oz. = English 2 pints = English quart

1000 gr. = 1 litre — 35 Imp. fl. oz. = 33½ U.S. fl. oz.

750 gr. = ¾ litre — 26¼ Imp fl. oz. = 25½ U.S. fl. oz.

20 Imp. fl. oz. = English pint = 19 U.S. fl. oz.

500 gr. = ½ litre — 17½ Imp. fl. oz. = 17 U.S. fl. oz.

16½ Imp. fl. oz. = 16 U.S. fl. oz. = U.S. pint

10 Imp. fl. oz. = English ½ pint = 9½ U.S. fl. oz.

8⅓ Imp. fl. oz. = 8 U.S. fl. oz. = U.S. ½ pint = U.S. cup

5 Imp. fl. oz. = 1 glass = English ¼ pint = gill = 5 U.S. fl. oz.

100 gr. = 1 décilitre — 3½ Imp. fl. oz. = 3⅓ U.S. fl. oz.

1 Imp. fl. oz. = 1 liqueur glass = 1 U.S. fl. oz.

 # HERBS AND SEASONINGS
USED IN CHARCUTERIE

The Garlic Family between them—garlic, onion, shallot, leek, and chives—provide gradation of oniony flavor from strong to mild:

Garlic. French *ail*, pl. *aulx* (*Allium sativum*). The cloves (*gousses d'ail*), i.e., the clustered bulbs, of this most pungent of cooking plants will multiply in the northern garden. But originally from central or western Asia, the garlic does better in the sunnier and drier climate around the Loire or in Provence, and cloves brought home from a French market stall are more powerful, as well as cheaper. English prejudice against garlic may originate in the fact that it is less easy to grow in the north than the related onion and shallot.

Onion. French *oignon* (*Allium cepa*). Onion and garlic are two of the basic culinary plants of the Indo-Europeans, and have traveled with them—like the eating of the pig—from their ancient homeland, which was probably western Asia. No wild form of the onion is known. Onion and garlic alike were anciently applied or eaten against a multitude of ailments.

Shallot. French *échalote* (*Allium ascalonicum*). The familiar small cluster onions, which derive their name, according to Pliny in his *Natural History*, from Ascalon in Palestine. They are a variety of the onion anciently developed in cultivation.

Chive. French *ciboulette, cive, civette* (*Allium schoenoprasum*). Native in dry places around the northern world, chives do well in the garden, and look well. The tufts of leaves can be snipped and snipped for cooking, the small bulbs rapidly renewing the supply. See *Fines herbes.*

Leek. French *poireau* (*Allium porrum*). Like the onion, the leek is not known in a wild form. Easily grown in northern climates, the leek, like carrot and onion, is an invaluable source of flavoring for *court-bouillon* (see page 46).

Allspice. See *Peppers.*

Anise. French *anis* (*Pimpinella anisum*). An umbelliferous herb, like coriander, parsley, and chervil. The flavor in English cake-making is taken from the seeds; but this Mediterranean annual, which is easy to grow, is used fresh in pâtés, as well as salads and omelettes.

Basil. French *basilic* (*Ocimum basilicum*). From the warmth of Asia, basil can only be cultivated with us as an annual, in good summers. It does better in a greenhouse. Used fresh it is the best of all herbs, particularly with tomatoes—even dried it makes a useful addition to the seasonings of a *court-bouillon.*

Bay leaves. French *laurier* (*Laurus nobilis*). The fact that the French for the sweet bay is *laurier* sometimes leads to a dangerous misidentification in cookery books, *laurier* being translated as laurel—as if it were the poisonous, broad-leaved cherry-laurel of shrubberies, so useful for asphyxiating moths and butterflies in jam jars. The sweet bay tree—from the Mediterranean—is not entirely hardy with us, and may be killed or severely cut back if sharp frosts continue. The dry leaves do not keep their flavor for very long. See *Bouquet garni.*

Bouquet garni. The invaluable small bunch or faggot of herbs added to most meat cookery in France—tripe, stews, soups, stock, *rillettes*—and removed at the last moment before serving. The usual herbs are bay leaf, sprig of thyme, and sprig of parsley, tied together with thread. Appropriate and seasonal additions are often made.

Caraway seeds. French *carvi*. The dried seeds of *Carum carvi*, another umbellifer grown without difficulty as an annual or a biennial. Caraway is sometimes found in England as a naturalized plant. Used in *charcuterie* in Alsace and the Franche-Comté.

Cayenne pepper. See *Peppers.*

Celery. French *céleri* (*Apium graveolens var. dulce*). Celery tops, as well as stalks, are a pleasant addition to stews, *court-bouillons,* and tripe dishes. Out of season, celery seeds and celery salt (seeds powdered with salt) are a good substitute. *Un pied de céleri* = a head of celery.

Chervil. French *cerfeuil* (*Anthriscus cerefolium*). Hardy annual, as easily grown as parsley, to which it is related; does best when planted for early summer or autumn. See *Fines herbes.* The little sprigs of leaves are known, in France, as *pluches.*

Chives. See *Garlic family,* above.

Cinnamon. French *cannelle.* The bark of the cinnamon tree (*Cinnamomum zeylanicum*), native of India and Malaysia, best bought in sticklike rolls, as the inferior bark is used for powdered cinnamon. An ingredient, together with cloves, pepper, and nutmeg, of the *charcuterie* spice-blend *quatre-épices* (see below). In Les Landes sausages and black puddings are much flavored with cinnamon.

Cloves. French *clous de girofle.* Dried flower buds of the clove tree (*Eugenia aromatica*), a native of the Moluccas, now commercially grown on the east coast of tropical Africa, notably in Zanzibar and Madagascar. An onion stuck with cloves is an invariable ingredient of *court-bouillon* and stewed meat dishes. In powder form it is used, together with cinnamon, pepper, and nutmeg, in the *charcuterie* spice-blend *quatre-épices* (see below).

Coriander. French *coriandre* (*Coriandrum sativum*). Umbellifer-ous annual herb from southern Europe easily grown from spring sowings for its fragrant seeds, which impart a faintly orange flavor to meat dishes. Particularly successful with pork. Much used with sausages and black puddings.

Cumin seeds. French *grains de cumin.* The seeds of *Cuminum cyminum,* a small umbelliferous annual from the Mediter-ranean, grown from spring sowing. Delicious in sausages or in *choucroute.* It is not often used in England, except in curry powder.

Fennel. French *fenouil* (*Foeniculum vulgare*). Has a traditional association with fish—also unfortunately with that nastiest of childhood medicines, liquorice powder, which is flavored with fennel seeds. Once that distaste is overcome if not for-gotten, the finely divided leaves of fennel give a delicious flavor when sprigged into or rubbed over pork before roast-ing (page 229), or when fried with potatoes as an accom-paniment to pork. This umbelliferous perennial is easily grown in the garden, where it likes all the sunshine available, though it is not particular about soil. The wild fennel of the seaside is identical in kind and flavor.

Fines herbes. A mixture of fresh, chopped herbs, including chervil, watercress, chives, tarragon, and parsley. Sometimes it means little more than parsley, once it included cultivated mushrooms. *Fines herbes* are used as a garnish, or in very quickly cooked dishes like omelettes; the little bunch of herbs used in prolonged cooking is known as a *bouquet garni* (q.v.).

Garlic. See *Garlic family,* above.

Ginger. French *gingembre.* The dried rhizomes or rootstocks of the common ginger (*Zingiber officinale*), a native of the Pacific, now widely grown in tropical lands. Used in *charcu-terie,* in powdered form, both on its own and in the blend *quatre-épices* (q.v.).

Juniper berries. French *baies de genièvre* or *de genèvrier.* Bush or small tree, the juniper (*Juniperus communis*) is not so common in Great Britain; preferring chalk or limestone, the hard little blue-black fruits, which ripen after two or three years, are more fragrant in the warmer limestone areas of France, where in half an hour one can pick enough to last (they keep their flavor well) for a long while. They impart a unique flavor to pâtés, brawn (headcheese), and salt pork, as they do to gin, in French, *genièvre.* Available from Elizabeth David Ltd., 46 Bourne Street, London S.W.1.*

Leek. See *Garlic family,* above.

Mace. See *Nutmeg,* below.

Marjoram. See *Sweet marjoram,* below.

Mustard. French *moutarde.* Made chiefly from the seeds of black mustard (*Brassica nigra*) mixed with the seeds of white mustard (*Brassica hirta*); mustard is grown all over Europe, Russia, and North America, but chiefly and best in the United Kingdom. English mustard is usually sold in powdered form, ready to be mixed at home with water or milk. French mustard, sold in a ready-mixed paste, is blended with verjuice (the juice of unripe grapes) or unfermented wine, and spices; this is best bought by weight in French grocers and brought home in vast quantity, in bottling jars, for use in the kitchen. Small pots of some of the fine Dijon and Bordeaux blends may also be bought for table use, at a lower price than you would find them in London or in American cities. Mustard is used a great deal with pork in France—a piquant contrast to trotters (pig's feet), *fromage de tête*

---

* In the U.S., I am told, juniper berries are available at many local fancy-food stores.

(headcheese), pig's ears, and roast loin, as well as more conventionally with ham. A successful ingredient in glazes for roast meat.

Nutmeg, French *noix de muscade,* and *Mace,* French *macis,* comes from the hard seed of the tree *Myristica fragrans.* The very pretty scarlet aril surrounding, like a tight skin, the seed or nutmeg itself, provides mace—usually sold in powdered form in our country*; it is a useful spice with pork, with its flavor of both nutmeg and cinnamon. Never buy ground nutmeg, except as a component of the *charcuterie* spice-blend *quatre-épices;* it soon loses its flavor this way, and is little trouble to grate in the small amounts required. The tree is a native of Molucca, like the *clove* (see above), but is now widely grown, particularly in the West Indies.

Onions. See *Garlic family,* above.

Paprika. See *Peppers,* below.

Parsley. French *persil* (*Petroselinum crispum*). Biennial; and uncommonly rich in vitamin C—though it is probably more for its flavor that French housewives place bowls of chopped parsley on the table at mealtimes. Pliny described it, in the first century A.D., as a plant used by everyone. The most necessary herb next to garlic, and one which needs to be grown—fortunately it is one of the easiest of plants—in quantity, spring, summer, and autumn. The curly leaved varieties (*persil frisé*) seem to have more flavor than the flat-leaved parsleys, and cannot be mistaken for useless or poisonous relatives. Dried parsley is of little use. *Persillade,* literally a garnishing of chopped parsley, is extended to mean the dish which is garnished in this way—for instance, *persillade de boeuf.* The most striking use of parsley is in *Jambon persillé de Bourgogne* (recipe, page 213), where it is used by the handful to marble the pinkness of the ham with its bril-

---

* Mace in chip form is also available in the U.S. in many fancy-food shops and even in some supermarkets.

liant green. Remember that parsley stalks give as much flavor as the leaves, so that they can quite well be used in a *bouquet garni* (q.v.). See also *Fines herbes.*

Pepper. French *poivre.* Long the most prized of all spices, the tropical fruits of the pepper vine *Piper nigrum* were used both by Greeks and Romans. Black pepper (*poivre noir*) is the whole fruit, shell and all, and has the most aromatic flavor; white pepper (*poivre blanc*), used in powdered form in *boudins blancs,* etc., is stronger, the fruit minus the shell— a difference already described by Pliny.

N.B. Never buy black pepper in large quantities—or ground (*en poudre*), as it loses its flavor very quickly. It is useful to have a very little white pepper, however, in the store cupboard in powder form. Peppercorns (*poivre en grains*), both black and white, are easily obtainable from good chemists—like many other spices.*

Allspice. French *poivre de la Jamaïque, toute-épice.* So called because it was deemed to convey in one the qualities of nutmeg, cinnamon, and cloves. The dried fruit of the allspice tree or pimiento tree—*Pimenta officinalis*—from Jamaica. Not to be confused with the blend of spices known as *quatre-épices* (see below), though it provides a useful substitute in England where *quatre-épices* is not generally available.

Cayenne pepper. French *poivre de Cayenne.* Of different origin from black pepper, being the powdered fruit of red peppers, various hot varieties of *Capsicum frutescens,* coming from warm countries including those in South America and the West Indies. Use with discretion in pâtés, *andouillettes,* and sausages.

---

* In America peppercorns and other spices are available in most supermarkets, in fancy-food stores, and in the foreign markets of some cities.

Paprika. French *paprika.* Again of different origin from black pepper, being the powdered fruits of red peppers from milder varieties of *Capsicum frutescens,* cultivated extensively in the warmer parts of Europe. An essential ingredient of Hungarian goulash, but a useful and decorative pepper in *charcuterie.*

Sweet pepper. French *piment doux.* Whole fruit of the milder varieties of *Capsicum frutescens,* grown widely in warmer parts of Europe. The green fruits, easily available in English and American greengrocers' shops, soon ripen to red in a warm kitchen. Use crushed in *andouilles* and sausages.

Pistachio. French *pistache.* The pale delicately flavored nut of *Pistacia vera,* an Oriental tree much grown around the Mediterranean. Like the truffle, an optional extra frequently used in *charcuterie* for the contrast of texture and color it provides, over and above its delicious light taste. Unlike the truffle, it is quite reasonable to buy in our country and the United States, shelled and ready for use in *fromage de tête,* pâtés, and galantines.

Quatre-épices is a French blend of four spices—pepper, nutmeg, cloves, and either cinnamon or ginger—for use principally in *charcuterie.* It is not on general sale in England or America, but if you have not brought any back from France you can quite easily mix your own, and keep it in a well-lidded jar:

Pepper, 7 parts; nutmeg, cloves, cinnamon, 1 part each.

Every big spice merchant has his own blend, so the proportions can vary—though pepper is always the main element. *Larousse Gastronomique* gives this:

White pepper, 125 grams (4¼ oz.); cloves, 10 grams (2 teaspoons); ginger, 30 grams (1 oz.); nutmeg, 35 grams (1¼ oz., scant).

The disadvantage of mixing your own is that you will have to use commercially powdered spices, if you want a very fine powder. An electric coffee grinder does quite a good job on cloves and white peppercorns.

Apart from its conventional use in *charcuterie* (sausages, pâtés, *rillettes,* pig's-head recipes, trotters [feet], black puddings, etc.), add it to a mustard–and–brown-sugar glaze for baked ham, seasoned fresh pork with it an hour or two before cooking, and sprinkle some into mashed potatoes to be served with *fromage de tête,* trotters, sausages, etc.

Saffron. French *safran.* The dried orange stamens of *Crocus sativus,* the lilac-flowered saffron crocus which originated in Asia Minor, formerly grown at Saffron Walden and at Stratton in Cornwall (hence the saffron cake and buns of Cornwall and Devon). Saffron is now available in Great Britain and the United States, and care should be taken to buy it in the form of dried stigmas (a deep-red hairy mass—expensive at first glance, it actually goes a long way), so that you are quite sure what you are really buying. Much French saffron comes from around Boynes in the Gâtinais, the district immediately to the south and southeast of Pithiviers (Loiret).

To use the dried stigmas, you mix a pinch of them with a tablespoon or two of stock, water, or white wine, according to the dish. They need crushing down, then leave them to steep and impart their brilliant color to the liquid.

Sage. French *sauge* (*Salvia officinalis*). This small bushy native of the Mediterranean is easy to grow in England.* Once established, it provides leaves for the kitchen virtually the year round, year after year. In France there is no sage-and-onion stuffing to accompany roast pork, though it is added to pork stuffings for pâtés and galantines occasionally. More usually it flavors wine vinegar, or a *court-bouillon,* or young peas and beans—but always very discreetly. Try it with pork

---

* Or in the U.S., if you have a garden; if you do not, you can order fresh sage—and other fresh herbs—from Stillwater Gardens, Salisbury, Connecticut, or the House of Herbs Farms, Salisbury, Connecticut.

sausages or *crépinettes* (page 117), but always fresh; dried sage improves nothing.

Salt. French *sel.* The best salt to use is bay or sea salt (*sel marin*). This can be obtained at some expense at health-food grocery stores, or direct by post from the Maldon Salt Company, Maldon, Essex, and from Tidman & Son Ltd., 91 Old Church Road, Chingford, E.4.* If you live in London, you will be able to buy more cheaply the gray *gros sel* in Soho or Scottish sea salt from Elizabeth David Ltd., 46 Bourne Street, S.W.1.† Once you have used unrefined rock and sea salt, you will never return to the commercially adulterated powders on sale in every grocer's shop—the flavor has an extra fruity spiciness that improves the simplest dish of boiled potatoes. Buy a salt mill for table use, though many people like the crunchy texture of the crystals as they are. Salt for preserving and curing (see page 177) must be unadulterated. Blocks of rock salt are perfectly adequate, but sea salt makes a more interesting brine. If you go to France with a car, fill odd corners with polythene bags of Breton sea salt on sale everywhere; it works out at a fifth of the price of Maldon or Tidman salt.

Saltpeter, or **Potassium Nitrate.** French *salpêtre, nitrate de potassium,* is important in the making of brine because it gives meat (ham, Bath chaps, etc.) an attractive rosy appearance, when otherwise it would be a murky grayish-brown. It has no value whatsoever as a preservative, and should be used in tiny quantities as it will harden the meat, a tendency which is counteracted by the addition of sugar to the brine. Buy it in small amounts from the druggist, as it is very damp-absorbent, and keep any left over in a screw-topped glass jar.

---

* In America, sea salt is available in local fancy-food stores or from the House of Herbs Farms.

† Coarse crystal salt—sometimes called Kosher salt, I am told—can be bought in most American markets.

Shallot. See *Garlic family* (page 25).

Sweet marjoram. French *marjolaine* (*Majorana hortensis*). Highly aromatic, but not the same plant as the aromatic wild marjoram of chalk countryside, though related. A tender perennial herb from southern Europe which can be grown as an annual in northern English gardens—though chancy most seasons.* Use in galantines and game pâtés, sausages, stews, and *court-bouillon.*

Sweet peppers. See *Peppers*, above.

Tarragon. French *estragon* (*Artemisia dracunculus*). A perennial, originating in eastern Europe and western Asia, which dislikes damp and is not too easy to maintain in most English gardens. Keep a branch in a bottle of wine vinegar for use in vinaigrette and piquant sauces. Chop with a *fines herbes* garnish. Best of all with chicken in a *poulet à l'estragon*, but good too in chicken galantine or with rabbit. Use fresh if possible†; remember that the dried form is very concentrated.

Thyme. French *thym* (*Thymus vulgaris*). Garden thyme, the fairly bushy little perennial and more or less evergreen herb, originally from southern Europe. The cook's great standby, particularly in winter, and it can be grown at home on a windowsill. Use in forcemeat, pâtés, sausages, and with rabbit, and in *bouquets garnis* (see above).

Wild thyme. French *serpolet* (*Thymus serpyllum*), the wild thyme of downlands, is also used to flavor *charcuterie*. It is similar to the garden variety.

Truffles. French *truffes.* This black underground fungus rootled up by trained dogs and pigs from beneath oak trees, is the

* In America, potted marjoram plants can be ordered from Stillwater Gardens, Salisbury, Connecticut.
† Available fresh in local U.S. markets for a short time during the summer.

most delicate and expensive of all seasonings. At its best the truffle is bought fresh in Périgord, after the first frosts—but most of us have to be content with the tiny, luridly priced cans on sale at superior grocers shops. There is no doubt that even when tinned, they raise good pork dishes into the exceptionally memorable class. Expensive everywhere, it is still worth buying the tiny round tins in France where they are much easier to find, and 50 per cent cheaper than in England.* The white Italian truffle is delicious too, but in a different way, and not suitable for use as a seasoning in prolonged cooking.

Wine vinegar, or **Cider vinegar.** French *vinaigre de vin,* or *de cidre.* Both are preferable to the brutishly strong English malt vinegar—especially with *charcuterie* and fresh pork recipes, and accompanying vinaigrette sauces. If the wine recommended for many of the dishes in this book is not available, a dash of good vinegar will often improve the flavor. Keep a bottle of wine vinegar flavored with a branch of true tarragon. Stretch your vinegar by pouring in the strained dregs of a bottle of wine. Many recipes give too much vinegar—start off by using half the quantity specified, then add more to taste. Vinegar, of course, is a good preservative: if you haven't got a refrigerator and cannot cook meat straightaway, it will keep better and improve a flavor in a marinade of oil, vinegar, and spices. See *Marinade* (page 66).

---

* In America, they are even more expensive—$3.00 for a tiny can of two truffles.

 SAUCES AND RELISHES

COOKED SAUCES AND RELISHES

Allemande

This is a thick coating sauce, and a very useful cream sauce too, if you omit the second long cooking process.

2½ cups good chicken stock
4 tablespoons (½ stick) butter
4 tablespoons flour
2 egg yolks

½ cup cream or 6 table-spoons unsalted butter
Mace, or lemon juice, or tomato paste, or onion or mushroom purée

Heat the stock in one pan, whilst you make a *roux,* by melting the butter and stirring in the flour, in another. Add the hot stock gradually and leave the sauce to bubble gently away to half quantity, giving an occasional stir with a wooden spoon.

Transfer to a basin over a pan of hot water, beat in 2 egg yolks carefully, and add cream or unsalted butter. Keep the hot water at a simmer and go on cooking the sauce until it is very thick indeed, almost a paste.

Flavor with mace or lemon juice, as appropriate, or tomato paste, or onion or mushroom purée. Roll small skewers of meat (kebabs) in this sauce when almost cold, then in beaten egg and bread crumbs, before deep-frying.

Albuféra

4 tablespoons (½ stick) butter
4 tablespoons flour
2½ cups good chicken stock, heated
Up to 1 cup cream

1 pimiento, canned, drained and mashed with 4 tablespoons (½ stick) unsalted butter
½ beef bouillon cube

Make a *roux* with the butter and flour, add the heated stock carefully, and cook the sauce down gently until it is reduced by half. Add the cream. Just before serving stir in the mashed pimiento and butter and half a beef bouillon cube. Keep the sauce just under the boil until these are blended in.

A delicious sauce with a joint of salt pork.

Apple Chutney: see Apricot Chutney

Apple Purée, or Sauce

1 lb. crisp eating apples
4 tablespoons (½ stick) butter

Dash of powdered cloves, or grated nutmeg, or lemon juice

Peel and core the apples, cut them into pieces. Melt the butter in a heavy pan, add the apples, and cover. Cook very gently until the apples are soft, shaking the pan from time to time.

No water should be needed, and *no sugar.*

Finally mash the apples to a purée and season. Serve with roasted pork or glazed salt pork, black puddings, and sausages. See *mayonnaise Suédoise.*

Apples, Spiced

2½ cups dark brown sugar
1 cup white wine vinegar
8 cloves and ½ stick of cinnamon

1–2 lbs. apples, peeled and
cored

Bring the sugar, vinegar, and spices to the boil, and simmer the apples in it until just tender but not collapsed.

Pack the apples into a large sterilized bottling jar, pour over the spiced syrup, and seal. Leave for at least one month before using.

This recipe is delicious made with whole unpeeled crab apples, or Siberian crab apples, or peaches, or pears.

Apricot Chutney

1 lb. dried apricots or 2
lbs. fresh, weighed when
pitted
1 lb. onions, sliced (about
3½ cups)
1⅛ cups raisins
2½ cups white wine vin-
egar
2½ cups dark brown sugar

4 level tablespoons salt
½ lb. preserved ginger
1 level tablespoon mustard
seed
1 level teaspoon cayenne
pepper
½ level teaspoon turmeric
Grated rind of an orange,
juice of an orange

Put all these ingredients into a pan and cook gently to a soft mash. Add 4 ounces shelled walnuts. Keep at least one month before using with cold salt pork, or ham.

(For apple chutney use 2 lbs. apples, weighed when peeled and cored; substitute almonds for walnuts.)

Apricots, Spiced

Use fresh apricots, and follow the recipe for spiced apples.

Aspic Jelly

The best way to produce meat jelly is by simmering gelatinous meats and bones, plus a small amount of shin of beef—gelatinous again—to produce a good color.

Calf's foot is the classic ingredient, but pig's trotters (feet) are more easily available and do very well. Put them into a large pot and add, for instance, a poultry carcass, a veal knuckle bone, the bones from a rolled loin of pork, as well as ¼ to ½ lb. of shin of beef. For extra flavor add an onion or two, each stuck with 3 cloves; also carrots, a *bouquet garni*, garlic, pepper, but *no salt whatever*.

Cover with water and simmer for at least 4 hours, or until the foot or trotters are cooked enough to eat. Remove them and serve in one of the ways suggested on pages 271-3.

Leave the broth to boil on over a high heat, without a lid. The more you reduce it, the firmer the jelly will set.

Strain off the liquid, and leave it to set.

Turn it out next day and decide whether it needs *clarifying* —which is perfectly simple, so don't lose heart. For 5 cups of jelly, beat 1 egg white to a light froth that just holds its shape, and crush the shell. Put the jelly into a large pan—one that holds nearly twice as much liquid as the amount of jelly being clarified—and add the crushed shell.. Set the pan over a low heat, whisk in the white as the jelly liquefies, and bring slowly to the boil, whisking all the time. Reduce the heat to keep the liquid at a simmer for 10 minutes. Turn the heat off, and don't move the pan for 10 minutes. You will find that a thick, murky crust has formed including the egg and all the little nasty bits that were clouding the jelly.

Line a colander with a piece of cheesecloth, which should be tied in place over the handles, and suspend it over a bowl. Pour the broth gently through and leave it to drip. Don't help it along by stirring or squeezing.

Flavor with Madeira, or sherry; try a bare tablespoon first, don't overdo it. Or lemon, or sherry, or a dash of white wine vinegar.

NOTE: Jelly does not keep well, particularly in summertime. Any aspic-covered dishes should be eaten within 3 days (refrigerator stored), or 2 days (cold larder), and preferably eaten at one sitting. A large ham, for instance, could be ruined by sour jelly. This also applies to sauces containing aspic, a coating mayonnaise, for instance, or *chaudfroid* sauce.

If you do keep jelly, boil it up every 2 days and keep it simmering gently for an hour.

Quick Aspic

If you really must have a quick aspic jelly, powdered gelatin can be used. The result is much more gluelike, but will do, if flavored with discrimination.

2 beef bouillon cubes for 4½ cups, dissolved in only 2 cups of hot water or good meat stock (not salty)

2 envelopes unflavored gelatin (2 tablespoons)
1 teaspoon white wine vinegar, or lemon juice
1 tablespoon Madeira

Dissolve the gelatin in the hot water, add the flavorings to taste, and leave to set.

When either of the above jellies are still liquid, but on the point of setting and cold, they can be brushed onto a ham, or into a mold, as appropriate.

Béchamel

Sauce béchamel is the most betrayed of all sauces. The chief culprits are the English, who combine unspecified fat, too much flour and thin milk, or milk and water, then serve up the lumpy result as white sauce. On Good Friday it may be adorned with a flicker or two of parsley, fitting companion to boiled cod.

The correct basic ingredients are butter, flour, and hot rich milk—these and none other.

Various seasonings may be added; cream, egg yolks, chicken stock, mushrooms, crayfish, lemon juice may be used to build up other sauces from this simple and useful base, but butter, flour, and milk are the starting trinity.

Melt 4 tablespoons butter in a heavy pan, but do not let it brown. Add 4 tablespoons flour slowly, stirring it in with a wooden spoon. Cook very gently for 2 minutes, whilst 2½ cups of good milk (whole not skim) is heated in another saucepan until it is hot but not boiling.

Amalgamate the milk with the *roux* carefully, stirring continuously to avoid lumps. Take time to do this, removing the pan from the fire every so often to pour in more of the milk, then returning it to cook slowly together.

(Should lumps appear, beat with a rotary whisk [beater], or in an electric blender.)

Continue to cook over a gentle heat until you obtain the desired thickness. This is best done in a double boiler, or in a basin set over a pan of simmering water. Then you can leave the sauce to reduce gently for an hour or more, which improves the flavor. Season with salt, pepper, nutmeg, etc.

If you want to keep *sauce béchamel*, run some melted butter over the top to prevent a skin from forming. A buttered paper laid on the top works quite well too.

Bercy

This sauce is made in very small quantity to go with grilled pork (or other meat), liver, and so on. If you have no time to produce a concentrated meat glaze (see *Espagnole* sauce), make *sauce bercy* when you have some rich meat jelly from a roast joint. Alternatively, again, add ¼ lb. (1 stick) butter.

Cook 2 tablespoons of chopped shallots or scallions in 1 tablespoon of butter until golden-brown. Add ½ cup of white wine and boil down, until there is about half the quantity of liquid left. Add ½ cup meat jelly. Season with salt and pepper if necessary, and a squeeze of lemon. Finish with a large teaspoon of finely chopped parsley.

If you feel obliged to stretch this sauce, add a cup of *velouté* sauce. But it is much better in concentrated form.

See butters, bercy; also *sauce à l'échalote*.

Bigarade

This sauce is normally served with duck but is in fact delicious with salt pork that has been finally glazed with a mixture of French mustard, orange juice, brown sugar, and marmalade.

When the meat has finished glazing, transfer the juices to a small pan and add ½ cup of white wine to them. Boil down, then add 1 teaspoon of cornstarch mixed to a smooth paste with ½ cup of the liquid the pork was simmered in. Add the juice of two oranges, and some of the peel cut into small strips. Taste, and season with a little lemon juice if necessary.

Brown Sauce: see Espagnole

Butters

Compound butters, *beurres composés*, are served in small pats on grilled meat, or else used as a final enrichment and seasoning for sauces. The particular flavoring is mashed with the butter, then chilled.

Bercy, 2 tablespoons of chopped shallots, cooked down in ½ cup white wine, with 4 tablespoons meat jelly added. Reduce to a strong essence, and mash into the butter whilst just warm.

Colbert, parsley, tarragon, and lemon juice, particularly tarragon.

Maître d'Hôtel, parsley and lemon juice.

Moutarde, French mustard.

Paprika, paprika pepper.

Pimiento, mashed, canned pimiento, or crushed, blanched fresh sweet pepper.

Ravigote or *Chivry*. Blanch equal quantities of chives, parsley, tarragon, and chervil for 2 minutes in boiling salted water. Drain in a sieve, run under the cold tap, and pat dry in a muslin cloth. Blanch a chopped shallot for 2 minutes— about 2 tablespoons. Pound ingredients in a mortar, adding the butter.

There are many more butters of this kind. You can invent your own, but the above are the most useful with pork.

Beurre manié is a useful way of thickening a sauce at the last moment, but be sure not to let the sauce boil again once it is added. Knead some butter into flour, forming little balls, in the proportions of 3 to 4.

A quantity of 3 tablespoons of flour to 4 tablespoons of butter is a useful amount.

Beurre noir is butter cooked in a pan to a rich deep brown, *not black*. *Noisette* means cooked to a golden-brown. Capers, lemon juice, and parsley are often added, and a little vinegar which has been swilled round the buttery pan at the end.

Charcutière (*The Charcutier's Wife's Sauce*)

One of the delicious piquant sauces that go so well with pork. This one is distinguished by the use of sliced rounds of gherkins. See also *sauce piquante* and *sauce Robert*.

2 tablespoons butter	½ lb. tomatoes (about 2 tomatoes)
4 shallots or 2 scallions, chopped	1 teaspoon sugar
2 tablespoons flour	Gherkins and *fines herbes* to finish
½ cup white wine	Salt, pepper
½ cup white wine vinegar	
Stock to about 2½ cups	

Sauté the shallots or scallions in the butter until golden and translucent, sprinkle on the flour, and cook until the mixture is a pale coffee color. Stir in the wine and vinegar, then the stock, until everything is smoothly amalgamated.

Leave the sauce to cook down on a low heat, until it is the desired consistency.

Meanwhile cook the tomatoes and sugar to a purée, and sieve into the onion and wine sauce toward the end of their cooking time. Taste and season. Just before serving, add the gherkins, sliced, and the *fines herbes*.

Pour into a very hot sauceboat; to accompany grilled pork chops arranged around a pyramid of firm, mashed potatoes.

au Cidre

Never be tempted to use (or drink for that matter) a beverage sold widely under various brand names suggesting a connection

with cider. It is nonalcoholic, gassy, and oversweet, turning to a
bitter nastiness when cooked. Unless you live in Somerset or
Devon, good bottled cider with an alcoholic content can be quite
expensive: wine merchants stock it. It is worth finding out if
any pub near you sells draught cider, which comes a lot cheaper
than, say, Merrydown vintage cider.*

4 tablespoons chopped
 onions
4 tablespoons (½ stick)
 butter, melted
4 scant tablespoons flour

½ cup good dry cider
2½ cups liquor from boil-
 ing the ham
Salt and pepper

Simmer the chopped onions in the melted butter until golden
and soft. Sprinkle on the flour, cook until deep golden. Stir in
the cider, then the ham liquor, and simmer gently until the
sauce is reduced to the right consistency. Season with salt and
pepper. Make this an hour before the ham is cooked, so that the
sauce can simmer very gently.

Court-bouillon

Ideally these ingredients should simmer for ½ hour before adding the meat—trotters (feet), pig's head, ears, etc.—and if you
later require the stock for jelly, omit the flour. This is added to
keep the meat white rather than grayish-brown, but is obviously
unnecessary if the meat has been salted in a brine containing
saltpeter, or a pinch of saltpeter is added to the *court-bouillon*
during the cooking.

* American cider in general is reportedly even worse than our poor
brands. In the U.S., bottled English cider is very expensive and quite hard
to get—it is available, I am told, in some liquor stores and occasionally in
fancy-food shops. Dry white wine could be substituted, adding 2 tablespoons of applejack if you have it on hand.

5 cups water

2 medium onions, each stuck with 3 cloves

2 medium carrots, sliced

Bouquet garni

1 clove garlic

1 stalk celery, or celery leaves, or celery seed

1 cup white wine, or ¼ cup white wine vinegar

2 heaped tablespoons flour, or a good pinch saltpeter

8 peppercorns, crushed but not ground fine

Other spices to taste

Mix the flour with a little water to a smooth paste, put with the rest of the ingredients in a large pan. Simmer for ½ hour before meat is put in to cook. A little salt may be added, according to the recipe, but not if you want to reduce the stock later on for jelly or sauces.

à la Crème (*la Sauce Normande*)

There are many versions of cream sauce; if you use cider (see *sauce au cidre*) as well as cream, it is known inevitably as Normandy sauce—where cider, butter, and cream reach their pitch of perfection.

White wine, eggs, and changes of herbs can vary the final result. Tarragon, for instance, makes it the perfect sauce with chicken; this version with cider, or the piquant *saupiquet* version with white wine (on page 57), goes well with ham:

1 medium onion, chopped (about ¾ cup)

4 tablespoons (½ stick) butter

2 heaped tablespoons flour

½ cup good dry cider (or dry white wine), heated

½ cup appropriate stock, ham liquor e.g., heated

Powdered cinnamon, grated nutmeg, salt, pepper

Extra butter, up to 4 tablespoons (½ stick), cut into small pieces (or 2 egg yolks)

½ cup heavy cream

A little lemon juice

Cook the onion gently in the first 4 tablespoons of butter until it is melted and gold. Add the flour and cook for 2 minutes slowly. Stir in the heated cider or wine and stock. Cook down a little, until it is the thickness you require. Season, beat in the small pieces of extra butter, or egg yolks, and reheat without boiling. Just before serving add the cream and lemon juice to taste.

NOTE: Be sure to serve cream sauce in a very hot sauceboat, with very hot plates.

Chaudfroid

2 cups *velouté* sauce, made with chicken stock, hot
½ cup firmly jellied stock or aspic jelly
Appropriate flavoring (Madeira, sherry, white wine, mushroom essence)
Additional extras—2 tablespoons cream and 1 egg yolk

Add the jellied stock to the hot *velouté* sauce and boil down over a good heat, until the result coats the back of a wooden spoon. Flavor appropriately, adding the cream and egg yolks if liked. Unsalted butter can be used instead of cream.

Coat the ham or other meat with the sauce when it has quite cooled but before it has set.

If you are making this for the first time, and are not sure about the consistency, cool a little of it in the freezer to test.

NOTE: You can also make this sauce with a brown stock and *Espagnole* sauce, half and half, or one third to two thirds, *or*, very simply, combine thick cream with concentrated aspic jelly.

Cornichons: see Charcutière

Demi-glace: see *Espagnole*

Diable

2 heaped tablespoons finely chopped onions or shallot
½ cup wine vinegar
1 cup white wine
1 cup *Espagnole* sauce

or 1 cup beef or veal stock, well flavored, and a knob of *beurre manié*, made with 3 tablespoons flour and 4 tablespoons (½ stick) butter

Cook the onions, wine, and vinegar until there is hardly any liquid left. Add the *Espagnole* sauce or stock, and bring to the boil. Do not strain.

Add the *beurre manié* at the end, and reheat the sauce carefully for 3 or 4 minutes, without boiling.

NOTE: English-style, you can add a little tomato paste and Harvey's or Worcester sauce (Worcestershire sauce).

Serve with chops, ham, salt loin of pork.

Duxelles

This is a useful mushroom forcemeat, a dry forcemeat, which can be incorporated in pâtés, or laid inside pastry for meat cooked *en croûte—jambon de Reims en croûte* (page 195) or *jambon à l'anglaise,* or *cervelles de porc en chausson* (page 262).

A quantity can be made, and stored for future use. It can also be turned into a sauce by cooking it up again with some white wine and cream, or by adding a quantity of *Espagnole* sauce, or some good stock and a final thickening of *beurre manié* (qq.v.).

4 tablespoons (½ stick) butter	fine and left on a cloth to drain
1 medium onion and 2 shallots, chopped	Salt, pepper, mace to flavor
½ lb. mushrooms, chopped	4 tablespoons chopped parsley

Melt the butter, simmer the onion and shallots gently until they turn gold. Add the mushrooms, seasonings, and parsley. Cook slowly until the liquid has evaporated completely. This means you have to keep stirring toward the end, so that the mixture doesn't burn.

Leave to get cold, and pot.

NOTE: The name was given in honor of the seventeenth-century Marquis d'Uxelles, by the very great chef La Varenne, to whom we also owe the earliest really practical cookery books.

à l'Échalote

A form of *sauce bercy.*

Chop 4 shallots and cook them with 8 tablespoons of white wine vinegar until there is only a tiny amount of liquid left. Add some good concentrated beef stock and simmer for an hour. Thicken finally with *beurre manié* (q.v.), making sure that the sauce cooks without boiling afterward. Finish with chopped parsley, salt, and pepper to taste.

Espagnole or Brown Sauce

Sauce Espagnole is one of the basic sauces, used as it is, like *sauce béchamel,* or added to various ingredients to make other sauces, also like *sauce béchamel.* In great restaurant kitchens, where large quantities of these sauces are required, their preparation is long and so is the list of ingredients.

Its beautiful flavor does need some attention in producing the stock. Using a beef bouillon cube cuts the time required—and the expense, and is not altogether to be despised—but for a really good *Espagnole* sauce try the following method:

———• *Stock* •———

2 onions, chopped (about 1½ cups)
2 carrots, chopped (about 1½ cups)
Lard or butter
2 lbs. shin of beef, cut in large pieces, say 3 or 4
¾ cup red wine

Garlic, *bouquet garni*, peppercorns
1 knuckle of veal
Bones from a poultry carcass
and/or ham bone
and/or pork bones

Fry the chopped onions and carrots in some lard or butter, and, as they cook down and turn color, add the shin. Brown it on both sides, pour in the red wine, and add the peppercorns, garlic, and herbs. Bring back to the boil and then transfer to a large pot. Pack in the other bones, and cover with water. Put on the lid and barely simmer on the side of the stove or in a very low oven overnight. *Do not be tempted to add any salt.*

(If you want to make some meat glaze, say for *sauce bercy* in a day or two, keep back half the liquid when you make *Espagnole* sauce next day. Reduce over a good heat, until it is brown and treacle-thick (molasses-thick). This is why you do not add salt to the stock. Keep it in a pot, with a covering layer of melted lard.)

———• *Sauce* •———

4 tablespoons (½ stick) butter

4 tablespoons cornstarch, 2 tablespoons flour
5 cups stock

Melt the butter, stir in the cornstarch and flour. Cook for 2 minutes, then add the stock gradually to avoid lumps. Boil this gently for 2 hours or more on the side of the stove, or over a low heat, until it is the consistency you require.

Season appropriately.

NOTE: *Demi-glace* sauce is made by reducing 1 cup of *Espagnole* and 2 cups of stock still further. Flavor with Madeira.

The real excellence of these brown sauces lies in the long, long simmering.

aux Fines Herbes

Assemble a good handful of chopped *fines herbes* (page 28). If you have no chives, substitute a finely chopped shallot.

Put them in a pan with ½ cup white wine, and boil down until there is just a little liquid left. Add about 1 cup of *Espagnole* sauce. Cook gently together, strain, and serve with a fresh sprinkling of chopped *fines herbes*.

French Dressing: see *Vinaigrette*

Madère

Espagnole sauce, flavored with Madeira.

or

Remove the ham or salt pork from the dish in which it has been glazing. Stir 6 tablespoons of Madeira into the juices and bring to the boil. Add 1 cup of *sauce Espagnole*. Alternatively add 1 cup of good beef stock (bouillon cube), and thicken finally with *beurre manié* (page 44). Remember not to let it boil again, but cook slowly for the sauce to thicken.

or

(Elizabeth David's quick recipe.) Slice an onion and a

carrot thinly. Let them melt in 2 tablespoons butter in a heavy pan. Add 1 cup of water, a chopped tomato or 2 tablespoons of tomato paste, 1 tablespoon of meat glaze (page 50), or a bouillon cube, a *bouquet garni,* and leave to cook for 20 minutes.

Mix 1 tablespoon of flour with a small glass of water. Pour through a strainer into the sauce, stirring until it thickens. Strain into a clean pan. Add ¼ cup of Madeira.

Melt 4 tablespoons (½ stick) butter in a small pan. Let it turn golden, but be careful not to let it catch. Stir into the sauce. This, as Mrs. David observes, is what gives a characteristic flavor.

Meat Glaze: see Espagnole

Mirepoix

The name given to the dice of onions, carrots, celery, leeks, and salt sowbelly or bacon, sweated in butter and flavored with a *bouquet garni,* that forms the basis of brown sauces, stews, and braising, or is used as a garnish.

Mornay

Béchamel sauce, gently reduced in a double boiler or a basin set over boiling water, flavored with cheese and nutmeg, mace, or cayenne. Use Parmesan if you are able, or a well-flavored English or Canadian Cheddar.

Moutarde

Make a *sauce béchamel,* but substitute the liquid from boiling ham, salt pork, or trotters (feet) for milk. Keep the sauce to the consistency of light cream.

Beat 2 egg yolks in a bowl with 2 heaped tablespoons of French mustard, a dash of vinegar, 2 tablespoons of cold water, and 4 tablespoons (½ stick) of butter, cut into small dice. Pour on some of the hot sauce, beating carefully, then return to the pan and cook slowly *without boiling,* stirring all the time with a wooden spoon until the sauce is the right thickness—heavy cream this time. Add 2 tablespoons of chopped parsley before serving.

Normande: see *à la Crème*

Peaches, Pickled: see *Apples, Spiced*

Pears, Pickled: see *Apples, Spiced*

au Persil

To a beautifully made *béchamel* sauce, add plenty of chopped parsley just before serving.

Good with trotters (pig's feet) or with salt pork.

Périgueux

Madeira sauce with the addition of truffles.

Any reference to Périgueux on a menu means the inclusion

of truffles in the dish. *Périgourdine* means truffles and foie gras; *sauce périgourdine* is Madeira sauce with truffles and foie gras added.

Curnonsky* gives this version of *sauce Périgueux*, which is made with white wine, rather than Madeira, and *sauce Espagnole*.

Chop 2 or 3 shallots, and fry them to gold in a little fat—goose fat, preferably.

Add slightly more than ½ cup dry white wine, and set the mixture alight with ¼ cup *eau-de-vie* or brandy. Don't forget to warm the brandy first.

In another pan fry an onion, sliced, in some more fat. When it changes color, add some flour—about 2 tablespoons; let the mixture cook for 2 minutes, then stir in 2½ cups warm stock. Cook for 5 minutes.

Add the shallot and wine mixture, and leave the sauce to simmer for 2 hours at the side of the stove, or over a low heat. Stir it frequently.

If you are using fresh truffles, peel them and add the peelings to the sauce. With canned truffles, chop them, and leave them to one side.

Strain the sauce, add the truffles, heat through without boiling for 5 minutes, and serve in a very hot sauceboat, with ham or a fine joint of salt pork.

NOTE: Also served with fillet steak and poultry.

Piquante

Prepare like *sauce à la charcutière*, but omit tomato purée, and finish with a mixture of tarragon, parsley, chervil, paprika, capers, and *only a few gherkins*.

* *Recettes des Provinces de France* (1962).

Poivrade

Another hot, piquant sauce that goes well with pork.

2 tablespoons butter
6 tablespoons chopped carrots
4 tablespoons chopped onions
2 tablespoons chopped shallots
2 tablespoons flour
½ cup red wine
2 tablespoons wine vinegar
Bouquet garni

3 cloves
8 crushed peppercorns
6 crushed juniper berries
1 cup good stock, with a little meat glaze, if available
Freshly ground black pepper
Salt to be added, as necessary

Melt the butter, and fry the chopped vegetables gently until they turn golden-brown. Stir in the flour, then the wine and vinegar, herbs and spices. When it is well amalgamated, stir in the stock slowly and the meat glaze. Simmer for at least an hour over a low heat—a bubble from time to time is about right.

Strain the sauce into a clean pan, and taste. Add plenty of freshly ground black pepper and taste again. Add salt if necessary.

au Porto

Espagnole sauce (page 50), flavored with port, and often embellished with truffles and chopped mushrooms, sautéed in a little butter. Serve with ham.

See also *sauce madère* (page 52).

Robert

"It is my wish," said the Queen, ". . . to have my granddaughter served up with Sauce Robert."

An old sauce, with a literary history beginning with Rabelais and continuing well with Perrault's wicked mother-in-law. Delicious, too, with pork.

4 tablespoons (½ stick) butter	Dash of lemon juice
2 heaped tablespoons flour	½ teaspoon granulated sugar
3 large onions, chopped (about 3 cups)	1½ tablespoons French mustard
2 cups good stock	Chopped tarragon and parsley to finish
Dash of wine vinegar	

Melt the butter, cook the onions in it until they turn golden-brown. Stir in the flour, cook for a few moments, then gradually add the stock, still stirring. Let it cook for at least ½ hour very gently, better still an hour. Flavor at the end with the vinegar, lemon juice, sugar, mustard, and salt if necessary. Finally add a sprinkling of tarragon and a little parsley.

Roux

The name given to flour cooked with melted fat, usually butter —the start of many sauces.

Saupiquet

Here is a beautiful piquant sauce, superb with ham in this version, from *French Provincial Cooking,* by Elizabeth David:

4 shallots
¾ cup wine vinegar
6 crushed juniper berries
4 tablespoons (½ stick) butter
4 tablespoons flour

1 cup good beef stock, heated
¾ cup white wine
Up to 1 cup heavy cream, heated to boiling point
Extra butter to finish

Chop the shallots very finely, and put them in a small heavy pan with the vinegar and juniper berries. Boil until there is no liquid left, but don't burn the shallots.

Meanwhile in another pan melt the butter and make a *roux* with the flour. Cook until it is a pale coffee color. Pour in the heated stock slowly, stirring until the mixture thickens. Add the wine, then the shallots. Cook gently for ½ hour, removing any scum that rises to the surface.

Sieve the sauce into a basin over a pan of simmering water, add the bubbling cream, which you have heated to boiling point, then the extra butter.

The sauce will now keep hot until you want it. "It will be a beautiful pale coffee-cream colour, smooth, but not very thick."

Sainte-Ménéhould

As might be expected, an accompaniment to pig's trotters (feet) and ears *à la Sainte-Ménéhould*.

4 tablespoons finely chopped onions
2 tablespoons finely chopped shallot
2 tablespoons butter
½ cup white wine
¼ cup white wine vinegar
1 cup good beef stock
Bouquet garni

2 tablespoons flour, kneaded with 2 tablespoons butter
1 good teaspoon French mustard
Chopped gherkins, parsley, tarragon, chervil
Freshly ground black pepper, salt

Sauté the onions and shallot in the butter until soft. Add the wine and vinegar and cook until no liquid remains. Add the beef stock and the *bouquet garni*. Simmer for ½ hour at least. Finally thicken with the *beurre manié*, being careful not to let the sauce boil afterwards but cook gently.

Finish with the mustard, gherkins, chopped herbs, pepper and salt.

Soubise

A beautiful golden bland onion sauce, delicious with pork.

4 tablespoons (½ stick) butter

4 tablespoons flour

½ cup cold water

1 lb. yellow onions, chopped finely (about 3½ cups)

A dash of white wine vinegar

Salt, pepper, and nutmeg or mace

A little stock may be necessary, or juice from the pork

Make a *roux* with the butter and flour, cooking until it is very pale coffee color, no more. Add the cold water, and then the chopped onions, vinegar, pepper, and a little salt.

Cover closely and cook on a low heat for a good ½ hour. Stir from time to time, but the onions should provide enough juice to keep the sauce from burning. If extra moisture is required use stock or the juice from roast pork.

Go on cooking until the onions have melted into a thick cream of a sauce. They won't need to be sieved. Flavor with nutmeg or mace.

A lighter but not so delicious *soubise* sauce can be obtained by stewing 3 large chopped onions in 4 tablespoons (½ stick) of butter, sprinkling on a tablespoon of flour, and then adding 2 cups hot milk. Flavor finally with salt, pepper, and nutmeg or mace.

This is in effect an onion-flavored *béchamel* sauce.

Spiced Fruit: see *Apples, Spiced*

Suprême

Take equal quantities of the simplified *velouté* sauce on page 61 and chicken stock, and boil them down in a heavy pan until they are reduced by half. Add cream toward the end of this process. Finish the sauce with unsalted butter.

Use, say, 1 cup *velouté*, 1 cup stock, ½ cup cream, and a final 4 tablespoons (½ stick) butter.

Taste and adjust the seasoning if necessary.

Serve with brains, kidney, and so on, as well as the conventional chicken.

Tomate

One of the most useful sauces of all, particularly delicious if you can flavor it with fresh, chopped sweet basil.

4 tablespoons butter or olive oil	2 level tablespoons sugar
4 tablespoons chopped onions	Salt, plenty of freshly ground black pepper
2 cloves garlic, chopped	*Bouquet garni*
2 heaped tablespoons flour	2 tablespoons tomato paste
1 lb. tomatoes (or use a 1-lb.-3-oz. can)	2 tablespoons wine vinegar
½ cup red or white wine	Freshly chopped basil, or tarragon, or parsley

Cook the chopped onions and garlic gently in the butter or oil. Sprinkle on the flour, and when it has cooked in add the wine. This will make a small amount of thick sauce.

Add the tomatoes, cut in half (no need to peel), the *bouquet,* and sugar. Put the lid on the pan and cook for an hour slowly—longer, if you like.

Strain through a sieve, rubbing the tomato pulp through as well, into a clean pan. Flavor with tomato paste, vinegar, and extra salt, pepper, and sugar as required. English tomatoes need a great deal of additional seasoning, more than American ones.

Serve with a sprinkling of chopped herbs, a good sprinkling. This sauce should be very rich and spicy, with the fresh contrast of herbs.

Velouté

Velvety sauce. One of the basic sauces; forming with *sauce Espagnole,* or brown sauce, and *sauce béchamel,* or white sauce, the trio of the *grandes sauces* from which so many other sauces derive. *Velouté* sauce is a *béchamel* sauce made with hot veal or chicken stock instead of milk. Mushrooms are a characteristic additional flavoring. Like the other two *grandes sauces, velouté* gets better in flavor and smoother in texture with long, long gentle cooking.

———————

UNCOOKED AND OIL-BASED SAUCES

Mayonnaise

Do not be frightened at the thought of making mayonnaise. Provided eggs, oil, and bowl are at warm-room temperature, and you do not try to rush the early stages, you are bound to succeed. Large quantities of mayonnaise are usefully made in an electric blender, or with an electric mixer. But for small family amounts, many people prefer a bowl and wooden spoon as the flavor really does seem to be better when mayonnaise is made this way. A heavy mortar is sensible; a pudding basin or mixing bowl needs a tea towel (dish towel) twisted round the base to keep it steady, otherwise you will be following the bowl round the kitchen as you beat. A French friend uses a fork and a shallow soup plate with great success.

1 egg yolk	1 teaspoon French mustard, heaped
½ cup oil, olive, walnut, or vegetable oil	Good pinch of salt
	2 tablespoons wine vinegar

Beat the egg yolk well with the mustard and a bare teaspoon of the vinegar. It will thicken a little.

Add the oil slowly, drop by drop, beating all the time. It is useful to have a "mayonnaise boy" at hand to drip in the oil— a favorite job with children, who are fascinated by the magic transformation. As the mayonnaise thickens, the oil can be added in slightly larger quantities. But be cautious.

(If the mayonnaise becomes too thick, add a little more of the vinegar, or a bare teaspoon of hot water at a time, until the consistency is more manageable.)

(If by sad chance the mayonnaise curdles, add 2 tablespoons of boiling water and beat. If this doesn't succeed, put a fresh egg yolk into a clean basin and start again, pouring the curdled mayonnaise onto the second yolk drop by drop.)

Finally taste the mayonnaise and adjust the seasonings. You may or may not require the rest of the vinegar.

Lemon juice is often used instead of vinegar. In Denmark a very little curry powder is added at the beginning, ½ teaspoon to 1 yolk of egg; this is occasionally pleasant with cold pork as a change. Children particularly enjoy mayonnaise flavored with tomato paste and chopped parsley.

Coating Mayonnaise

Although mayonnaise spreads quite well as it is, the addition of cold but unset aspic jelly (page 40) makes it a great deal easier to manipulate smoothly. Add 8 tablespoons of jelly to ½ cup of mayonnaise, and use the mayonnaise before the jelly has time to set firmly. See *chaudfroid* (page 48).

Mayonnaise Suédoise

As far as cold pork (and duck) is concerned, this is the best variant of mayonnaise:

Add an equal quantity of cold apple purée to the mayonnaise. If the purée has been made with cooking apples, be careful not to oversweeten.

Flavor carefully with horseradish, grated or in cream (see *raifort*), and *vin rosé*.

Tartare

Sauce tartare is either a vinaigrette or mayonnaise sauce seasoned with finely chopped shallots, *fines herbes*, capers, and gherkins.

A vinaigrette basis is best when the sauce is served with hot gelatinous meat like trotters (feet), pig's ears, and pig's head.

Use a mayonnaise basis for serving with cold meat (or fish).

Rémoulade

This is a type of mayonnaise, but 2 hard-boiled egg yolks are added.

Pound the hard-boiled yolks in a mortar and mix them to a stiff paste with 1 raw egg yolk, 1 teaspoon French mustard, salt, pepper, ½ teaspoon sugar, ½ teaspoon wine vinegar and, if you like, ½ teaspoon of curry powder.

Add ½ cup of oil drop by drop, being careful that it is at room temperature, as if you were making mayonnaise.

Season with a *ravigote* (bundle) of green herbs, chopped, and extra vinegar to taste.

Delicious with cold ham, salt pork, and pork.

Verte

Sauce verte is a pretty accompaniment to cold ham or salt pork. It is a mayonnaise (page 61), colored and flavored with blanched green herbs, which are then drained and pounded.

A mixture of parsley, chives, tarragon, chervil, sorrel, and spinach, according to what is available, is tied together and plunged for 2 minutes into boiling water.

Drain well, pound in a mortar, and add to the mayonnaise. If you are using an electric blender for the mayonnaise, you do not need to pound the herbs; just drain them well and let them cool a little.

If you grow sorrel or have bought some fresh, the blanching process can be eliminated. Put 3 or 4 leaves into the electric blender, set it going, and add the mayonnaise. The result will be a very fresh green, with a clear taste. No other herbs are needed.

Raifort

Horseradish sauce is delicious with sausages, particularly when they are being served with a hot potato salad. Most English recipes include a quantity of vinegar, malt vinegar at that. Lemon juice is a much better idea.

2 rounded tablespoons freshly grated horseradish or drained bottled horseradish

½ cup heavy cream

1 teaspoon granulated sugar

Salt, pepper, and lemon juice to taste

Whip the cream so that it is evenly thickened but not stiff. Fold in the horseradish, then the sugar and a dash of lemon juice. Taste and season.

NOTE: A good hot horseradish sauce (for salt pork or hot ham) can be made by adding the cream to 1 cup of *béchamel* sauce in a double boiler. Make very hot, but do not boil. Add the horseradish at the last moment and season quickly with lemon juice, sugar, salt, and pepper.

Vinaigrette

Universal French dressing for salads of all kinds, usually made in England with far too much malt vinegar, which is stronger and harsher than wine or cider vinegars, and to be avoided. Many cookery books give the proportions of 1 part vinegar to 3 parts oil, without warning about the different strengths of various vinegars, but this is too strong. I find 1 part wine or cider vinegar (or lemon juice) to 5 or 6 parts of oil is more satisfactory.

Seasonings vary according to the salad, the time of year, and individual preferences. Here is a guide:

2 tablespoons wine vinegar
1 teaspoon granulated su-
gar
1 good teaspoon French
mustard
10–12 tablespoons oil
(preferably olive oil)

Plenty of pepper, freshly
ground
Plenty of parsley, chopped
1 clove of garlic, crushed
2 tablespoons chopped
shallots or scallions

Mix vinegar, sugar, and mustard together till it thickens. This happens quickly. Stir in the oil and add the seasonings to taste—don't be afraid of the raw shallots or scallions.

To this vinaigrette basis, you can add many things:

à la Grecque. Add 2 tablespoons tomato paste.

Ravigote. Add a bundle or *ravigote* of green herbs, chopped fine

—parsley, tarragon, chervil, chives, watercress can be included for instance.

Next, stir in some capers and a small chopped gherkin or pickled cucumber.

The result should be thick and piquant, to contrast with the gelatinous meats (trotters, pig's ears, pig's head) it usually accompanies.

Two chopped anchovy fillets are often added as well.

See *sauce tartare.*

Marinade

To marinade a piece of meat is to leave it for some hours, even days, in a mixture of wine or vinegar and oil, heavily seasoned with spices and herbs.

The process has three effects—it gives added flavor, it tenderizes the meat, and it keeps the meat in good condition, a poor man's refrigerator.

Apart from cheaper cuts of meat for stewing or cooking as kebabs, legs of mutton and pork are often marinaded to give them the flavor of venison and wild boar respectively. In this case the marinade is cooked first, then the meat rests in it for 2 to 4 days.

But first the simple uncooked marinade:

¼ cup chopped carrots (1 medium carrot)
½ cup chopped onions (1 large onion)
2 stalks of celery, chopped
2 cloves garlic, crushed
3 sprigs thyme
3 sprigs parsley

1 bay leaf
6 black peppercorns, crushed, and any other spices you like—e.g., juniper berries, coriander seeds, *quatre-épices*
1 cup dry white wine
½ cup of oil

Use a deep dish that only just holds the meat; mix all the ingredients given above and pour over the meat in the dish. Cover and leave for at least 4 hours, better still 12—or according to the recipe. The marinade can be strained and used as basting liquor when the meat is cooking, or to make a sauce. Turn the meat in its dish from time to time, so that it becomes impregnated by the flavors of the marinade.

Provided you keep a fair amount of wine, vinegar, or cider, the other ingredients can be varied a great deal both in kind and proportion.

The cooked marinade:

½ cup chopped onions (1 large onion)
½ cup chopped carrots (2 medium carrots)
2 stalks celery, ¼ cup celeriac, or 1 teaspoon celery seeds
3 cloves garlic
Oil or lard
Bouquet garni

Extra parsley
2 sprigs rosemary
8 crushed juniper berries
8 coriander seeds
10 crushed peppercorns
3 teaspoons salt
2½ cups white wine, cider, or red wine
½ cup wine vinegar

Brown the vegetables in oil or lard, including the chopped garlic. Add all the other ingredients and bring to the boil. Let it get cold. Skin the leg of pork (or mutton), score the fat lightly, and turn it over in the marinade twice a day, for 2 to 4 days according to the weather. Watch the humidity—a coolish muggy day or a damp cool larder do as much harm to meat, from the keeping point of view, as higher but dry temperatures.

The meat should be braised on a bed of vegetables, browned lightly in butter first (see *mirepoix*), with the marinade poured over, plus 5 cups of stock. Cover and cook in a slow oven for about 4 hours.

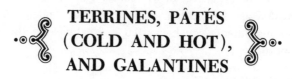

TERRINES, PÂTÉS
(COLD AND HOT),
AND GALANTINES

TERRINES AND PÂTÉS

What is a terrine, what is a pâté?

A meatloaf is a terrine, a pork pie is a pâté. But only from an academic point of view. Nowadays the words pâté and terrine are used interchangeably by French and English alike.

Terrine, with the same origin as our English *tureen,* means something made of earth, of *terra.* Nowadays a deep, straight-sided oval or oblong dish, and stretched to include its contents.

Pâté shares a common Romance origin with English words such as patty, pastry, and paste, and with Italian and Spanish words like *pasta.* Even though derived from the Greek verb, πασтειν, "to sprinkle," it early acquired cereal connotations. Sometimes pâtés are hot, sometimes cold. Pastry is kept mainly for hot *pâtés* (what we call pies), and for the finest cold pork-based *pâtés,* or game terrines. Flat strips of pork fat preserve moisture and flavor in more humble mixtures.

Many modern English cookery books give excellent recipes for making pâtés. *Pâté maison* is on the menu in many English (and American) restaurants. It is the first thing that travelers in France think of buying for a lunchtime picnic. In the midday shade of a walnut tree, or poplars bordering a canal, two or three pâtés are laid out on the cloth, with new crusty bread, good butter, fruit, cheese, and wine—not always very good wine perhaps, but very good pâté, and each day's choice differing in flavor from the one before.

I am not thinking of exotics—the Pithiviers lark pâté, for instance, the truffled foie gras pâtés of Périgord, or the superb range of Battendier's game pâtés in Paris—but of the simple pâtés produced in unique variety in every village in France above the size of a hamlet.

Our small market town of Montoire, with its 2,708 inhabitants, has four *charcuteries*. There are three pâtés on sale daily (the number increases dramatically at the great Feasts and on Sundays) in each shop, *pâté de foie, pâté de campagne*, and *pâté de lapin*. But none of them are quite the same, although the four *charcutiers* are using roughly similar recipes. So there is an immediate choice of twelve. Our own village of 549 inhabitants produces two pâtés—not counting *rillettes*, and *fromage de tête*, and *hure* (pages 334, 248, 251, respectively) which further extend the picnicker's choice.

When you go into a strange *charcuterie*, be brave. Take your time and buy small amounts of all the pâtés. There will not be sulks and sighs *à l'anglaise*—nor murmurings from the other customers behind. An enterprising greed is the quickest way to any French person's generosity and kindness. Often persistence is rewarded by kindly hand-outs of *saucisson* and black olives to small daughters and sons.

All pâtés have a basis in the pig (though with the mousse-like ones it is a tenuous connection, rather than a solid basis). Hare and game pâtés, for instance, often consist of small pieces or strips of the name creature layered with a pork forcemeat. As they cook slowly, pâtés have a permanent basting from the bards of pork fat which line the dish.

Variety, as I have said, is infinite. By the addition of different alcohols, different combinations of spices and herbs, orange juice and rind, an egg, a little flour, some truffle parings, one recipe can be stretched interestingly over months. You can chop the meat larger or smaller, or grind it. You can layer larger pieces with a virtual mousse. You can pour off the fat after cooking and substitute a jelly made from game bones or flavored with Madeira, or port, or lemon juice. You can alter the flavor by keeping the pâté for a couple of days (indeed you should do this) or for weeks (run a good layer of lard or butter over the top) not in the deep freeze but just in the cool.

This sounds expensive, and the very best pâtés are; on the other hand I make a cheap pâté, which is always appreciated:

2 lbs. meat, equally fat and lean, cut from half a pig's head
2 oz. lean bacon (about 1½ thin slices)
Extra pieces of fat cut from the head, to put on top
¼ cup Madeira, sherry, or a little brandy plus wine
1 large egg

½ lb. onions or shallots, chopped (1¾ to 2 cups), softened in butter
1½ tablespoons each of flour, herbs, pepper and salt, plus 1 teaspoon of lard for greasing the pot or terrine
Strips of fat back, or bacon that has been blanched

Grind the meat twice, stir in flour, onion, alcohol, egg, and seasonings. Grease the terrine, pack in the meat, set in a pan of hot water coming halfway up the side of the terrine, and bake in a moderate oven for 1½ hours with strips of fat on top, and a lid of aluminum foil. Keep for 2 days in a cool place, under a light weight.

What could be simpler or cheaper? As in all *charcuterie*, the performance is not difficult, but care and judgment are at a premium. The most amateur cook can turn out a good pâté, once these four points are understood:

1 · As much fat meat as lean, including the lining strips of fat.
2 · Avoid bacon in large quantities.
3 · Counteract crumbling when cold by the use of egg, a little flour, and jelly, and by cooling under a weight.

4 · Avoid overcooking. The pâté is done when it appears to be floating in its own fat, or when a knitting or larding needle is stuck in the middle and comes out clean.

PORK TERRINES

Pâté de Campagne

BASIC METHOD

1½ lbs. lean, boned shoulder of pork (*épaule*)

3 oz. veal, ham, or lean beef

½ lb. leaf lard (*panne*)

½ lb. fat back (*gras dur*), cut into strips, or bacon, blanched

½ lb. pork belly, or sow-belly (*lard de poitrine*)

½ lb. onions, chopped (2 cups)

6 tablespoons butter or lard

½ cup dry white wine

2–3 oz. brandy, Calvados, *marc*, or *eau-de-vie*

2 level tablespoons flour

1 large egg, beaten

Seasonings—salt, pepper, *quatre-épices*, nutmeg, mace, crushed juniper berries, thyme, parsley, garlic, etc.

If the butcher won't cut the fat back into thin slices, and you can't do it without slicing yourself, cut it as thin as you can safely manage, then beat it out with a wooden mallet. Salt and pepper lightly, leave in the cool. Caul fat, softened in tepid water, is a good substitute.

Chop all the other meat finely. Put it through the grinder if you must, but the ideal is very small dice. Mix in the seasonings you have chosen, and the alcohol, and leave to marinade overnight.

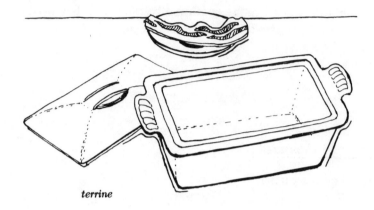

terrine

Next day cook the onions gently in the butter or lard until they are a golden hash. Do not brown them.

Beat the flour and egg together to a smooth paste, and add with the onions to the meat mixture.

Grease a terrine with lard. Any ovenproof dish will in fact do—there is no need to buy one of those dramatic dishes with dead hare lids and simulated pastry sides. Provided it holds 5 cups, it doesn't matter what shape it is. If you like, you can divide the mixture between several smaller dishes.

Some people line the terrine next with short-crust pastry, and cover the meat with a decorated pastry lid. But unless you want that kind of a showpiece (which adds considerably to your labor), a lining of pork fat strips is quite enough. (See raised pies, page 100.)

Stand the terrine in a larger pan of hot water, which should come about halfway up the side, and bake in a slow oven for 1½–3 hours, according to the depth of the dish: small but deep dishes of pâté take longer than wide shallow ones. Oven temperature should be about 340°F. The pâté is done when it appears to swim in fat, quite free of the sides of the terrine; you can also test it with a metal knitting or larding needle—if it comes out clean, the pâté's cooked.

The seasoning of pâtés is a personal affair, but allow for the fact that foods to be eaten cold need more seasoning than foods to be eaten hot. It's prudent to try out a small rissole (fried or baked) before irrevocably committing the pâté to the oven. Should you have overdone the seasoning, add more chopped meat, or—in desperate situations—some bread crumbs.

Fill the terrine absolutely full, and mound over the top— it will shrink in the cooking. Lay a lattice of fat pork strips on top and cover with foil.

You can also cook pâtés like steamed puddings, on top of the stove. If you want an addition to the store cupboard, try bottling the pâté in preserving jars like fruit. It needs 2 hours' cooking. This is widely done in France.

Pâté can be served straight from the cooking dish. If you do this, remove the foil 20 minutes before the end of cooking time so that the top can brown appetizingly. Cool for an hour, then weight it gently.

Remember that it will taste better the next day.

For very elegant meals, the pâté is finished with meat jelly. If there is much fat, pour it off, add the jelly in a liquid state, and don't weight the pâté until the jelly is beginning to set. Be careful to eat the pâté within three days if you have a refrigerator, within 2 days at most if you haven't, for jelly sours quickly. Turn to page 40, aspic jelly, for the recipe—flavor finally with Madeira or port.

If the pâté is to be the main dish of a meal, serve a green salad with it, and some small pickled gherkins. In France crusty bread is always served too, but English factory bread is flabby —so is American commercial white bread—and needs toasting, or, better still, baking in thin slices to a golden-brown crispness.

Although bottling is the best way of keeping pâté, it also keeps well under a ½-inch layer of lard, in a cool, dry larder. A month is a safe length of time. To do this, allow the pâté to cool for an hour, then weight it not too heavily (a dish with

MAKING A PÂTÉ

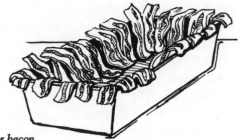

line terrine with fat strips or bacon

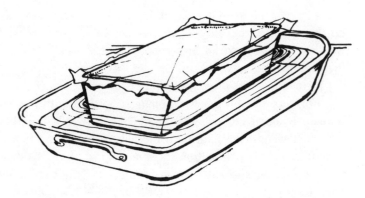

put in pan half full of water, cover with foil

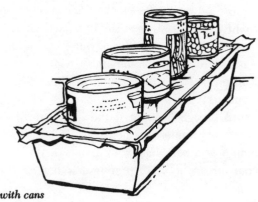

cooked pâté weighted with cans

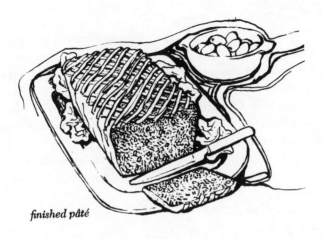

finished pâté

a couple of tins on top, or a foil-covered board). Next day melt plenty of good-quality lard and pour it over the pâté, so that it is completely covered to the depth of half an inch. When the lard has set cover it with aluminum foil, smoothing it on right close to the fat. Then put another piece of foil over the top, as if you were finally covering a jam pot.

Pâté de Foie de Porc

1½ lbs. pig's liver, weighed when hard bits are removed
1½ lbs. sowbelly, salted in mild brine for 12 hours (page 191)—*or* 1 lb. fresh sowbelly, ½ lb. streaky bacon
½ lb. leaf lard

Strips of hard fat back to line terrine and cover *or* a large piece of caul fat
1 large egg
3 tablespoons flour blended with ½ cup dry white wine
Seasonings to taste

Follow the preceding recipe.

Pâté de Foie Fine

1 lb. pig's liver
½ lb. lean veal (fillet), weighed without bone (*rouelle de veau*)
½ lb. cooked ham fat, or very fatty ham
2¼ cups fresh white bread crumbs soaked in a little milk
2 large eggs
¼ cup brandy or other hard liquor

½ cup chopped parsley
Salt and spices according to taste, including a bay leaf
¾ cup onion melted in some lard (*do not brown it*)
Plenty of fat *bardes* to line the terrine and cover

Grind the meat finely—mix everything together, except *bardes* and bay leaf.

Whirl in the electric blender, if you have one, or put through the grinder again.

Finish according to the BASIC METHOD, laying the bay leaf on top of the final cover of fat.

Pâté de Foie

(Very simple, suitable for children's sandwiches.)

¾ lb. pig's liver
2 lbs. sowbelly
½ cup chopped onions, melted in butter

1 large egg beaten with 2 heaped tablespoons flour
Salt, parsley, spices
Strips of pork fat to line and cover, or caul fat

Grind or chop the meat. Mix everything together except the strips of pork fat to line the terrine.

Finish according to the BASIC METHOD.

Fromage de Foie d'Italie

½ lb. pig's liver
1½ lbs. sowbelly
½ lb. leaf lard
Strips of pork fat or caul
fat to line terrine and
cover
1 large egg

4 tablespoons flour mixed
with ⅓ cup dry white
wine
¼ cup brandy or hard
liquor
Salt, spices, parsley

Grind the meat, except for the fat strips, then mix it in the electric blender with the other ingredients. If you cannot do this, grind the meat several times as finely as you can.

Finish according to the BASIC METHOD.

Pâté for Picnics

James Beard gives this recipe of his mother's in *Delights and Prejudices*. I have reduced the quantities, and do not restrict its consumption to picnics.

———→ *Forcemeat* ←———

½ lb. chicken livers, stiffened in 4 tablespoons
(½ stick) butter
1 lb. fillet of veal, weighed
without bone
1 lb. lean sowbelly
½ onion, chopped (about
⅓ cup)
1 large egg

3 cloves garlic
1½ tablespoons salt
½ teaspoon ground black
pepper
5 oz. brandy
½ teaspoon thyme, ¼ tea-
spoon savory, a pinch
of nutmeg and ground
clove

Make the forcemeat first. Whirl the livers in the blender with the egg, garlic cloves, the ½ onion, and ¼ cup of the brandy. If you don't have a blender, you will have to chop it all finely.

Grind the veal and sowbelly, and mix all the ingredients for the forcemeat together by hand.

Filling

1 lb. cold tongue	Bacon strips, blanched, to
½ lb. leaf lard	line and cover
plus	

Cut the filling into long strips (⅜ inch thick for the tongue, ¼ inch thick for the pork fat).

Line the terrine with the bacon strips (or fat pork *bardes*). Lay in a layer of forcemeat, then a layer of tongue-and-pork-fat strips. Repeat, then cover with a layer of forcemeat. Cover with more bacon or *bardes*. Bake (in a *bain-marie*—in other words a pan quarter filled with hot water) for 2½ to 3 hours at 325°.

Cool and serve in thin slices. It will keep in a refrigerator for a week, but wrap it in foil to keep it moist.

NOTE: This demonstrates the method used for many game pâtés—layers of a fine forcemeat alternating with strips of solid meat. Here is an even grander recipe, from the Restaurant Cazalis at Chartres:

Le Pâté de Viande de Chartres

———➤ Forcemeat ◄———

1 lb. lean picnic shoulder of pork	2 tablespoons cognac or other brandy
1 lb. lean veal fillet	¼ cup port
½ lb. chicken livers	5 egg yolks
1½ lbs. hard fat back	1 cup cream
1½ oz. spices	Salt, pepper

——— *Filling* ———

½ lb. tongue
½ lb. ham
¼ lb. veal fillet
¼ lb. hard fat back

} All cut in strips and marinaded for 2 hours in some brandy

——— *Also* ———

1½ lbs. puff pastry

Line the terrine with pastry, keeping back enough for the lid (see also raised pies, page 100). Layer forcemeat, filling, forcemeat, filling, and finally forcemeat, as in the preceding recipe. Put on the pastry lid and decorate. Do not stand in a pan of water, but bake in a slow oven for 2 to 2½ hours, protecting the top when necessary with greaseproof paper.

When the pâté is quite cold, pour in meat jelly (page 40) flavored with port. Do this through a funnel by way of vents in the pastry lid. Or remove the lid carefully with a sharp, pointed knife, so that it can be replaced tidily when the jelly has been poured over the filling.

RABBIT, POULTRY, AND GAME PÂTÉS (PÂTÉ DE LAPIN, DE POULE, DE DINDE, D'OIE, DE CANARD, DE GIBIER)

RABBIT PÂTÉS

In early October, we are honored—and appalled—by an invitation to inspect the finest rabbits in the *vigneron's* hutches, so that a proper choice may be made for the wine-harvest lunch pâté. The ritual victim is then fed, and fed. Ten days later, feeling squeamish, the women in the family sit in the Beaubrun's cool, pale-green kitchen, chopping and mixing the ingredients for the pâté, while Fernande Beaubrun prepares the *poule au riz* which will be eaten afterwards. In the vineyard beyond the village, Maurice Beaubrun works hard with preparations for the next day's work, cursing cheerfully—and filthily—under his breath. There is much excitement, particularly if the summer has been hot and the grapes are sweet and full. Because of these associations perhaps, this is, to me, the best of all pâtés:

Pâté de Vendange

2½ lbs. rabbit meat, weighed without bones
2 lbs. fat sowbelly
½ lb. lean veal or ham, uncooked
1 lb. onions, chopped (about 3½ cups)
Plenty of garlic and thyme

Salt and pepper
About 1 cup *rosé* or white wine
¼ cup *marc* or brandy
Extra fat back, cut in strips, to line the terrines
3 tablespoons flour
2 eggs

Chop or grind the rabbit, sowbelly, and veal. Mix in the chopped onions and seasonings, and pour on the wine and brandy. Leave, if you can, to marinade for 4 hours.

Line the terrines with the strips of fat pork.

Make the flour into a cream with some of the marinading liquor, beat in the eggs, and add to the meat and onions.

Pack into the lined terrines, cover with a layer of strips of fat. Seal on the lids with a flour-and-water paste, stand them in pans of hot water, and cook in a slow oven for 3 hours. Let the pâtés cool for 5 hours with the lids still in place.

Pâté de Lapin (a second method)

2½ lbs. rabbit, weighed
  after boning
½ lb. veal, weighed after
  boning
¼ lb. ham
¼ lb. lean sowbelly

¼ lb. hard fat back
Strips of fat back to line
  pot
2 tablespoons brandy
Herbs, spices, salt

———•➤ The Stock ➤•———

The rabbit bones, skin from
  the belly, and the ham
1 veal bone or beef bone
2 carrots
3 large onions
1 leek

1 cup water
1 cup dry white wine (or
  rosé)
Pepper and *bouquet garni*
  and spices
NO SALT to start with

Ask the butcher to chop the veal or beef bone. Put all the ingredients for the stock into a pan, simmer for an hour, then boil hard to reduce by half—which is why you do not add salt until the very end.

Of course this stock can be made in advance and simmer for longer.

All the meat—except for the lining strips—can be ground. Alternatively you can lay aside some nice pieces of rabbit and veal, and grind the rest. If you follow the latter method, you will layer forcemeat and pieces in the terrine, starting and ending with forcemeat.

Mix the brandy and seasonings with the forcemeat. Leave in a cool larder for an hour or two (preferably two), whilst the stock is finishing.

Line the terrine with fat, put in the meat, cover with a layer of fat and pour in the stock. Cover with aluminum foil, and bake for 2 hours standing in a pan of water in a slow to moderate oven.

For poultry and game pâtés, many French recipes insist that the final flavor is better if you do not remove the lid of the terrine until the pâté is quite cold. Baking pâté in a pastry case is said to conserve the flavor too. You will often notice in French restaurants and *charcuteries* that it is the finest pâtés, and the most expensive, that have received this treatment. Lark pâtés from Pithiviers, duck pâtés from Amiens, for instance.

However, I think that a double layer of aluminum foil, pressed and tied firmly onto the terrine, is the simplest and most efficient way to seal in the flavors. And in the matter of game and poultry pâtés, I leave the foil lid completely undisturbed until the pâté has cooled for several hours. This differs from the finishing of pork pâtés, which have their foil lids removed 20 minutes before the end of cooking time so that the tops brown nicely.

Pâté .de Lapin (a third method)

1 lb. rabbit, weighed when boned

1 lb. veal, weighed when boned

1 lb. sowbelly, weighed when boned

½ lb. hard fat back

6 oz. scraps of meat, left from the weighing of rabbit, veal, and pork, made up with ham

Onions melted in lard or butter, parsley, thyme, garlic to taste

Salt and pepper

Chop and spice the first three ingredients.

Make a good reduced stock with the bones, and wine, as in the previous recipe.

Cut the hard fat back into small dice—*do not grind*. Grind the onions and meat scraps, if you have any, together; mix in with fat back, add herbs and seasonings.

Grease a terrine thoroughly—no lining strips of fat, this time —with either butter or lard. Lay in a layer of rabbit-veal-pork, then a layer of the onion-fat mixture. Do this once again, then cover with a final layer of the rabbit, etc. Pour over the reduced stock, and fix the lid onto the terrine with a flour-and-water dough. Cook as for the previous recipe.

NOTE: This recipe can be adapted to suit goose, duck, game, instead of rabbit. There should be equal quantities of whatever creature you choose, veal, and sowbelly. Vary the other ingredients accordingly.

Terrine de Lapin

I find that this is the most successful hot rabbit recipe, as well as one of the simplest. It is, in effect, a hot pâté or pie—which I have put here as it does not require pastry, as most hot pâtés do.

1 rabbit
Plenty of strips of hard fat back
Plenty of chopped onions— about ½ to ¾ lb.
2 medium carrots, chopped

Plenty of thyme
Garlic, spices, salt and pepper, according to taste
Dry white wine or *rosé*
¼ cup brandy or *eau-de-vie* or *marc*

Joint the rabbit, then cut the joints into suitable serving pieces. Do not bone.

Line the terrine with strips of fat, as if you were going to make an ordinary pâté.

Put in a layer of rabbit, then a good layer of chopped vegetables, thyme, spices, and so on, then a few strips of fat —no need to cover the layer completely. Then another layer of rabbit, the rest of the vegetables and spices, then a complete cover of strips of fat. Pour in enough dry white wine or *rosé* to come about halfway up the meat, and ¼ cup brandy or *eau-de-vie* or *marc*.

Fix the lid on with flour-and-water paste, or use a double layer of foil as a lid, stand the terrine in a shallow pan of hot water, and cook in a slow oven for 2 hours.

Serve with boiled potatoes and a plain green salad to follow. This recipe sounds disgustingly fatty—but it isn't. The best flavor is obtained by using a wild rabbit (*lapin de la garenne*).

———•◦•———

CHICKEN AND TURKEY PÂTÉS

It is not worth making a chicken pâté with a battery hen.* Try and choose a hen you know—or that the poulterer knew— had once run around in a yard, scratching in the grass and weeds, pecking up good corn and generally improving its post-mortem flavor. In other words an honest boiling fowl—which you in America would call an old hen, cock, or rooster. If you are using a turkey, or part of a turkey, round about Christmas, it should be quite easy to get a well-flavored bird; the kind that hang up plucked, except for a few throat and head feathers, rather than the kind in a polythene bag in the deep freeze. Battery turkey is slightly more worth using than battery chicken—but only marginally so, and considering the expense of such a large bird I would not bother with it.

Pâté de Poule, or de Dinde

½ lb. nice pieces of chicken or turkey breast

2 lbs. boned chicken or turkey, taken from the rest of the bird

½ lb. picnic shoulder of pork

½ lb. hard fat back

½ lb. veal

½ lb. ham (if you can't get veal, use ¾ lb. each of pork and ham)

Strips of hard fat back to line and cover the terrine, or caul fat

1½ tablespoons salt

Pepper, *quatre-épices*, or other spices to taste

¼ cup brandy

2 large eggs

* "Battery" is the English derogatory and descriptive adjective for chickens bred under factory conditions, rather than in a farmyard where they can run about and be fed on corn. In the author's opinion these chickens are fattened too quickly, killed too soon, and have no flavor.

Put aside the pieces of breast and the strips of fat, whilst you grind the rest of the meat and mix it together with the seasonings, eggs, and brandy.

Line the terrine with strips of fat, layer in the forcemeat and pieces of breast, starting and ending with forcemeat. Cover with a layer of strips of fat, and a double foil lid. Set the terrine in a shallow pan of hot water, and cook in a slow oven (325°F.) for 2 to 3 hours according to the age of the chicken. If you are worried about its antiquity, try the pâté after 2 hours with a metal knitting needle. It will come out clean if the pâté is cooked. Turkey should be ready after 2 hours. Cool under a light weight.

Pâté de Poule, or de Dinde (a second recipe)

Breast of chicken (or turkey) cut in nice pieces (about ½ lb.)

2 lbs. boned chicken (or turkey)

1½ lbs. lean pork

1½ lbs. salted fat sowbelly (or 1 lb. salted lean sowbelly, plus ½ lb. hard fat back—or ¾ lb. streaky bacon, plus ¾ lb. hard fat back)

Strips of hard fat back or caul fat to line and cover

Pepper, salt (be discreet, in view of salt pork)

6 heaped tablespoons parsley, chopped

Quatre-épices, or spices preferred

10 juniper berries, crushed

Eau-de-vie, marc, vodka, or brandy

Follow the method of the previous recipe.

The following three pâtés are delicious, but I doubt I would make them unless I had an electric blender. If you are a patient siever, or "Mouliner," you might like to try them but it is certainly hard and heating work.

Chicken-Liver Pâté

Elizabeth David's version, quoted from *A Book of Mediterranean Food*, is the most popular with our visitors. I do it in the blender, however, putting the liquid from the pan in first then tipping the lightly cooked livers onto the fast whirling blades. Half quantities and a little more butter do very well—however the quantity can be divided amongst several small pots, covered with ½ inch of melted butter, and a foil lid, for eating on different occasions.

"Take about 1 lb. of chicken livers or mixed chicken, duck, pigeon or any game liver. Clean well and sauté in butter for 3 or 4 minutes. Remove the livers and to the butter in the pan add a small glass of sherry and a small glass of brandy. Mash the livers to a fine paste (they should be pink inside) with plenty of salt, black pepper, a clove of garlic, 2 oz. of butter [4 tablespoons], a pinch of mixed spice and a pinch of powdered herbs— thyme, basil and marjoram. Add the liquid from the pan, put the mixture into a small earthenware terrine and place on the ice.

"Serve with hot toast."

Le Gâteau de Foie Blond de Poularde de Bresse au Coulis de Queues d'Écrevisses

This famous but, as Elizabeth David says, "virtually uncookable" dish, was originally described in *La Cuisine au pays du Brillat Savarin*, by Lucien Tendret, published in 1892. The combination of chicken liver and shellfish may sound odd—but it works.

½ lb. chicken livers
⅛ lb. beef marrow
2 tablespoons concentrated jelly or juice from roast beef

⅜ cup milk
2 whole eggs plus 2 egg yolks
½ clove garlic, pepper, salt

Whirl the ingredients in an electric blender; otherwise pound the livers, mix in the other ingredients, and put through a sieve. You should end up with a thick cream. Pour it into a well-oiled soufflé dish or pudding basin, leaving plenty of room for the mixture to rise without spilling over. Cover with foil, tied on with string, and stand on a rack in a pan of cold water, coming halfway up the side of the dish. Bring slowly to just below the boil—a shudder should be heard from time to time, that's all; leave to simmer for 1½ hours.

Meanwhile make the sauce:

20 freshwater crayfish	2 egg yolks
6 tablespoons (¾ stick) softened butter	¼ lb. mushrooms, chopped small, cooked in a little
½ cup heavy cream	butter (about 1 cup)

Whirl the first four ingredients, cook them slowly in a basin over a pan of hot, not boiling, water. Stir from time to time, but provided you keep the temperature of the hot water below boiling point you will not need to hang over it. At the very last moment, when the *gâteau de foie* is turned out onto a hot serving plate, add the mushrooms to the sauce and pour over the *gâteau*.

Pâté de Dinde et Foie de Porc

If you are roasting a large turkey, catch it before the legs are quite cooked and save them until you can make this pâté. Use butter to roast the turkey, and keep its liver to one side.

Cut the meat off the turkey legs and weigh it.

———→ *Add* ←———

⅔ of the weight in pig's liver	Strips of fat pork to line and cover the terrine
⅔ of the weight in fat sow-belly (salted or fresh)	Parsley, spices, garlic, salt and pepper to taste
⅔ of the weight in the fat from roasting the turkey	1 bay leaf
Turkey liver	¼ cup *eau-de-vie,* brandy, vodka, or *marc*

Because the turkey is half-cooked, this pâté does not spend so much time in the oven, and the oven should not be quite so warm. Grind both livers and sowbelly, cut turkey into ¼-inch dice. Put the alcohol and half of the turkey fat, melted, into the electric blender and spoon the minced meat in. Whirl everything as smooth as possible, adding a little more turkey fat and seasonings to taste. If you don't care for the thought of tasting, bake a little in the oven and try that. Add diced turkey.

Line the terrine with the strips of fat pork, pour in the mixture, cover with more strips, and a double layer of foil as a lid. Set the dish in a shallow pan of hot water and bake for ¾ to 1 hour at 310°.

Like the chicken-liver pâté, this one improves with a day or two's keeping. If you want to keep it longer run melted butter over the top to a depth of ½ inch.

Serve with hot toast, or bread baked in the oven in crisp slices.

———•◆•———

PÂTÉ DE FOIE GRAS, AND GOOSE PÂTÉ

I suspect that some of the emotion turned against factory-farming in our country is stimulated by the tastelessness of the result. Were battery chicken as delectable as foie gras, what then?

Consider the French and foie gras—"Les oies sont des animaux rustiques par excellence qui coutent peu à nourrir" (and they also like to overeat, so they are easily fattened) "et permettent de preparer de succulentes charcuteries dont la finesse et la délicatesse sont d'une renommée mondiale." In other words the goose supplies a comfortable combination of gastronomic excellence, thrift, and *la gloire*.

Professor Zeuner considered that there is no evidence for or against the statement that the goose was the earliest bird to be domesticated. The word for goose in all Indo-European languages is the same, but it is the Romans who seem to have been the first to attempt a foie gras on modern lines, and they liked to buy a special breed of geese from Germania and Belgian Gaul, which were driven in slow herds over the Alps to Rome. Recent estimates and experiments suggest that this was a six months' walk.

The foie gras goose is much larger than our common gray farmyard goose or your domesticated American goose, and provides far more fat, in which the famous *confits d'oie* are preserved (page 330), as well. The names of the two related breeds, Toulouse and Strasbourg, give an indication of the best areas in which to find good foie gras. Geese are fed intensively on a diet of hard-boiled eggs, soaked bread crumbs, potato mash, skimmed milk, oats, and barley mash—in other words, the antique diet of cereal mushes fed to Penelope's geese in Homeric times. But the process of *gavage* is a modern one, comparatively speaking, whereby the enlargement of the goose's liver is completed by funneling a mash of maize into the creature's throat. The funnel is thoughtfully provided with a rounded rim, so that no injury occurs. The fattening geese are also kept in a confined space at a steady temperature. Sometimes with their feet nailed down.

Foie gras is enormously expensive, whether you buy it in Strasbourg or Fortnum and Mason's.* Supported by its essential ally, the truffle, you may see it for sale in Périgueux in January or February, in its unprepared state.

Pâté de Foie Gras aux Truffes

Soak a fine foie gras (they can weigh up to 3½ lbs.) in cold water overnight, after you have carefully removed any dark greenish parts stained by contact with the gall. Next day dry it very carefully with a cloth, slice in half and trim to a good shape. Make little slashes with the point of a sharp knife, so that small pieces of truffle can be inserted. Season with salt and pepper, and marinade for an hour at least in some brandy or good *eau-de-vie* or Madeira.

* Or in an American fancy-food store or butcher.

Meanwhile make the forcemeat. The proportions of sow-belly, liver trimmings, and truffles vary a great deal in different recipes—they can be 6 : 1½ : 1, or 1½ : 6 : ½. The mixture should be bound with an egg and seasoned.

Line a terrine with thin strips of pork fat or blanched bacon. Lay in one third of the forcemeat, then half the liver; then another third of the forcemeat, the second half of the liver, and finally the last of the forcemeat. Pour over the marinade juices, cover with foil, and cook in a slow oven in a shallow pan of hot water for 2 to 3 hours according to the depth of the terrine.

Foie Gras en Brioche

Truffle and marinade the foie gras as in the preceding recipe.

Meanwhile make a *brioche* dough and as it rises bake the foie gras for 15–25 minutes, according to size, in a slow oven, wrapped in a piece of caul fat. Let it cool down until it is warm, then line the mold you intend to use with the *brioche* dough, put in the foie gras, and make a lid of dough. Leave it to prove and bake at 400°. Before you put it in the oven brush over with beaten egg and water for a good glaze. This is a good recipe for stretching foie gras, if you have individual popover tins or the fluted French *brioche* tins. Of course they will not take so long to cook—20 minutes for the small ones, and 40 minutes for the large.

See *saucisse en brioche* (page 164) for dough recipe.

Pâté d'Oie

Supposing you have the whole goose, you could make a goose-neck sausage (page 124), an *halicot* of the wings, feet, and carcass, some *confits* (page 331), and this terrine:

2 lbs. goose meat (include
 the heart and lungs)
Goose liver (foie gras)
1 lb. veal, weighed without
 bones
1 lb. sowbelly, weighed
 without bones

Truffle parings
2 large eggs
¼ to ½ cup of brandy,
 eau-de-vie, or Madeira
Salt, pepper

Make a forcemeat from all the ingredients except the liver,
though the trimmings from the liver may be included. Line the
terrine with strips of pork fat, arrange the forcemeat and liver,
and cook as in the first recipe for *pâté de foie gras*.

I have made this terrine successfully, though less exotically,
with a common goose, and an ordinary goose liver.

Foie Gras aux Raisins

Marinade the foie gras in Madeira, after seasoning it well, for at
least an hour. Wrap it up well in some caul fat and put it into
an ovenproof casserole. Pour over the marinade juices, put the
lid on and cook in a moderate oven for 30 to 40 minutes, pouring
on a little more Madeira after 15 minutes. Prepare some grapes
by peeling and pipping them, and add them to the foie gras
after you have poured off the juice and removed the fat.

Pour back the juice, and cook the foie gras in a slow oven
for a further 20 minutes.

Alternatively you can fry slices of foie gras in butter, and
serve them on slices of fried bread, decorated with peeled and
pipped grapes. Keep them hot in the oven while you dilute the
pan juices with a Frontignan or Muscadel wine. Pour over the
slices of foie gras.

If you are lucky, you may find these dishes on a menu in
the Languedoc, made with either goose or duck liver.

DUCK PÂTÉS

Duck pâtés vary from the usual layered forcemeat and meat style of game and poultry pâtés, to a virtual galantine (page 111) in which the skin is stuffed with fine forcemeat and liver or foie gras. In France ducks are fed, like Toulouse and Strasbourg geese, with a maize mash until they reach 9 or even 11 lbs. The liver weighs up to 1½ lbs. in the largest birds, and its flavor is said to be even more delicate than that of *foie gras d'oie*. However, it has the great disadvantage of dissolving into fat when cooked, far more than goose liver does. Any *foie gras d'oie* recipe can be used.

Good-sized deep-freeze ducklings can quite well serve for the following recipes. But don't expect the full flavor of the best duck pâtés made in France, at Amiens for instance, or in Normandy at Duclair or Rouen, or in Languedoc.

Terrine de Canard

2 lbs. boned duck, including the heart
The duck liver
½ lb. boned veal
½ lb. sowbelly
Strips of pork fat or blanched bacon to line terrine
2 oz. truffles (optional)

2–3 oz. Madeira or brandy, or both
1 large egg
Salt, pepper, thyme, parsley
(¼ cup orange juice and some grated orange rind can be used)

Cut some of the duck flesh into nice strips or dice, and leave them overnight in the alcohol, and orange juice if used, together with seasoning.

Next day prepare the forcemeat with the rest of the duck, the veal, and the sowbelly, ground or chopped finely. Bind with the egg, season with salt and pepper, and herbs.

Line the terrine with strips of pork fat or bacon. Lay in a layer of the forcemeat, then a layer of the marinaded duck, the liver cut into pieces, and the truffles. Repeat this, and cover finally with a layer of the forcemeat. Cover with strips of pork fat, and a foil lid, and cook for 2 hours in a slow oven in a shallow pan of hot water.

—— *Either* ——

Cool for at least 5 hours, without removing the lid; cover with ½ inch of lard and the pâté will keep for weeks in a cool, dry place.

—— *Or* ——

If you want to serve the pâté almost immediately, pour off the fat as soon as it is cooked and replace with a well-flavored jelly made from the duck bones. Add some Madeira or brandy to it, and some gelatin if it doesn't set well—test this by preparing the jelly the previous day and leaving it to set overnight. Take no chances.

Pâté de Canard

1 duck, with its liver, and
extra livers or foie gras
2 lbs. lean pork
½ lb. fat sowbelly
Truffles (optional)

2–3 oz. brandy or Madeira
1 large egg
Salt, pepper, and *quatre-
épices* or mixed spices

Bone the duck (or persuade the butcher to do this for you), and remove as much of the flesh as possible without tearing the skin. Leave the legs alone.

Chop or grind the duck meat and the pork, leaving it for 2 hours to marinade with the brandy or Madeira and seasonings. Bind with the egg.

Lay the skin of the duck out flat, inside up, and put half the forcemeat in the middle, flattening it out. Next put a layer of the duck liver and foie gras and truffles. Then the rest of the force-meat. Pat this into a nice shape, so that the livers, etc., are completely enclosed in the forcemeat, then wrap the skin round and sew it into shape. Grease a terrine and press the duck gently into it, easing in the legs, so that the whole thing lies tidily. Cover with strips of fat pork, then a foil lid. Bake in a moderate oven for 1½ hours.

Serve quite cold.

Pâté de Canard d'Amiens

1 duck, with its liver
Enough short-crust pastry to line and cover the dish, made with half as much butter as flour, and cold water to mix, plus a pinch of salt for flavor
2–3 oz. foie gras (or ¼ lb. chicken livers)
Truffles (optional)
1 lb. sowbelly
½ lb. rabbit
½ lb. lean pork

½ cup meat jelly or good stock
½ cup Madeira
½ cup brandy
2 medium eggs
Salt, pepper, thyme, bay leaf
¼ lb. mushrooms
2 to 3 tablespoons butter
Enough strips of pork fat to cover the bottom of the dish

Ask the butcher to bone the duck; or do so yourself by cutting it along the back, and easing the flesh carefully off the bones without breaking the skin. You need a small sharp knife with a good point.

Make the short-crust pastry.

Make the forcemeat. Chop the mushrooms small and cook them down in 2 to 4 tablespoons of butter. Chop the livers, truffles, pork, rabbit, and mix them all together. Heat the *eau-de-vie* or brandy in a small pan, set it alight, and pour it over the chopped meat, etc. Add the mushrooms, eggs, meat jelly, Madeira, seasonings, and herbs. Whirl it in the. Food Processor or blender, or put it twice through the finest blade of the grinder to get it as smooth as possible.

Stuff the duck with a third of this forcemeat, or a little less, and fold it over into shape.

Line the terrine with pastry, lay on it a layer of strips of pork fat, then some of the forcemeat and the duck. Pack the rest of the forcemeat round and over the duck, covering finally with a few fat strips of pork and a pastry lid. Make a hole in the middle, and decorate suitably. Brush with egg. Bake in a moderate oven for an hour and a half, placing greaseproof paper over the crust if it colors too quickly.

Make a good jelly from the duck carcass and pork bones, flavoring it with Madeira. Pour this into the pâté through a funnel next day and leave to set.

NOTE: You can make a very attractive-looking pâté by not using the terrine. Cut two pastry ovals larger than the duck, which should be completely covered with the forcemeat before being laid on one oval, and covered by the other; press the pastry edges firmly together, decorate the top and make a hole in the middle. Brush with egg and bake.

It should need about 1½ hours, and will have to be protected by a double layer of greaseproof paper. Pour in the jelly next day.

This is the old way of making the Amiens duck pâté; though the duck was not boned, but three-quarters cooked before the pâté was put together. Nowadays boning the duck makes the whole thing much easier to deal with, both from a cooking and from an eating point of view.

———•◆•———

GAME PÂTÉS

The great area for game pâtés in France is the Orléanais, covering much of the departments of Loir-et-Cher, Eure-et-Loir, and Loiret.

Partridge (*perdreau*), lapwing (*vanneau*), larks (*alouettes* or *mauviettes*), thrushes (*grives*), and hares (*lièvres*) with "golden coats, the colour of ripe corn," fatten on the wide corn-fields of the Beauce which stretch from Blois to Chartres, and on the abundant vineyards of the Loire. So if you are by good fortune in these golden, blue-skied districts after the corn and wine harvests, in October, look for the game pâtés of Chartres, the very famous lark pâtés of Pithiviers, and the thrush pâtés of Gien, because you will not be able legally to make them for yourself when you return home.

A little further south the Sologne shelters the finest game in all France, in the meres and woods which replace now its ancient, ague-ridden marshes. There you might find woodcock (*bécasse*) on the restaurant menu, the finest of game birds.

At Christmastime, you will find a magnificent choice of game pâtés in Paris and other large towns, at the leading *charcuteries*. But for most of us in England, Scotland, Wales, and Ireland, it comes down to the pigeon (*pigeonneau*, U.S. squab), or hare, with an occasional grouse (*tétras*) or capercaillie, pheasant (*faisan*), or partridge (*perdreau*). Pâté is an excellent way of serving an elderly bird—particularly if you have a number of guests, who would otherwise not get more than a mouthful. Very small amounts of game can be neatly diced and mixed into a very smooth forcemeat of equal quantities of lean and fat pork, but here is a slightly more elaborate and traditional method:

Game Pâté

Bone your animal, setting aside the nicest pieces to make a layer or two later on in the terrine. Weigh the rest, making it up to 1½ lbs. with veal. Add 1½ lbs. hard fat back and grind finely.

Bind the mixture with 3 eggs, and as much brandy as you can muster up to a good ½ cup. If you're short on spirits, make up the volume with dry white wine, or stock made from the bones of the game. Season with salt, pepper, spices, thyme, parsley, and crushed juniper berries. Leave in a cool place for several hours or overnight. Line the terrine (6-cup capacity) with strips of pork fat, layer forcemeat and game pieces, beginning and ending with forcemeat. Put a few fat strips on top, and a foil lid. Stand in a pan of hot water and bake for 2 to 2¾ hours. Cool under a light weight. Keep for 24 hours.

Gâteau de Lièvre

Here is an old recipe for a hare pâté. Try it if you are having a large party, but it is prudent to bake the mixture in several terrines rather in the one large stewpan recommended, then you can run a layer of lard over any you do not use at the time, and keep them for several weeks.

"Chop all the meat of a hare, and of a rabbit, half a leg of mutton, two pounds of fillet of veal or fresh pork, and two pounds of beef suet; season these with pepper and salt, fine spices pounded, chopped parsley, shallots, a quarter of a pound of pistachio nuts peeled, about a pound of raw ham"—use uncooked gammon (prosciutto, etc.)—"cut into dice, half a pound of truffles or mushrooms also cut into dice, six yolks of eggs, and one glass of good brandy; garnish a stew-pan all round with slices of lard, put all your preparation close into it, and cover it over with slices of lard"—i.e. hard fat back, not the modern lard but the French *lard*—"also, rather thick; stop the pan all round with a coarse paste, and bake it about four hours; let it cool in the same pan, then turn it over gently; scrape the lard quite off, or leave a little of it, and garnish it with any sorts of colours; or to make it more even, and to give it a better form, cover it over with hog's lard or butter, in order to garnish it with different colours according as your taste shall direct."

Game pâtés can be tackled quite a different way, as these two recipes from *French Provincial Cooking*, by Elizabeth David, show:

Terrine de Gibier (Game Pâté)

"A wild duck (mallard), 1½ lbs of fat pork, ¼ lb fat, mild bacon, seasonings and white wine as above" (¾ cup).

"The orthodox way to make a game pâté is to strip all the flesh off the bird in its raw state. It is a tedious, wasteful process until you have done it many times, so it is permissible to half roast the bird, let it cool, and then remove and mince [grind] or chop the meat.

"Put your duck, therefore, to roast for 20 minutes or so in a medium hot oven. When cool remove all the meat and discard the skin, but be careful to preserve as much as possible of the juices which run out during the process. Chop or mince [grind] the meat coarsely. Blend it thoroughly with the minced [ground] pork and 2 oz of the fat bacon, cut into little cubes, and which supply the squares of fat characteristic in these home-made pâtés. Add the seasonings and the wine . . ." and cook in a pan of water in the usual way for 1½ hours, at 310°F.

"Any game birds can be turned into pâté in this way, allowing approximately the equivalent weight in pork of the uncooked weight of the bird. So instead of one mallard you would need three teal, or two stewing partridges, or two large pigeons [squab in U.S.], which make a cheap and excellent pâté. A domestic duck, being so fat, needs only a small proportion of pork, or a mixture of pork and veal.

"For a *terrine de lièvre* or hare pâté, also allow equal proportions of fat pork, or even a little more, for hare is very dry, and the flavour too needs softening to make a successful terrine."

Terrine de Porc et de Gibier (Pork and Game Pâté)

"Here is a pâté on a somewhat larger scale, suitable for a party or for a buffet supper. It will be sufficient for twenty to twenty-five people, and is all the better for being made three or four days in advance.

"Quantities are 2 lbs each of belly of pork and leg of veal (the pieces sold by some butchers as pie [stew] veal will do, as these are usually oddments of good quality trimmed from escalopes and so on), ½ lb of back pork fat, and 1 wild duck or pheasant. For the seasoning you need 2 teacups [1 cup] of dry wine, 1 tablespoon [2 U.S. tablespoons] of salt, 8 to 10 juniper berries, 1 large clove of garlic, 10 peppercorns, 2 tablespoons [½ cup] of stock made from the duck carcase with a little extra white wine or Madeira.

"Mince [grind] the pork and the veal together, or to save time get the butcher to do this for you. Partly roast the duck or pheasant, take all the flesh from the bones, chop fairly small, and mix with the pork and veal. Add 5 oz of the fat cut into little pieces, the garlic, juniper berries, and peppercorns all chopped together, the salt. Pour in the white wine, amalgamate thoroughly, and leave in a cold place while you cook the duck carcase and the trimmings in a little water and wine with seasonings to make the stock. Strain it, reduce to 2 good tablespoons [½ cup], and add to the mixture (if it is necessary to expedite matters, this part of the preparation can be dispensed with altogether; it is to add a little extra gamey flavour to the pâté).

"Turn into a 3-pint [8-cup] terrine; cover the top with a criss-cross pattern of the rest of the pork fat cut into little strips. Cover with foil. Stand in a baking tin containing water, and cook in a low oven, Gas No. 3, 330°F. [330°F. in U.S.], for two hours. During the last 15 minutes remove the paper, and the top of the pâté will cook to a beautiful golden brown.

"One wild duck or pheasant to 4 lb of meat sounds a very small proportion for a game pâté, but will give sufficiently strong flavour for most tastes. Also the seasonings of garlic, pepper, and juniper berries are kept in very moderate proportions when the pâté is for people who may not be accustomed to these rather strong flavours, and with whose tastes one may not be familiar."

RAISED PIES

If you would like to make a setpiece of a pâté, line the terrine with short-crust, puff, or hot-water raised pie pastry, and decorate the lid with crescents and diamonds in the French style, or roses and leaves. If you want to do this, a hinged mold makes the job easier and the final result prettier. They are used in France for pâtés like the one from Chartres on page 78, or for the small lark pâtés to be bought in the autumn in Pithiviers, just as they are for the traditional English pork and raised game pies. Grandmothers can sometimes supply them, or good, old-fashioned kitchen-equipment firms. Some hinged molds are provided with a base, others have to be used on a baking tray. A cheap alternative is a cake pan with a removable base—but then the pie will lack its flamboyant molding.

Finer pâté recipes provide ideas for the filling, or the sweetbread recipe on page 261. The mixture must justify the presentation. Think of most commercial pies on general sale in our country: hopes raised by a golden exterior are sadly disappointed at the first mouthful. For this reason it is worth making your own pies at home with a straightforward, well-seasoned pork mixture of good honest excellence:

Raised Pork Pie

For an oval mold, 4 inches deep, 8½ inches long by 5½ inches across.

—→ Jelly ←—

2 lbs. pork bones, plus a veal knuckle bone or a pig's trotter (foot)
1 medium-sized carrot

1 medium-sized onion stuck with 4 cloves
Bouquet garni
Peppercorns

—→ Filling ←—

2½ lbs. boned shoulder pork or neck, with nearly as much fat as lean meat
½ lb. piece of lean bacon

Sage, or other fresh herbs
Salt, pepper, spices
½ lb. thinly cut back bacon (Canadian bacon) slices

—→ Pastry ←—

1¼ lbs. flour (4¼ cups)
7 oz. water
9 oz. lard

1 teaspoon salt
3 level tablespoons confectioners' sugar

Deal with the jelly first—it can be made the night before, if you like, or else fit in the preparation of the filling and pastry-making, while it simmers. Put the bones and vegetables into a large pan, cover with water and bring to the boil. Fix on the lid and leave to bubble gently for 3 hours. Be sure to add no salt. After 3 hours, strain off the liquid into a clean pan and boil it down hard to about 2½ cups. Season with salt, pepper and a little lemon juice, and put it in a cool place to set.

For the filling, grind ½ lb. of the pork and ¼ lb. of the lean bacon finely together. Cut the rest of the pork into ½-inch cubes, and brown gently in their own fat for 15 to 20 minutes. Cut the rest of the lean bacon into slightly smaller pieces than the pork, put them into a pan, barely cover with cold water, and bring to the boil; drain, mix with the browned cubes of pork, season, and leave in a cool place.

Traditionally the pastry is made on a marble slab. I find a big bowl, or the electric mixer, less messy. First the dry ingredients are sieved together into a mound, in which a well is made. Bring the water and lard to the boil in a saucepan and pour it slowly into the well, mixing everything together with a wooden spoon (or the electric beater). Knead this hot dough until smooth. It needs to be malleable, but not so hot and soft that it slips down the mold when you try to pat it into place.

To assemble the pie, grease the hinged mold and put the lump of pastry into it, keeping aside enough for the lid. Now gently but firmly smooth it up the sides of the mold, paying attention to the crevices and shapings so that they are evenly covered. Cracks must be avoided. Line the pastry with the thinly cut back (Canadian) bacon slices. Put half the ground pork and bacon as a bottom layer and fit in the seasoned cubes. Don't thrust them in or they'll dent the pastry walls. Cover with the other half of the ground meat, doming it gently above the rim of the mold—this gives a pleasantly rounded form to the pastry lid, before the meat shrinks inevitably in the cooking.

Brush the pastry rim with beaten egg. Roll out the pastry lid and fix into place, with a knocked-up edge. Make a central hole, just large enough to take a small kitchen funnel, through which the jelly will be poured in later on. Keep the hole open during baking with a roll of paper, or a pastry rose with a stem, which can be gently removed when the pie is baked. Brush the top with

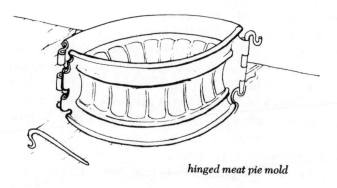

hinged meat pie mold

beaten egg, put on the other decorations and brush them with egg too. Lay three thicknesses of greaseproof or brown paper on top of the pie, and bake at 300° to 320° for 1½ hours. The paper stops the lid of the pie browning too vigorously.

Let the pie cool in a larder for 45 minutes before removing the hinged mold. If you do this too soon, the sides sink outwards in a spare tire, and crack. Brush the sides with beaten egg and return to the oven for them to glaze (protect the top again with paper).

The pie should cool for 2 hours before adding the jelly; it will still be warm enough to absorb it evenly. If you've made the jelly well in advance, reduce it to a semi-liquid state by standing the bowl in some hot water for a few seconds, stirring all the time to keep it smooth. Remove the paper roll or rose from the pie, and pour in the jelly through a funnel or in careful spoonfuls. Serve the pie cold. You will find that the meat has taken a pinkish tinge from the saltpeter used in curing the bacon, and is appetizingly marbled with firm jelly.

HOT PÂTÉS OR PIES

Any pâté mixture can be baked in pastry and served hot as a pie. If you do this, omit the usual lining of pork fat in strips. The sausage-meat recipes on pages 151–5 provide ideas for simpler mixtures. The secret of a good pie is the seasoning, this needs courage and judgment; the rest of the process is easy enough.

Gâteau à la Berrichonne

Once in Paris, near the Palais Royal, we bought a solid-looking but delicious wedge of an enormous wheel of a pie. It was made quite simply of a pork forcemeat or sausage meat baked in flaky pastry, resembling our English fidget pies (sausage meat, layered with grated apple, grated onion, and grated potato in various combinations, which I can thoroughly recommend) but altogether lighter. This is understandable as no rusks or cereal are used in the manufacture of French sausage meat, and more attention is paid to the seasonings. The pork had also spent a few hours in brine (page 200), which gave it a pinkish salt-peter glow.

Use a deep pie plate, so that you are able to have a good inch of filling.

If you use a 9-inch pie plate, you need 1 lb. puff pastry, and 1½ lbs. meat (boneless) for filling. The simplest way in England or America is to buy ½ lb. fat pork, ¾ lb. lean pork, and a generous ¼ lb. of lean bacon (the bacon cure will impart a pinkish appearance to the uncured meat). Alternatively, buy neck or shoulder pork that has a high proportion of fat to lean (about 40 per cent fat to 60 per cent lean), and ask the butcher to put it in brine for a few hours—or brine it yourself. This very mild curing improves the flavor. (*If the butcher has salted the pork for you,* try out an experimental rissole first, before grinding the bulk of the meat. If it's too salty, put the rest of the meat into a pan of cold water, bring gradually to the boil and simmer for 2 minutes. *If you use the mild brine* on page 191 you don't need to do this.)

Grind the meat. Season with parsley and thyme, salt, and freshly ground pepper. Add some *quatre-épices*, or mace, but the predominant seasoning should be herbs, and 2 to 4 table-spoons of fine bread crumbs. If you are making an enormous cartwheel of a pie for a party, you will need proportionately more bread crumbs—⅓ cup to every ½ lb. of meat is about right.

Line the pie plate with just over half the pastry and brush it with white of egg. This keeps it from becoming too soggy. Pack in the filling, cover with the rest of the pastry, decorate, knock up the edges and brush with an egg-yolk-and-water glaze.

Bake in a hot oven for 15 minutes at 425°F., then reduce

the heat to 355°F. for a further half an hour. If your pie is enormous, give it an hour at the reduced temperature, covering the pastry after the first 15 minutes with greaseproof paper.

NOTE: You can layer the meat with grated apple, onion, and potato as they do in the north of England. Some people add defrozen uncooked peas, so that a whole meal is eaten in a convenient form—ideal for picnics, and it tastes nicer warm than very hot. Good solid open-air food, though I always omit the potato as that makes it too solid for most people these days.

GAME AND POULTRY PIES

If you want a more elaborate hot pie, you should layer the forcemeat with strips or small dice of meat (rabbit, hare, chicken, goose, game); or else make small *ballottines* of birds or a larger one of a duck and encircle with forcemeat inside the pastry, like the Amiens duck pâté on page 94. The thing to remember is that for a dry-fleshed animal, a hare for instance, the proportion of fat to lean meat in the forcemeat must be 50/50. For goose or duck, it can be 40/60. Anything extra you can afford to add in the way of truffles or foie gras will turn a good game or chicken pie into an experience long remembered. Everybody has their own preferences for different seasonings. Elizabeth David is a devotee of juniper berries, several cooks I know swear by grated orange rind and juice; at the sight of a rabbit I think of thyme, and when March comes hares require spices and port and hard liquor and red-currant jelly or chocolate.

Pâté Chaud de Ris de Veau, or d'Agneau

Here is a hot pâté of delicate flavor, whose ingredients are within the range of nearly every supermarket-goer. The result, though, does not betray its origins.

1 lb. sweetbreads (calves' or lambs')
Chicken stock
Lemon juice
¾ lb. lean pork (or veal and pork), weighed without bone
¾ lb. hard fat back
2 large eggs, beaten
2 tablespoons flour
½ cup heavy cream
¼ lb. mushrooms

4 tablespoons (½ stick) butter
Seasonings: salt, pepper, and thyme
Enough pastry to line and cover, made of:
2¼ cups flour
10 tablespoons butter and lard combined, or just butter
2 level tablespoons confectioners' sugar, pinch salt, cold water

Stand the sweetbreads in cold, salted water for an hour. Then simmer them for 15 to 20 minutes in chicken stock, sharpened with a little lemon juice. Drain and take off the gristly hard bits and divide them into smallish pieces.

The forcemeat can be made whilst the sweetbreads are soaking. Grind the pork and fat as finely as you can. Add beaten eggs, flour, and cream. If you have an electric blender, whirl the mixture in this. Season with salt and pepper and thyme.

Slice the mushrooms (more than ¼ lb. does not hurt, and if you can use field mushrooms, or even better *trompettes des morts* [*Craterellus cornucopioides*], the flavor will be greatly improved). Fry them lightly in butter. If you have plenty, mix half into the forcemeat after it has been whirled in the blender.

Now assemble the pie. Line a pie dish with pastry, then line the pastry with a thick layer of forcemeat, keeping aside enough to cover. Next put in the sweetbreads and mushrooms, and cover with the last of the forcemeat. Put on a pastry lid, decorate, knock up the edges, and brush with egg-yolk–and–water glaze. Bake in a moderate oven for an hour, protecting the pastry lid with greaseproof paper if necessary.

------•-•-•------

GALANTINES

The derivation of the word "galantine" is obscure. Snow-drops, rushes with aromatic roots, Chinese galangale (a mild spice of the ginger family), gelatin, and the popular fish galen-tines of the Middle Ages have all assisted, incongruously, in the speculations. But from a *charcuterie* point of view, the word takes on interest in the mid-eighteenth century, meaning then "a particular way of dressing a pig," along the lines of the recipes given on pages 246 and 253. By the turn of the century, "galan-tine" was used in France in its modern sense to describe a cold dish of chicken, turkey, etc., and veal, boned, stuffed, simmered in a cloth and pressed, making an elegant appearance swathed in and surrounded by its own jelly. Although talking of fish, Chaucer nicely described the emotions a galantine in its jelly might arouse:

> Was never pyk walwed in galauntyne
> As I in love am walwed and y-wounde.

Such enthusiasm is particularly delightful to the cook, because a galantine is not at all a difficult dish; its preparation is lengthy, but the result is never in question. Like pâté, it should be pre-pared at least a day in advance for all the ingredients to settle down together and mature.

In the *charcuterie*, the galantines look like pale-colored pâtés, with a geometric patterning of fat, truffles, pistachio nuts, tongue, foie gras, and jelly. From a commercial point of view, it is necessary to prepare them in long metal loaf pans, rather than with boned birds, so that every customer's slice has its exact share of all the good things. I find these galantines dis-appointing very often. Their almost classical intarsia prepares one for a supreme experience, and of course one is let down. Galantine of rabbit or pig's head is inevitably prepared in this way, but for attractiveness and flavor, poultry, veal, and game galantines should be tackled like this:

Galantine de Poulet

BASIC METHOD

A chicken, weighing about
4 lbs. when dressed

———— Forcemeat ————

1¼ lbs. lean meat (pork,
pork and veal, or veal
and ham)
1 lb. hard fat back

¼ lb. streaky bacon
2 eggs
Herbs, spices, salt, and
pepper

———— Optional Salpicon ————

Pistachio nuts, blanched
¼ lb. cold pickled tongue
¼ lb. ham fat or pork fat
Truffles

Foie gras
Liver from the chicken
Brandy, Madeira, sherry,
or *eau-de-vie*

———— Stock ————

Calf's foot or pig's trotters
(feet)
Veal, ham, or pork bones
An onion stuck with 4
cloves

1 carrot
Bouquet garni
1½ cups dry white wine
Stock made from chicken
cubes

Choose a mature bird. Battery chicken is useless, as flavor
is needed.

Cut the flesh from neck to tail down the back, and by using a very sharp knife to scrape the flesh off the bone, you will
not find it difficult to achieve a flat, if locally lumpy, oblong of
bird. Do not pierce the skin, though this can be remedied by
removing a piece of flesh from, say the leg, and laying it over
the small tear. The worst part is the legs. Take your time, and
gradually pull the muscles and skin off inside out, as your knife

loosens them from the bone. Lay the final result, skin-side down, on a clean cloth and distribute extra bits of flesh over the thinly covered parts. But don't get fussy and niggly with it. Sprinkle on some salt and pepper, leave in the cool.

Put the carcass on to boil in a large pan, together with a calf's foot or pig's trotters, a ham bone if you have one, an onion stuck with 4 cloves, a carrot, *bouquet garni,* and a mixture of wine and stock. Any other scraps of pork skin, or pork, veal, or poultry bones, would not come amiss. You need as good a stock as you can make.

Assemble any attractive bits and pieces that you can manage —the liver of the bird, foie gras, truffles, pistachio nuts, cold tongue, cold ham, ham fat or pork fat—and decide whether you are going to make a formal arrangement or whether you are going to dice these and mix them right in with a fine forcemeat. This collection of larger pieces is know as a *salpicon.* Leave them to marinade in some brandy or Madeira or sherry.

Make the forcemeat—as fine as you can—of *equal parts of lean and fat meats.* Pork entirely, with a little bacon, if you like; or lean veal and lean ham and fat pork; or the lean flesh from an extra bird and veal or pork or both, and an equal quantity of fat pork. You need about 2 lbs. for a 4-lb. chicken, correspondingly more for a turkey, less for a partridge or pheasant. Bind with 2 eggs; season with salt, pepper, herbs, spices, according to your preference and the creature concerned.

I don't advise the use of shop-bought sausage meat ever. It's too stodgy. If you can't face the tough grinding required, ask the butcher to do it for you.

If you want to include the *salpicon: either* add it to the forcemeat, stirring it in well, so that you have an evenly marbled mass to lay on the boned chicken, *or* put two layers of it, attractively arranged, between three layers of forcemeat, on the boned chicken.

If you are omitting the *salpicon,* lay the forcemeat by itself on the chicken.

The next step is to wrap the back edges up and over the forcemeat, etc., and sew it into a rough chicken-shape. Wrap this tightly in cheesecloth and tie the ends securely.

Meanwhile the stock ingredients have been bubbling away. Let them have 2 hours before adding the bird, which also requires 2 hours once the liquid has returned to the boil. Keep it simmering gently, not galloping.

Take the pan off the heat, but don't remove the chicken for another hour. You have to squeeze a good deal of liquid out of it, so you don't want it too hot. On the other hand, don't squeeze it dry either, and don't put too heavy a board and weight on it— you want a succulent galantine. Forget about it overnight.

For the jelly, you use the simmering liquid. Strain it and taste. Reduce if necessary, or zip it up with extra seasonings, lemon juice, Madeira, port, sherry. Leave it in a bowl to cool— it will be much easier to remove fat from jelly than from liquid.

If the liquid doesn't jell, or doesn't jell firmly enough, add powdered gelatin (1 envelope [1 tablespoon] to 2 cups).

If the jelly is murky, clarify it (page 41).

Next day unwrap the chicken, very carefully, remove the white thread, and put it onto a wire rack over a dish. Melt a little of the jelly until it just runs and brush it over the bird. You can then put some decorations on, once the jelly has reset. Brush on another layer to hold the decorations. When that has set, transfer the chicken to the final serving dish. Arrange round it chopped jelly, holding back some to whip into mayonnaise (page 41).

Everyone has their own ideas on decoration. But I would recommend the abstract and simple—tomato flowers and cucumber leaves raise suspicions that the cook has got something to hide. Picot-edged oranges and daisied eggs are for spoiling the fun at nursery tea parties, where chocolate biscuits and sardine sandwiches would be much more welcome, and at wedding receptions, where one begins truly to understand how England acquired her unenviable gastronomic reputation.

Galantine de Veau

Breast of veal, large flat piece, bones removed

—•— *Forcemeat* —•—

½ lb. lean pork, ground well (or pork and veal, or veal and ham)
½ lb. fat pork, ground well
2 eggs
Pistachio nuts } optional
Truffles

Plenty of herbs, but don't muddle them—either parsley, or basil, or marjoram
Salt, pepper

—•— *Stock* —•—

Veal bones, pork bones
An onion stuck with 4 cloves

1 carrot, chopped roughly
Salt, pepper

You can follow the Ligurian style with advantage, by folding the breast of veal in half and sewing up two of the sides. The forcemeat is put into this pocket, or *cima*, and then the third side is sewn up.

Let the stock simmer for a good hour before you put the veal, wrapped in a cloth, in to cook. It will need 2 hours of very gentle simmering.

Follow the method for galantine of chicken, but let it cool completely in the liquid. Glaze with jelly only: this dish is not usually decorated.

Galantine de Faisan
(de Dinde, de Pigeonneau, de Pintadeau)

Follow the BASIC METHOD, but adjust the quantity of forcemeat to the size of the bird. Ideally there should be an extra bird to hand so that the forcemeat can be made of half pheasant, half fat pork. With a turkey this is easy, as there is plenty of meat on the one bird for you to remove some for the stuffing. But an all-pork forcemeat will be delicious enough, if the extra game can't be managed.

Galantine de Cochon de Lait

1 suckling pig, boned, except for head, trotters (feet) and tail

———— *Forcemeat* ————

1 lb. meat from the suckling pig
1 lb. lean veal
1 lb. hard fat back
1 whole egg, plus 2 egg yolks

Truffles, if possible
1½ cups bread crumbs, soaked in a little milk, then squeezed
Salt, pepper, spices, parsley

———— *Salpicon* ————

The liver of the suckling pig

¾ lb. hard fat back, cut in finger strips
½ lb. ham, cut in strips

———— *Stock* ————

2½ cups dry white wine
5 cups water
3 large carrots, sliced (about 2¾ cups)
2 large onions stuck with 4 cloves each

2 bay leaves, sprig thyme, parsley
2 pig's trotters (feet), or a calf's foot
Veal bones, pork bones
Pig's skin

Follow the BASIC METHOD.

Simmer for 4 hours, turning the pig over at half-time. Do not glaze, but serve surrounded with chopped jelly, made from the stock.

Galantine de Porc

See page 253, but use a fresh picnic shoulder of pork, boned, rolled, and tied. Finish with plenty of parsley mixed in with the chopped meat.

 # SAUSAGES AND WHITE PUDDINGS, OR BOUDINS BLANCS

Sausage, *saucisse, saucisson* derive ultimately from the Latin *salsus*, "salted," probably by way of a Late Latin word, *salsicia*, something prepared by salting. The Romans are, in fact, the first recorded sausage makers, their intention being—as the derivation suggests—to preserve the smaller parts and scraps of the pig for winter eating. Though unwise to say so in a Frenchman's hearing, the Italians are still the supreme producers of dried and smoked sausages. They use beef as well as pork, but not usually donkey as some Frenchmen firmly believe.

For the fresh sausage, France is the country. It is still an honorable form of nourishment and pleasure there, protected by law from the addition of cereals and preservatives, produced in ebullient variety—both regional and individual—by thousands of *charcutiers*. In other words, the French sausage is freshly made, well-flavored, and, apart from seasonings, 100 per cent meat. Inevitably you pay more than in England or the United States, but the money is better spent. For picnickers the sausage is an ideal alternative to pâtés; cook it in foil in hot wood ashes, or unwrapped on a metal grill. At the weekends, look out for the light puff-pastry sausage rolls, *friandises,* and on Sundays for the luxurious *saucisse en brioche* (recipe, page 164), which can be bought by the piece—though if you want to be sure of it, order on Thursdays, no later.

Although the meat is basically pork, from neck and shoulders and sowbelly, a resourceful use of seasonings (spices, onions, sweet peppers, chestnuts, pistachio nuts, spinach, quite large amounts of sage or parsley, champagne, truffles) produces a variety of sausages that an English or American traveler going through France for the first time may find bewildering.

Making a good sausage is a simple affair, though you mightn't think so from the nasty pink packages sold in grocer's and butcher's shops in our country—and the equally tasteless concoctions in plastic packages which you have in the United States, I am told. If you haven't an electric mixer with a sausage-making attachment, or a hand sausage-stuffer: prepare the mixture and take it in a bowl to your butcher for him to put into skins; or else buy a good-sized piece of caul fat as well as the pork and make *crépinettes*—little parcels of sausage meat wrapped in beautiful veined white fat and either fried or grilled; or *gayettes;* or faggots, which closely resemble *gayettes.* Some cookery books suggest frying the meat in a rissole shape, with perhaps an egg-and-bread-crumb coating, but *crépinettes* are a more succulent solution.

First of all, though, sausage meat. It is so simple to buy the necessary lean and fat pork and put it through the grinder that I cannot see why butchers find it worth their while to sell prepared sausage meat, with its high proportion of cereal and its poor seasoning.

Sausage Meat (*Chair à Saucisse*)

—•— *Either* —•—

1 lb. lean pork from neck or shoulder
½ lb. hard fat back
1½ tablespoons coarse salt
½ teaspoon *quatre-épices* or spices to taste

Freshly ground black pepper
Plenty of parsley, or sage, or thyme

Put the lean and fat pork through the grinder once, or twice, according to the texture desired. Season.

———•► *Or* ◄•———

1 lb. lean pork from neck or shoulder	Freshly ground black pepper
1 lb. hard fat back	Plenty of parsley or sage or thyme
1½ tablespoons coarse salt	
1 teaspoon spices or *quatre-épices* or just cinnamon	

Prepare as above.

———•► *Or* ◄•———

½ lb. lean pork from neck or shoulder	½ lb. hard fat back or bacon fat
½ lb. veal	Seasonings to taste

———•► *Or* ◄•———

½ lb. poultry or game	½ lb. hard fat back
¼ lb. lean pork	Seasoning to taste
¼ lb. veal	

NOTE: If you want to bind these sausage meats or force-meats (*farces*), say for stuffing a bird or making a pâté, remember these proportions.

To 1 lb. of meat (lean and fat) add:

1 whole egg	Optional extras:
1½ tablespoons coarse salt	¼ cup brandy
1 level teaspoon spices	⅓ to ⅔ cup bread crumbs

SAUSAGES WITHOUT SKINS

CRÉPINETTES

BASIC METHOD

Ingredients for one of the above sausage meats, plus a piece of caul fat.

You will find that the caul fat is stiff, and easily torn if you try to pull it out. Soak it in a little tepid water with a tablespoon of vinegar; when the mixture is prepared and it becomes pliable, and it is easily cut into rough 4- or 5-inch squares with a pair of kitchen scissors. Lay one of the squares over your hand, put a lump of sausage meat in the middle, and wrap it up. The conventional shape is a flattish, rather round-angled triangle or oval about ½ inch thick. See that the edges overlap each other nicely. Continue until you've used all the mixture.

The *crépinettes* are now ready to be fried, or else brushed with melted butter or beaten egg, rolled in white bread crumbs, and grilled.

Crépinettes aux Pistaches

To 1 lb. of sausage meat, add 2–3 oz. of blanched pistachio nuts. Follow the BASIC METHOD.

crépinettes

Crépinettes aux Marrons

To 1 lb. of sausage meat, add ¼ lb. of roughly chopped chestnuts —not too fine, or you lose the mealy chestnut texture. (Slash ½ lb. of chestnuts, put them on a baking tray and leave in a hot oven for 10 minutes before shelling them.) Follow the BASIC METHOD.

Crépinettes aux Cumin

To 1 lb. of sausage meat, add the flesh of 1 red pepper, which has been well seeded, then blanched for 5 minutes in boiling water, and roughly chopped, plus 2 cloves of garlic, crushed, and 2 oz. cumin seeds. Follow the BASIC METHOD.

Crépinettes de Foie

Beautiful *crépinettes de foie* can be made from the livers of chicken and other poultry, game, and so on. The heart could be added too. Weigh the liver and heart.

To each ⅛ lb., add:

3 oz. fresh hard fat back
   or ham fat
¼ lb. finest fresh pork tenderloin or mild ham
1 small egg
2 tablespoons thick white
   sauce

Salt and fine white pepper
Parsley or a dash of Ma-
   deira or brandy
Squares of caul fat
Truffle parings (optional)
White bread crumbs

Grind the meats well. Beat the egg and add not quite all of it to the meat, with the white sauce. Season with salt, pepper, parsley or alcohol, and wrap in squares of caul fat. If you have some truffle parings, or truffles to spare, add them to the mixture when you make the actual *crépinettes*, in a central sandwiched layer surrounded by the forcemeat.

These *crépinettes* should be brushed with the remaining beaten egg, rolled in white bread crumbs, and gently fried in butter or fat from the bird. (If you want to put this mixture into sausage skins, don't fry the result. Leave them for 2 days in a cool, dry larder, then simmer them for 45 minutes in stock or water—prick with a needle as they rise to the surface. Eat them cold.)

GAYETTES DE PROVENCE

Gayettes, a French equivalent to English West Country faggots, are often to be found in *charcuteries* and homely restaurants in Provence and the Ardèche, where they make a speciality of *gayettes aux épinards* (recipe below). They look like faggots, very appetizing in their brown hummocky rows. Strictly for hungry picnickers on chilly days, when they taste delicious if you wrap them in a double layer of aluminum foil and reheat in wood ashes on the edge of the fire. The non-spinach *gayettes* are often eaten cold, in slices, as an hors d'oeuvre. I recommend black olives with them, and plenty of bread and unsalted butter.

1 lb. pig's liver
¼ lb. hard fat back
¼ lb. lean pork from neck or shoulder
Piece of caul fat
2 cloves of garlic, crushed

Salt, pepper, and spices to taste
Plenty of parsley or other herb, chopped
Lard or butter

Grind the meat, season, and wrap in pieces of caul fat—as for *crépinettes*, but *gayettes* are more the shape of small, round dumplings. Lay them close together in a greased baking dish. The oval yellow and brown French gratin dishes are ideal.

Melt a little lard or butter and pour over. Bake for 40 minutes in a medium oven. The top will brown nicely, and you can turn them over half-time, though this is not the conventional thing to do. Like faggots, *gayettes* are good-tempered—you can stretch the cooking time with a slower oven and raise the heat to brown them at the end. Eat cold, sliced, as an hors d'oeuvre.

Gayettes (*economical recipe*)

From the *charcutier*'s point of view, *gayettes* are a way of using up the pig's lungs and spleen. If you want to be really economical, you can do the same and ask the butcher for a mixture of liver, lights (lungs), and spleen, with more liver than anything else. Cut off all the gristly bits when you get home, weigh the result, and add one third of the weight in sausage meat (half fat, half lean pork).

Then follow the preceding recipe.

gayettes or boulettes

Gayettes aux Épinards

½ lb. Swiss chard leaves,
  or spinach, or perpetual
  (white) beet (*poirée*)
½ lb. spinach (*épinard*)
Butter or lard
Few leaves of garden sorrel
  (*oseille*)

½ cup flour
½ lb. sausage meat (half
  lean pork, half fat back)
A dash of hard liquor
Salt and pepper and spices
Piece of caul fat

Wash the beet greens and spinach, shake off as much water as possible, and put in a pan over a low heat with a knob of butter or lard. No extra water should be needed, if you keep the pan covered and shake well from time to time to prevent sticking. Drain well, and chop with the *uncooked* sorrel. Stir in the flour, then the sausage meat and seasonings. Finish like *gayettes de Provence*, but eat them hot.

NOTE: Frozen spinach does quite well, follow instructions on the package and dry thoroughly. Allow for different quantity.

If you can't get beet leaves, use all spinach and a stalk of celery chopped finely but not to a mush.

If you can't get sorrel, use a squeeze or two of lemon juice. Though I should say, go out and buy a packet of sorrel seed immediately. Once sown, it's there for ever, welcoming the spring with its clear sharp taste and lasting until the first severe frosts. Invaluable for soups, spinach purées, and sauces for veal or fish.

BOULETTES DE BRETAGNE

Boulettes are sold in Breton *charcuteries* and, as their name suggests, they are round like large bullets, resembling the southern *gayettes* or English faggots in appearance, though the meat mixture is a little different. They are eaten cold, sliced, with crusty bread or toast, like a pâté.

Piece of caul fat
1 lb. lean pork, boned⎫
¾ lb. fat pork ⎬ or 1¾ lbs. interlarded pork
¼ lb. lean bacon
Pepper, herbs, a little salt

Grind the lean pork, fat pork, and bacon together coarsely, or chop them by hand. Season the mixture, but don't use too much salt owing to the inclusion of the bacon.

Follow the *gayette* recipe for forming the *boulettes* and baking them.

———— • ◆ • ————

FAGGOTS

Whilst I am making *gayettes* (which keep well in a refrigerator, or under a ½-inch layer of lard), I often make a dish of faggots to be eaten hot from the oven at a hungry family lunch. Peas are the traditional accompaniment to this favorite Wiltshire dish; preferably *petits pois* cooked with a sage leaf or two, and finished with a sprinkling of chopped sage. And potatoes, boiled in their skins, then peeled and quartered. Homely perhaps, but most satisfactory, like the *gayettes aux épinards*.

The big *Oxford English Dictionary* gives the meaning of faggot as "bundle"—in this case a somewhat derogatory description of the ingredients—deriving from the Old French *fagot*. And what about *gayette*? Do both words come from *fegato*, the Italian for liver? But *fegato*, *fagotto*, *fagot*, or *faggot*, here's the recipe:

1 lb. pig's liver, or liver and
  kidney
10 oz. fat sowbelly, fresh or
  salted, *or* 6 oz. hard fat
  back and ¼ lb. lean pork

2 medium onions, chopped
  (about 1½ cups)
Sage leaves, crumbled
1 clove of garlic, crushed
Salt, black pepper

½ teaspoon mace, or nut-
meg and cinnamon
2 medium eggs, beaten
About 2 cups fresh bread
crumbs

Large piece of caul fat
2 tablespoons vinegar
A little well-flavored stock
or gravy left from a roast

Put the meat, ground, in a heavy pan with the onions, sage leaves, garlic, salt and pepper. Give it half an hour on a low heat, stirring occasionally to prevent it browning.

Drain off the juice into a small basin, mix the meat with the mace, beaten eggs, and enough bread crumbs to make a stiffish, easy-to-handle mixture. Taste and adjust seasoning. Put the caul fat into a bowl of tepid water with 2 tablespoons of vinegar, and cut, when pliable, into 5-inch squares, wrapping each one round a dumpling-sized piece of the meat mixture. Choose a shallow, attractive baking dish that can be put on the table, grease it with lard, and lay in the faggots, side by side, touching. Add the stock or gravy. They will need 40 minutes to 1 hour in a moderate oven. Halfway through pour off all the juice into the basin containing the juice from the first cooking. Stand in cold water, or put in the fridge, so that the fat rises and can be skimmed off; add the fat-free gravy to the dish 5 minutes before serving.

Faggots are very good-tempered too, provided you cook them slowly. The heat can always be raised at the end if they need further browning. You can eat them cold, sliced like the Provençal *gayettes;* or reheat them under a lid of aluminum foil.

Like *crépinettes* or sausages, you can keep them for weeks, without a refrigerator, by putting them in a clean dish after they are cooked, and covering them with melted lard to a depth of ½ inch. A sort of *confits,* in other words, like:

GOOSE-, DUCK-, OR TURKEY-NECK SAUSAGE
(*COU D'OIE, DE CANARD,* OR *DE DINDE FARCI*)

Buy your bird with the head on, or get the butcher to cut off the head just under the beak. Feel where the neck ends in the breast, and cut it off there. With the aid of a sharp knife, you will find it quite easy to strip the skin carefully off the flesh and vertebrae so that you end up with a tube. Alternatively you can slit the skin from top to bottom, so that you end up with a rough rectangle of skin.

Make a sausage meat to fit the occasion—either very simple, or with pistachio nuts, or truffles and foie gras—and stuff the neck. Tie it at both ends. Any scraps of meat from the neck can go in the sausage meat, scraps of ham and so on. If you have a rectangle, not a tube of skin, you lay the sausage meat on it, and perhaps put the creature's liver in the middle, completely enclosed by sausage meat. Sew the skin back into sausage shape with needle and "heavy-duty" white thread.

In France, on farms in the southwest, this stuffed neck would be cooked in goose fat with the rest of the bird, to go into the pot of *confits d'oie,* but for most people it is more convenient to poach the sausage in stock, very gently, for 40 minutes. Let it cool in the stock, dry and slice for an hors d'oeuvre. A very successful Christmas Eve or Boxing Night supper dish, but don't forget to remove the thread just before you slice it.

SMALL FRESH SAUSAGES
(*Saucisses de porc*)

Assuming that you have an electric mixer with a sausage-making attachment, it is the easiest thing in the world to make good sausages. (Otherwise a hand sausage-stuffer will do, or you must find a cooperative butcher to help.) Three things to remember—try to get meat from what is called "overweight pig," most pork on sale nowadays is from very young pigs bred for tender, lean, and rather tasteless meat, so tell the butcher that you want something a little older and with more flavor*; keep a high proportion of fat in the mixture, at least a quarter of the total weight of meat, and in some cases a half; and don't add cereals, rusk, or bread crumbs if you can help it, anyway never more than one tenth of the total weight of lean and fat meat together.

Skins, prepared from sheep and beef guts, are to be obtained from any butcher who makes his own sausages. They are preserved in salt, and will keep that way indefinitely. When you want to make some sausages, take a length or two and soak them overnight. Next day push one end of the length over the tap and run cold water through, wrinkle them on to the sausage-making attachment and there you are. Don't fill the skins too tightly or they'll burst, even if you prick them with a fork when they are fried. Hanging them up in a cool, dry place for 2 days is also a good idea—this gives them a chance to mature, as you will see if you try eating some immediately and some 2 days later.

All-meat sausages are naturally much less stodgy to eat, and make a great difference to dishes like *cassoulet,* home-baked beans and pork sausages, sausage rolls, or toad-in-the-hole, where the accompaniments are on the hefty side. *Saucisse en brioche* would be impossibly doughy with an English-style—or American-style—sausage, which habitually contains one third of its weight in cereals. If you have some sausage meat left over, prepare a *chou farci* (page 151).

Even if you aren't provided with a refrigerator or a deep freeze, you can keep sausages in lard, like the *confits* described further on, from page 331. Sauté them gently in a little lard until they are a good golden color, pack them into sterilized stoneware pots or large bottling jars, and cover them with melted lard to a depth of at least ½ inch above the highest sausage.

* You Americans do not have to do this—all U.S. pork is from what we call "overweight pig."

When the lard has solidified, cover with aluminum foil or seal. *Crépinettes* can be kept in the same way, for weeks, even months, in a cool, dry place. When you want to use them, stand the pots or jars in a very slow oven until the lard is melted. In theory you can remove the few sausages you require, push down the rest, and leave the lard to solidify again. But in practice, I prefer to use a whole pot at once—which means more pots and more lard. Incidentally the flavor of sausages kept in this way will be much better than the flavor of sausages kept in a deep freeze. As the preserved sausages are already cooked, they will need only the briefest frying to make sure that they are thoroughly heated inside and crisped up on the outside.

SAUSAGE RECIPES

Any of the mixtures given under "Sausage meat" (page 115) and "Sausages without skins" (page 117) can be used.

Saucisses de Campagne

These country sausages are very good in *cassoulets,* or in thick cabbage soups (*potées* or *garbures*), which are very popular in the French countryside in winter, being a complete meal in themselves (recipes, pages 168–75).

Ideally you need beef intestines for the skins, but most of us have to make do with the usual sheep guts. Anyway, ask for the widest sausage skins possible, not chipolata ones.

1 lb. lean pork from neck or shoulder
½ lb. hard fat back
About ¼ cup red wine
A good pinch saltpeter
1½ tablespoons coarse salt

¼ teaspoon granulated sugar
¼ teaspoon each of pepper and spices (*quatre-épices*)

Grind the meat, not too finely, and add the wine, saltpeter, and seasonings. Fill the skins, twisting them every 6 to 8 inches. Hang them in a dry, airy place (60°F.) for 5 days in cold weather, 3 days in cool but mild weather, and only 2 days in hot or very damp weather. (They will, in fact, keep in a really cool place, once dried, for several weeks.)

If you want to vary the seasonings, you could use savory, tarragon, garlic, thyme, wild thyme, chives, bay leaf, coriander, sweet marjoram, shallots, crushed juniper berries, parsley, pimiento, sage—anything, in fact, that appeals to you.

Poach these sausages in simmering water or stock for a quarter of an hour. If you are making a hearty vegetable soup, add them 20 minutes before the end. Remember to prick the sausages well before you put them in the hot liquid.

Saucisse de Toulouse

This is the famous sausage cooked in with *cassoulet* (page 168); it is also good with a hot potato salad, after brushing with melted butter and grilling, or simmering in water for 10 minutes.

1½ lbs. lean pork from neck or shoulder	1½ tablespoons granulated sugar (scant)
½ lb. hard fat back	1 pinch white pepper
1½ tablespoons coarse salt	1 pinch saltpeter

The distinguishing characteristic of this sausage is its coarsely chopped meat— grinding is too fine. Mix in the seasonings, and leave overnight in a dish with a lid (a Pyrex casserole is ideal). Next day stir the ingredients up well and fill the skins, using the very large-holed plate of an electric grinder with the sausage-making attachment. They are ready for use, but to my mind improve with keeping a day or two.

Elizabeth David suggests stiffening them by dipping into boiling water for a few moments, before frying or grilling. This is a good idea.

Saucisses au Foie de Porc

This is a heavier sausage, more like a black pudding. It goes well, too, with apple purée or apple rings lightly fried in butter.

1 lb. leg of pork, salted in
   brine for 3 days
1 lb. pig's liver
1 lb. hard fat back
½ lb. onions, chopped and
   melted in butter (about
   3 medium onions)

2 tablespoons coarse salt
1 teaspoon each of black
   pepper and *quatre-épices*
¼ cup Kirsch (Alsatian or
   German Swiss Kirsch-
   wasser)

Grind the liver two or three times, until you get a virtual purée. Put the lean and fat pork twice through the grinder. Mix in the cooked onions, which should have been reduced to a mash, and the other seasonings and Kirsch. Hang in a cool, airy place for 2 whole days, then poach in very hot but not boiling water for an hour. Prick them with a needle as they rise to the surface. Drain well, leave to cool, then fry lightly in butter or grill.

Saucisses d'Alsace-Lorraine

2 lbs. lean pork shoulder
1 lb. hard fat back
2 tablespoons coarse salt
A pinch of ground ginger

½ teaspoon each of pep-
   per, sugar, *quatre-épices*
   (cinnamon, nutmeg,
   cloves, pepper)
Good pinch saltpeter

Grind the meat and fat, season, and fill the skins. These are Christmastime sausages, and the chains are tied together at each end to form a circle, once you have twisted the sausages into 4-inch lengths. Dry them in an airy place (60°F.), hanging from a hook, for 24 hours. If you want to continue the festive tradition, brush a third of them with caramelized sugar or red food coloring, and wrap the rest in silver and gold foil. Hang them on the Christmas tree on Christmas Eve. Eat them for Christmas-night supper, simmered in stock or lightly fried, with a hot potato salad or potato purée.

Saucisses de Périgord

A more elegant festival sausage.

1 lb. lean pork
¾ lb. hard fat back
1½ tablespoons coarse salt
¼ cup dry white wine

½ teaspoon each of pepper, mixed spices or *quatre-épices*, sugar
Up to 2 oz. truffles

Grind the meat, mix in the rest of the ingredients, and stir well. Leave a day in a covered dish for the ingredients to blend their flavors well together, then fill the skins.

Saucisses au Champagne

The *charcuterie* textbooks say that this sausage, the finest of them all, should be made from the still-warm, freshly killed pig, so that the champagne can be really well absorbed. You must scald the grinder and basin, too, so that the meat won't lose temperature before you amalgamate it with the champagne.

It is excellent made with butcher's meat, for a special occasion.

1½ lbs. lean meat from the shoulder or leg

1½ lbs. hard fat back

2 tablespoons coarse salt

1 level teaspoon *quatre-épices*

5 oz. truffles

½ bottle (1½ cups) champagne

3 eggs, fresh-laid if possible

1 level teaspoon white pepper

Butter

Grind the meat finely, two or three times. Mix in all the seasonings, except the truffles, and stir in the champagne gradually. Finally add the truffles. Put into chipolata skins, twisting every 6 inches. Leave in a cool place, not a refrigerator, for two days to mature.

Melt some butter in a heavy pan, and fry the sausages gently to a golden-brown.

SMOKED SAUSAGES
(*Saucisses fumées*)

Unlike the *saucissons secs*, pages 134–41, the first four recipes require only a slight smoking, for flavor rather than preservation, so it would be all right to use the Abu Smoking Box, which gives no more—be warned—than a smoky taste and appearance. Alternatively if you want to experiment with proper smoking, say in an old farmhouse fireplace, or by means of a trench and crate (William Heptinstall's method, described in *Hors d'oeuvre and Cold Table*, Faber & Faber, though not altogether adequately from a complete novice's point of view), sausages are a good way of starting as they are reasonable to make. See page 203.

And of course you can always eat the sausages without smoking them. If you have a solid-fuel stove leave them hanging nearby to dry out, provided the temperature never rises above 70°F.; 60°F. is the ideal. This is quite successful with *chorizo*, a red peppery sausage of Spanish origin but very popular in

France, particularly in the southwest, as you would expect, where it is added to thick vegetable soups (*garbures*) and *cassoulet*, or served, after 15 minutes' simmering, with a purée of chick-peas. The peppery seasonings can be varied to taste.

Chorizos

1 lb. lean pork from neck or shoulder
½ lb. hard fat back
About ¼ cup red wine
1½ tablespoons coarse salt
¼ teaspoon granulated sugar
A good pinch saltpeter

1 whole red sweet pepper, on the small side, and 1 small chili pepper
¼ teaspoon spices
¼ teaspoon cayenne pepper
1 large clove of garlic, crushed

Cut the red and chili peppers in half, remove all the seeds carefully as well as the stalk, and put through the grinder (coarse plate) with the lean and fat pork. Add the rest of the ingredients, and fill wide sausage skins (1-inch diameter), twisting every 5 to 6 inches. Smoke lightly, or dry above the stove, at a temperature between 60° and 70°F., overnight.

Saucisses Espagnoles

1 lb. lean pork
1 lb. hard fat back
1½ tablespoons coarse salt
1 teaspoon *quatre-épices*

½ small sweet red pepper, crushed, or ½ teaspoon cayenne pepper
¼ cup raisins, chopped

Grind the meat (lean and fat), add the crushed pepper, seasonings, and chopped raisins. Fill the skins, twisting a 4- to 5-inch lengths, and smoke lightly. Use in the same ways as *chorizos*.

Saucisses Viennoises
(*de Vienne, Isère,* not *Vienna, Austria*)

½ lb. lean pork
½ lb. veal
½ lb. fillet steak
1½ tablespoons coarse salt

½ teaspoon each of cayenne pepper, saltpeter, and coriander
2 cups warm water

Grind the meat as finely as possible—twice through the machine at least. Add the seasonings and the warm water, stirring it in bit by bit. Fill wide, 1-inch-diameter sausage skins (beef skins are the ideal), smoke quickly, and simmer for 10 minutes in water just on the boil. Prick with a fine needle as the sausages rise to the surface. Eat with a hot potato salad, dressed with a horseradish-flavored vinaigrette.

Saucisses Allemandes (*Saucisses d'Augsbourg*)

2 lbs. lean pork from the neck
½ lb. hard fat back or fat bacon
Good pinch of saltpeter

½ teaspoon black pepper
1 teaspoon *quatre-épices,* or mixed cinnamon, nutmeg, cloves
2 tablespoons coarse salt

Grind the pork coarsely, season it, and finally add the fat back or fat bacon cut in very small dice—about ⅛ to ¼ inch, chopped rather than diced perhaps, but as regularly as possible. Fill the skins and dry in an airy place at a temperature of about 60°F. for 4 days. Smoke them lightly and quickly, then simmer for 15–30 minutes (according to the thickness of the sausage—beef skins, 1 inch diameter, are the best, but you may have to make do with the smaller sheep-gut skins).

If you are experienced in smoking meat, you might like to try the following two sausages, which are so popular in north-eastern France. Frankfurters are well-known in our country and yours, but not the cumin-flavored *saucisses croquantes*, though some delicatessens and butcher shops sell them under their German name, *knackwurst*.

Saucisses au Cumin, or Croquantes

1½ lbs. lean pork from shoulder or neck
1 lb. lean beef
½ lb. hard fat back
2½ tablespoons coarse salt
A scant teaspoon saltpeter

2 large cloves of garlic, crushed to pulp with a little salt
1 teaspoon black pepper
2 teaspoons chopped red pepper
2 oz. cumin seeds, crushed in the mortar

The beef has to be ground very finely indeed and seasoned with a little salt and the saltpeter; then the pork (lean and fat) has to be ground not quite so finely. Mix everything together very thoroughly, with an electric beater if possible, so that you can add 1 cup cold water gradually, whilst the meat is being stirred round.

Fill the skins, twisting them into 4- or 5-inch sausages. Smoke them for 2 days, after drying them in an airy place (60°F.) for 2 to 5 days, according to the temperature and the humidity. They can be kept in a very cool larder for some time.

When you want to cook them, put them into a pan of cold water and bring them slowly to the boil, or rather to the simmer. Leave for 5 minutes, then serve—if you are not quite ready, take the pan off the heat, but leave the sausages in the water to keep them hot.

Saucisses de Francfort, or *de Strasbourg*

1½ lbs. shoulder and leg
of pork, salted in brine
3 days if possible
1 lb. hard fat back
2 tablespoons coarse salt
1 heaped teaspoon white
pepper and coriander

(A tiny pinch of saltpeter,
if the meat is unsalted)
1 scant teaspoon of mace
or nutmeg and cinnamon
mixed

Grind the meat (lean and fat) twice—the first time fairly coarsely, then add the seasonings, grind again with a finer plate. Stir it well, whilst adding 1 cup of cold water—an electric beater, at a low speed, is ideal for this part of the operation.

Separate the skins into lengths between a foot and a foot and a half; fill the skins, tie them at each end, and twist them in the middle, to make two long, thin sausages each.

Hang them up to dry in a cool, airy place, where the temperature is about 60°F. at the most. Leave them for a whole day, then smoke them for 8 hours. If timing is awkward, leave them to dry for a longer rather than a shorter time. Eight hours' smoking should be enough to produce the deep, tawny brown frankfurter color.

You can keep them for several weeks. To cook, lower them into water at the simmer and leave for 10 minutes. After that time, draw the pan to one side to keep the sausages hot. Traditionally they are served with *choucroute* (page 162) or a hot potato salad.

LARGE SAUSAGES
(*Saucissons*)

On a row of hooks in the *charcuterie,* above the small, fresh sausages, the *boudins blancs* (page 147), and the *boudins noirs* (page 340), hang the medium-sized saveloy-type *saucissons,* for boiling and eating hot or cold (page 146). Beside them are ranged the very large keeping sausages (*saucissons secs*), which the *charcutier* sometimes makes himself, but which are usually supplied from a factory, as they are to delicatessen shops in England and the United States. They are easy to recognize, meshed in string, wrapped in gold, silver, and colored foils, and cheerfully labeled. Like the fresh sausage, they must be all meat, predominantly pork—if horse meat, for instance, is used, the label must say so. The more unfamiliar, black-skinned *andouilles*, or large tripe sausages (page 280), hang with them, slicing to a grayish-brown, beautifully marbled surface.

You can buy these sausages whole, for storing from hooks in your own larder, and in miniature, for modern, small-family convenience, but mostly they are sold in slices, by weight. Eat them as they are, with hunks of bread and butter; olives go well too and can be bought at most *charcuteries*. A good picnic idea is to heat through some garlic sausage (*saucisson à l'ail*) and a piece of *petit salé* (cooked, pickled pork, page 181) with a large can of pork and beans French-style (*cassoulet*).

In town *charcuteries* you will often find a variety of regional, national, and international *saucissons*. Forget about the ones you know. Buy 50 grams (just under 2 oz.) of as many as you can afford—if they are well wrapped, then rewrapped after the picnic, they will survive days of heat and car travel in good condition. Often there will be local names, so point and don't lose heart. French patience is endless in matters of food, even in busy shops. Explain that you would like to make an hors d'oeuvre of as many kinds of *saucisson* as possible, particularly *les spécialités de la région*. One name that we always remember is *gendarme*, given to flat, strappy, yellow-and-brown-speckled sausages in the Jura.

Buying *saucissons* in small quantities, whilst coping simultaneously with decimal weights and currency, one is only dimly aware of the high cost per pound. With an all-meat sausage you expect to pay more, but in the case of *saucissons secs* there is inevitably a good deal of shrinkage in the processes of drying and maturing, which pushes the price up higher still.

To make these sausages at home, you need skins made from the large intestine. If you have a farmhouse kitchen, with a solid-fuel stove and plenty of old hooks attached to the beams, you are well off because the *saucissons* need to be dried at a temperature of 60°F., and a steady temperature at that. You can store them in a cooler larder when the drying is completed, but once again they should hang so that air circulates all round them. Avoid a steamy, humid atmosphere.

As well as the right physical conditions, you need patience too, because this type of sausage needs at least a month in which to mature, whether or not it is smoked; some kinds need six months. They will be covered with white powdery flowers from about the sixth day, *"cette fleur est constituée par des micro-organismes de la famille des levures, qui préparent le climat idéal pour le développement d'autres microbes qui feront subir à la viande la transformation voulue d'onctuosité et de goût."* In other words, leave the white organism alone to do its work of maturing the sausage. Don't worry if the sausage shrinks, it will lose up to 40 per cent of its weight.

Saucisson Cuit au Madère

Here, first of all, is a large sausage that is neither dried nor smoked—in consequence it will not keep very long. Let it mature for 2 days, then eat it within 7 days.

1 lb. good lean center-cut pork loin	2 tablespoons Madeira
½ lb. hard fat back	2 oz. truffles (optional), chopped
2 tablespoons coarse salt	8–10 pistachio nuts, blanched
Pinches of white pepper, and spices, preferably *quatre-épices*	

Grind the meat (lean and fat) as finely as possible, two or three times. Season after the first time with salt and spices, then put through the machine again. Finally stir in the Madeira, the truffles, and the pistachio nuts.

Put into a nice piece of large intestine, tie each end. Wrap it in a fine muslin and tie it once again, like a parcel, not just at each end.

Simmer for 45 minutes, then hang it up to cool and dry. Tighten up the string and the cloth, and store in an airy place. Like the other *saucissons*, this one is sliced finely and served as an hors d'oeuvre.

Saucisson de Ménage, or de Campagne

This is the basic sausage mixture, left to dry and mature instead of being eaten straightaway like a small sausage. It is sliced, and served uncooked.

2 lbs. lean pork from neck or shoulder	4 tablespoons coarse salt
1 lb. hard fat back	1 teaspoon each of saltpeter, pepper, *quatre-épices*, sugar
1 clove of garlic, crushed	

Grind the meat (lean and fat) once, mix in all the seasonings, and the saltpeter, which will turn the sausage a rosy pink. Fill some large intestine, tying to make one or two sausages as you wish. Remember that they will shrink by about a third.

Hang in a steady, well-aired temperature of 60°F. for 3, 4, or 5 days according to the season. Keep them away from steam and direct sunlight. Remove them to a hook in a cool, airy place and don't be tempted to try them before a month is up. Better still, 2 or 3 months. When they start to shrink, squeeze them down from each end so that the inside is well compacted and easy to slice.

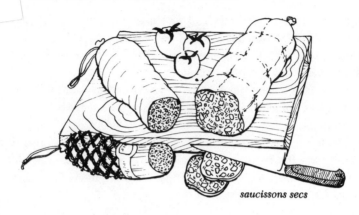

saucissons secs

Saucisson à l'Ail (Garlic Sausage)

2 lbs. lean pork from neck or shoulder
½ lb. hard fat back
2 tablespoons coarse salt
½ teaspoon ground black pepper, 1 teaspoon whole black pepper
½ teaspoon *quatre-épices*

A good pinch cayenne pepper
A small pinch saltpeter
2 tablespoons brandy, *eau-de-vie*, gin, vodka, or *marc*
1 clove of garlic, crushed

Grind the lean meat well, add the seasonings except for the whole black pepper and the hard liquor. Grind again twice.

Chop the pork fat into small dice, and add it together with the whole peppercorns and brandy to the ground lean meat. Mix it well together with your hands for 10 minutes. Fill the skins firmly, pressing the mixture down well. Hang from a hook, at an airy 60°F. for 4 days; then string and store at about 50°F. for 5 months.

Saucisson de Lyons (a)

There is not a great deal of difference between the large sausages of Lyons, Arles, Lorraine, and Burgundy. Sometimes beef is added to the pork, or a glass of liqueur, sometimes the fat is cut in strips, sometimes ground, but the method is the same, and after a maturing period the various types are all eaten raw, in thin slices, with bread, as an hors d'oeuvre or snack.

2 lbs. leg of pork, weighed without bone or fat	white pepper, *quatre-épices* or spices
½ lb. hard fat back (fat bacon will do)	2 tablespoons coarse salt
½ teaspoon each of white peppercorn, ground	1 tablespoon granulated sugar
	A pinch saltpeter

In this *saucisson* the fat is cut into nice little strips, and amalgamated with the finely ground and pounded lean pork, well seasoned and mixed. If you have an electric beater, it takes the hard work out of stirring the lean meat and spices, etc., together.

See that the fat is well distributed, but take care it isn't reduced to a hash like the lean pork.

Stuff the filling well down into the large beef intestine, tying it into 18-inch lengths. Leave in a cool, airy place, hanging from a hook, for 4 to 6 months. The temperature should be a steady 60°F. or a little under—no damp, or direct sunlight—for the first 3 to 6 days.

After 3 or 4 days, take the sausages down and tie them up firmly, so that they keep straight as they mature. Before you start, push the filling of each sausage tightly together from its two ends. Put four lines of string the length of the sausage, then wind the string round and round. Don't cut it into lots of separate bands of string, because you need to pull it up tighter during the long maturing time.

Now put the *saucissons* away in a dry, well-aired larder, hanging from a hook so that they have a good circulation of air all round them, and forget they are there—apart, of course, from an occasional restringing. If you are too impatient and try to eat the sausages too soon, they will taste horrible; so try to leave them for 6 months.

Saucisson d'Arles

2 lbs. leg of pork, weighed without bone or fat
½ lb. hard fat back (fat bacon will do)
¾ lb. lean beef
3 tablespoons coarse salt

1 tablespoon granulated sugar
1 teaspoon each of ground black pepper, black peppercorns, and *quatre-épices*

Follow the method of *saucisson de Lyons*, grinding the lean meat finely and keeping the fat in short strips.

Saucisson de Lorraine

1 lb. shoulder of pork, weighed without bone or fat
½ lb. lean beef
½ lb. fat from the neck
2 tablespoons coarse salt

1 teaspoon granulated sugar
½ teaspoon each of ground white pepper and *quatre-épices*

Follow the method for *saucisson de Lyons*.

Saucisson de Bourgogne

1 lb. lean neck or shoulder of pork, weighed without bone
½ lb. hard fat back (fat bacon will do)
2 tablespoons coarse salt

1 teaspoon ground white pepper
½ teaspoon *quatre-épices*
¼ cup Kirsch, *eau-de-vie*, *marc*, brandy, or vodka

Grind lean and fat pork together, stir, and season well. Then follow the method of *saucisson de Lyons*.

Saucisson à Trancher (*Slicing-Sausage*)

2 lbs. sowbelly, with roughly equal amounts of lean and fat
2 tablespoons coarse salt
1 teaspoon ground black pepper

1 teaspoon *quatre-épices* or spice mixture
2–3 cloves of garlic, according to taste
¼ cup chopped parsely parsley

Grind the meat well, flavor with seasonings, and fill large intestines, pushing the meat well down. Simmer for 2 to 3 hours in salted water, drain, dry, and hang up in a steady temperature at 60°F. for at least a month.

See also *saucisson d'Italie* (page 143).

————•◆•————

SMOKED SAUCISSONS
(*Saucissons Fumés*)

Saucisson de Ménage (or *de Campagne*) *Fumé*

Follow the ingredients and method for *saucisson de ménage* (page 137), adding another 2 teaspoons of sugar, another teaspoon of ground black pepper, and 2 more cloves of garlic.

Dry from a hook, at a temperature of 60°F. for 3 to 5 days, then smoke them until they are a beautiful deep yellowish-brown. This takes a few days. Hang in a cool, airy larder for a month.

Saucisson de Provence

2 lbs. lean pork from neck
or shoulder
⅜ lb. hard fat back
¼ lb. lean sowbelly
2 tablespoons coarse salt
1 teaspoon each of black

peppercorns, ground
black pepper, and
quatre-épices
2 teaspoons granulated
sugar
A pinch of saltpeter

Grind the lean pork and lean sowbelly well, add the fat, cut
in strips, and mix in the other ingredients. Dry from a hook, at
a temperature of 60°F. for 3 to 5 days, then smoke gently for
8 hours.

Saucisson au Foie de Porc

1½ lbs. lean pork (neck or
shoulder), weighed with-
out bone
1 lb. pig's liver
½ lb. leaf lard
1 lb. cooked tongue, cut
into small dice
¼ cup chopped onions

2 tablespoons coarse salt
3 oz. truffles, chopped
2 oz. pistachio nuts,
blanched
1 teaspoon each of ground
pepper and *quatre-épices*
Saffron dissolved in a little
white wine

Grind the meat, liver, and fat very small, add the tongue, season, stir well, and leave for a day in a covered dish.

Fill large beef intestine, pushing the meat mixture firmly
down. Tie at each end. Simmer in nearly boiling water for 45
minutes. Hang up to dry in a steady, airy temperature of 60°F.,
and leave for 5 weeks. Smoke it for a few hours—6 are recommended—after coloring the *saucisson* with some saffron dissolved
in a little white wine.

Saucisson d'Italie

This and the following recipe for *mortadella* are given in French *charcuterie* handbooks. Although they are Italian sausages by origin, they have become popular enough to be widely imitated in other countries.

1 lb. lean pork from neck or shoulder, weighed without bone
1 lb. lean veal
½ lb. hard fat back
½ pint pig's blood
2 tablespoons coarse salt

1½ tablespoons each of ginger, cinnamon, nutmeg
1 heaped teaspoon ground black pepper
2 cups dry white wine

Grind the lean meat; cut the fat into small dice, and add with the blood to the lean. Season. Stir in the white wine and mix everything well. This time the traditional casing is a pig's bladder, but use large intestine as an alternative.

Dry for 3 to 5 days, hanging from a hook, in an airy, steady temperature of 60°F. Smoke for 4 days over a smoldering fire of juniper branches. Brush over with olive oil and keep in a dry, cold place (40°–45°F.), still hanging up.

Leave to mature for at least a month.

NOTE: You can omit the smoking process, and leave the *saucisson* to continue drying on the hook for 2 months instead of 3 to 5 days.

Mortadelle

I always feel tempted in shops by the pale-pink sight of a *mortadella* sausage, studded with small cubes of white fat and peppercorns—but it never tastes as good as it looks. This recipe should produce a better result.

1 lb. lean pork, weighed
without bone
½ lb. hard fat back
¾ lb. salted fat back or fat
bacon

2 tablespoons of salt
1 level teaspoon each of
saltpeter, peppercorns,
and coriander

Grind to a close, fine mass the lean pork and fresh pork fat. Cut the salted fat into small cubes, and mix everything together. Lay a fine cloth on a strainer dish or grid, and let the mixture drain on it overnight. Traditionally again the casing is a pig's bladder, but you may find a piece of large intestine easier to come by. Tie the two ends and leave in an Italian brine for 10 days (5 only, if you are making it in large intestine).

Italian brine is made this way: put 1½ quarts of water on to boil with 2 heaped tablespoons saltpeter, 2½ lbs. sea salt (or *unadulterated* rock salt), and ⅛ cup of bicarbonate of soda. Stir everything well together and let it boil for a moment or two. Add 1½ quarts dry white wine and 1 oz. of mixed spices (peppercorns, cloves, some cinnamon), tied in a little cloth bag. Remove immediately from the heat and let the brine cool down completely before you put the *mortadelle* in. Take out the bag of spices. Whilst you have the brine, you could also cure a boned and rolled shoulder of pork or a leg (see page 200) in the Modena style.

After 10 days, remove the sausage, drain it well, and smoke for 4 days. It then needs cooking in nearly boiling water for 3 hours (1½ for smaller *mortadelle* sausages made in large intestine).

Drain it, dry with a cloth, and hang up for 30 days to mature.

Saucisson de Lyons (b)

Here is another version of the *saucisson de Lyons* (see also *saucisson de Lyons* [a], page 138) or *saucisson d'Arles* in that it contains beef. If you make it into large sausages, weighing about ⅞ to 1 lb. each, it is a good one to use for *saucisse en brioche* (page 164).

1 lb. lean pork, weighed without bone or fat	1 teaspoon whole black peppercorns
½ lb. fillet steak	¾ tablespoon salt
½ lb. back or Canadian bacon fat	Crushed garlic and chopped shallot to
½ teaspoon ground black pepper	taste: e.g., 2 cloves garlic and 4 shallots
	A pinch of saltpeter

Grind the pork and fillet steak together twice; get it as fine as you can. Pounding it with a pestle or beating it with an electric beater will reduce it to an even mass. Cut the bacon into small dice and mix it in evenly. Add the seasonings, the crushed garlic and the finely chopped shallots.

Leave the mixture in a cool place for 24 hours.

Fill the skins, tie them, and leave the *saucissons* in brine for 6 days—2 quarts of water brought to the boil with ½ lb. of bay or unadulterated rock salt, and ½ lb. of sugar (1¼ cups), and 1 heaped tablespoon saltpeter. Leave it to cool before pouring over the sausages, which should be placed for this purpose in a large glass or stoneware pot. Put a board on top, to keep the sausages entirely immersed. Cover the pot. Don't throw away the brine after 6 days, but turn to page 200, to see how else it can be used.

Drain and dry and smoke very lightly for 4 days. Hang them up to dry at a temperature of 60°F. Leave them to mature for at least a month, stringing and restringing as they shrink.

In the nineteenth century, sausages were hung up the farmhouse chimney to smoke very gently until they were dry and white. Then they were restrung, and dipped in a mixture of wine lees, boiled with sage, bay leaves, and thyme. A day or two on the hook to dry, and a month or two of maturing, wrapped in paper, in a box of wood ashes, and they were ready to eat.

For *saucisse en brioche,* you can treat this sausage as a *cervelas,* drying it for two days after the salting, then cooking for an hour, gently, in unsalted water.

———•–•–•–———

LARGE BOILING SAUSAGES, OR SAVELOYS
(*Saucissons-cervelas*)

As far as mixture goes, there is not much difference between these sausages and the smaller *saucisses* or the big *saucissons secs* and *fumés.* But for size and maturing, they are a halfway stage between the two. Choose skins that will give you a diameter of about 1½ inches, and as you fill them, twist every 8 to 12 inches; longer, if you want to bend them round and tie together at each end, in a loop. You can smoke them lightly, or not, as you please; you can salt them for 3 or 4 days in brine, or just hang them up in a cool place for 2 or 3 days.

This is the sausage you find on menus all down the eastern side of France. Served sometimes with a hot potato salad or *choucroute* (page 162), it has been simmered gently in hot water or red wine. Try seasoning the dressing of the potato salad with a little grated horseradish, or a spoonful of French mustard, or serve a proper horseradish sauce with it—½ table-spoon of grated horseradish beaten into a ½-pint carton of cream, with a little salt, sugar, and pepper to taste. Sharpen with white wine vinegar or lemon juice.

This sausage is also left to get cold, and then sliced and served as an hors d'oeuvre.

Saucisson-cervelas

Enough for 1-lb. sausage.

½ lb. lean pork from neck or shoulder, weighed without bone
¼ lb. fillet steak
¼ lb. fat bacon
¾ tablespoon salt

A scant teaspoon ground black pepper
½ clove of garlic, crushed
2 shallots, chopped
A small pinch of saltpeter

Grind the lean meat, add the seasonings, and grind. Chop the bacon into small dice, and mix in well. Fill the skin and tie at each end.

You can either hang up to dry in a temperature of 60°F. for 2 days, or salt in brine for 2 to 3 days; or use straightaway, though I think that it should be left for at least 24 hours for all the ingredients to blend their flavors well. It can be gently smoked for 6 hours.

Prick with a sharp needle and simmer in boiling water for an hour, or in red wine.

As the *cervelas* are not keeping sausages, you could use an Abu Smoking Box to give them a smoky flavor. If you want to conduct some experiments in smoking meat, this is a good recipe to try as nothing much is lost if the result is a failure.

———— ·•◆•· ————

WHITE PUDDINGS
(*Boudins Blancs*)

In contrast to the *boudins noirs* (page 340), these succulent creamy-white sausages are the dearest in the *charcuterie*. And also the nicest. The whitest of pork is used, or chicken, or occasionally rabbit, and cream, eggs, onions, and a few bread crumbs or ground rice to make the mixture as bland and smooth-textured as possible. Like the *boudins noirs,* they have been simmered by the *charcutier,* so all you have to do is fry them, or brush with butter and grill them. Provided you have a sausage-making attachment (or an obliging butcher), you can easily make these delicate *boudins* in England or the U.S. It's a good way of using up half a roast chicken, provided it was not reared in a battery. If you haven't got a ham or fish boiler with a strainer, use a metal salad shaker or "French-fry" basket for the simmering process. *Boudins* need to be lowered into the water, and lifted out, with the minimum of fuss and handling or they will burst.

Boudins Blancs de Paris

½ lb. roasted chicken or uncooked chicken breast

½ lb. best pork from the loin

1 lb. leaf lard and hard fat back

1 tablespoon coarse salt

1 teaspoon finely ground white pepper

1 teaspoon *quatre-épices* or other spices

¾ lb. chopped onions (about 3 cups)

¾ cup bread crumbs, soaked in about ¼ cup hot milk or cream

3 eggs

Grind the meat and fat as finely as possible, season with salt, pepper, and spices, and put through the grinder again with the onions. Add the bread crumbs and milk or cream, and the eggs. Beat well—use the electric beater if you have one—and fill the skins, but not too tightly or they'll burst in cooking. Tie into 6-inch sausages—twisting is not enough—with "heavy-duty" white thread.

Set a large pan on the stove with 5 cups of water and 2½ cups of milk. Bring it to the boil and lower the strainer tray or metal "French-fry" or salad basket of sausages into the hot liquid. Keep the temperature just below the boil or else they will burst, and prick them with a needle gently as they rise to the surface.

Twenty minutes of simmering should be enough, timed from when the liquid returned to just below the boil.

Raise the strainer tray carefully and leave it to drain completely over a bowl. Next day prick the sausages, brush them with melted butter, and grill them—or else fry them gently in butter. Serve with mashed potato.

Boudins Blancs du Mans

This is the usual *boudin blanc* mixture used by *charcutiers*, particularly in Anjou and Touraine.

½ lb. lean pork from neck or leg
1¼ lbs. fresh hard fat back
½ cup cream (light cream will do)
1 egg

1 tablespoon coarse salt
1 teaspoon fine white pepper and spices
1 medium-sized onion, chopped (about ¾ cup)
¼ cup chopped parsley

Follow the method for the previous recipe.

Boudins Blancs

If you have been using a lot of egg yolks, here is a good way of not wasting the whites.

2¼ cups milk
2 tablespoons ground rice
½ lb. pork loin or tenderloin
½ lb. white chicken meat
¾ lb. leaf lard

10 egg whites
1 teaspoon each of finely ground white pepper and *quatre-épices*
1 tablespoon coarse salt

Boil the milk, pour it onto the ground rice, stirring it well to avoid lumps, and return to the pan to cook gently until thick.

Grind the meat and fat two or three times, whirl it in the blender with a little of the milk and ground-rice mixture, or put it through a sieve. Mix the rest of the ingredients in thoroughly.

Finish according to the method of *boudins blancs de Paris.*

Boudins de Lapin, or de Lièvre

If you have rather a large hare or rabbit, set aside a joint or two for these delicious little *boudins.* Save the blood too, adding a drop of vinegar to prevent it from clotting before you use it.

1½ cups fresh white bread crumbs

½ cup milk

½ lb. rabbit or hare, weighed without bones

¼ lb. hard fat back

¼ lb. pork tenderloin

2 eggs

2 shallots and 1 medium onion, all chopped fine

3 tablespoons of blood and the rabbit liver

4 heaped tablespoons chopped parsley, chives, tarragon

1½ tablespoons coarse salt

½ teaspoon each of fine white pepper and *quatre-épices*

NOTE: You don't need skins for these *boudins,* though they can be made in conventional style with success.

First of all you need to make a thick paste of the bread crumbs and milk. Do this by boiling the milk in a pan, then stirring in the bread crumbs until the mixture is fairly solid. Cook slowly until the *panada* comes away from the side of the pan, leave it to cool completely.

Grind the lean and fat meat well together. If you have an electric blender, drop pieces of meat onto the whirling blades and moisten with one or both of the eggs as necessary. Beat this smooth meat mixture up with the cold *panada*—an electric beater does this well, and saves a lot of hard work.

Sauté the chopped onion and shallots in a little butter over a low fire. When they are a golden mush, stir in the blood and liver and go on cooking very gently.

Mix everything together, adding the eggs if you didn't use them earlier on. If you haven't a beater, squeeze and knead with your hands until everything is well amalgamated.

Make the mixture into little round balls, the usual meatball size, and drop them into simmering water to poach for 10 minutes. Drain, cool, coat with egg and bread crumbs, and fry in foaming butter. Serve with mashed potatoes.

------•◆•------

SAUSAGE RECIPES USING SAUSAGE MEAT

Saucisses aux Oeufs

A simple version of Scotch eggs, which makes an attractive hors d'oeuvre.

Make small flat cakes of sausage meat, just a little larger in diameter than an egg. Turn them in seasoned flour and fry gently in foaming butter. Drain well and cool.

Hard-boil some eggs, slice them, and lay one slice on each cake of sausage meat. Serve on a bed of young lettuce leaves, or watercress, and garnish with capers.

Chou Farci

BASIC METHOD

This is one of the great French standbys, and I can never think why, in our land of universal cabbage, it isn't an English national dish too. The stuffing can be varied in many unlikely but interesting ways. Here is the BASIC METHOD, followed by some suggestions for stuffing and accompaniments:

Choose a fine, large, crisp green cabbage.

Make your stuffing, based, usually, on sausage meat (or the ground remains of a joint of beef); be sure to spice it well with whatever you have to hand—and bind with an egg. Some cooked rice or bread crumbs make a good addition.

Plunge the cabbage, whole, into plenty of boiling salted water. Let it boil for 5 minutes. Don't overdo this, you want the cabbage to be pliable, not limp. Drain it well, and lay on a flat surface with plenty of room for maneuver.

Very carefully open the cabbage out, leaf by leaf, so that you can spread each one with a spoonful of the stuffing. Start in the middle and work outwards. Put the cabbage gently back into shape and tie it up so that it can't collapse all over the pan in the process of cooking.

If you have a deep earthenware pot into which you can fit a metal salad shaker or "French-fry" basket, this will make it very much easier to cook the cabbage and remove it in a good shape. I have also wrapped the cabbage in a string netted shopping bag.

On the other hand, if you can cook the cabbage in a pot you can bring to table, all that is required is an initial stringing up.

Having settled the method, put 2 cups of liquid into the cooking pot and then the cabbage. Add anything suitable you have by way of carrots, onions, leeks, pig's trotters (feet), small pieces of ham or bacon. The liquid can be half wine and half water with a beef or chicken cube, or stock thickened with a heaped tablespoon of flour dissolved in a tablespoon of butter or gravy left from the joint flavored with two thin curls of orange or lemon peel. Use your imagination and discretion.

Cover the cabbage with buttered or oiled paper, or some slices of all-fat bacon; put on the lid and cook very slowly for three hours at 320°F. This is a good-tempered dish, which can be cooked longer at a lower temperature to suit your convenience. Don't forget to remove the string before serving, dress with chopped parsley or marjoram, capers, a little chopped red pepper. Be sure, also, to correct the sauce if necessary, and skim off the fat.

If you want to make a really solid meal, add smoked sausages an hour before the end, or a piece of bacon. Frankfurters, or cooked *petit salé* (page 181), should be added 20 minutes before the end. In the last 5 minutes, slices of garlic sausage or salami can go in, or olives which have been desalted by a 5 minutes' soak in very hot water.

This dish is, of course, a meal in itself and needs nothing else to accompany it, apart from bread, toast, or fried bread.

NOTE: A number of suggestions are made above. Don't follow them all at once.

Chou Farci à la Provençale

¼–⅜ lb. very fat pork or bacon, diced and fried to pale brown
½ cup cooked rice
1 large onion, chopped and melted in butter
½ package frozen peas (or ½ lb. fresh, if available)
1 lb. sausage meat, well seasoned

½ lb. tomatoes, skinned and chopped
½ lb. spinach and a stalk of celery, chopped together, *or* ½ lb. chard, chopped, *or* a lettuce and a stalk of celery, chopped together
Egg to bind
Extra garlic, if there isn't any in the sausage meat

Follow the BASIC METHOD.

Chou Farci aux Câpres
(from Elizabeth David's *French Country Cooking*)

⅜ lb. ground pork or pork sausage meat
⅜ lb. chicken livers

2 cups bread crumbs
1 egg yolk
Seasonings, spices, herbs

Follow the BASIC METHOD.

Cook in a sauce made from ½ cup flour cooked in 4 tablespoons (½ stick) butter, and 1 cup stock or tomato juice.

Serve strewn with some capers and with a small glass of brandy poured over.

Chou Farci au Fromage

1½ lbs. sausage meat
1 large onion, chopped small (about 1 cup)
2 tablespoons chopped parsley
½ lb. mushrooms, chopped small (about 2 cups)

about ¼ cup additional chopped parsley
¼ cup grated Parmesan or well-flavored cheese

Follow the BASIC METHOD.

Cook in a sauce made of ½ cup flour stirred into 4 tablespoons (½ stick) melted butter, moistened with 1 cup tomato juice or an 8-oz. can of Italian tomatoes, sieved. Sprinkle the cabbage with more grated Parmesan and cover with pieces of fat pork or fat bacon.

Serve sprinkled with chopped parsley and the pieces of fat bacon removed. Have a bowl of grated cheese on the table.

Chou Farci aux Saucisses de Francfort

Two frankfurters per person, plus the following ingredients for the stuffing:

1½ lbs. sausage meat made from half-lean and half-fat pork

4 egg yolks
Salt and plenty of ground black pepper

Follow the BASIC METHOD.

Cook in 1 cup of stock, ½ cup of dry white wine, with a *bouquet garni,* an onion stuck with cloves, and a ⅜-lb. piece of salt pork.

Twenty minutes before the end, add frankfurters or other small smoked sausages. Pour off the sauce, skim off the fat, adjust the seasonings, and thicken with a tablespoon of cornstarch—or less, according to the amount of liquid. It should not be too thick.

Stuffed Cabbage Leaves

When the cabbage has been blanched, the leaves can be carefully broken off and stuffed individually. Tie carefully and braise on a bed of vegetables and diced bacon with 1 cup of liquid. An hour and a half will be long enough cooking time. See *potée* (page 173) and sausage-meat recipes on page 151.

USING SMALL SAUSAGES, FRESH, DRIED, AND SMOKED

Saucisses aux Tomates

This is a favorite Saturday lunch dish in France, made with long, chipolata-style, all-meat sausages; and the wonderfully flavored, large tomatoes you can buy there.

Butter and oil
3 cloves of garlic, chopped,
  plus 2 cloves, crushed
½ lb. onions, chopped
  (about 2 cups)

1½ lbs. sausages
1 lb. tomatoes, plus brown
  sugar for final flavoring
Salt, pepper, chopped parsley or basil

You need two large frying pans; alternatively you can prick the sausages and bake them in a greased dish in the oven, giving your full attention to the tomatoes.

Melt an equal amount of butter and oil together in one of the large pans, add the crushed garlic and the chopped onion. Cook slowly and gently for a quarter of an hour, whilst you get the sausages going in the other pan or in the oven.

Skin the tomatoes by pouring boiling water over them, cut them in half and add (cut-side down) to the pan of onions. Turn the heat up and brown the onions and tomatoes, or cook gently into a mush—whichever you prefer. Season enthusiastically with black pepper and brown sugar (only a very little if you are using French tomatoes). Finally add the 3 chopped cloves of garlic, stir them in but do not cook, put into a hot dish and lay the sausages on top. A last dressing of chopped parsley or basil, and serve very hot with plenty of bread.

Saucisses au Vin Blanc (or au Cidre)

This recipe greatly improves the flavor of commercial sausages, but is best made with an all-meat sausage of the size that goes 6 or 8 to the pound.

Prick the sausages, stiffen in foaming butter for 5 minutes.

Transfer them to an oven dish. Swill ½ cup of dry white wine or good cider round the buttery pan and pour over the sausages. Cook, covered, in a moderate oven. Allow ½ hour, but this is a good-tempered dish that can be hurried a little or slowed down.

Serve with triangular pieces of bread fried in butter.

If you want to make a fine dish, pour off the cooking liquid into a frying pan and reduce it hard over a good heat. Keep tasting. When it is concentrated and interesting, pour it onto a beaten egg yolk, whisking as you pour. Stir in 2 to 4 tablespoons of butter, cut into small dice, and finally a tablespoon of chopped parsley or sage. Provided you've kept the dish and the sausages very hot, you can pour the sauce over without reheating. If you have to reheat, do it over a pan of almost-boiling water so that it does not curdle.

Tuck the *croûtons* of bread round the edge of the dish, and decorate with some wedges of lemon.

Friandises (Sausage Rolls)

Make, or buy, some good puff pastry.

Roll out and cut into 4- or 5-inch squares, according to the size of the sausages.

Prick the sausages and blanch for 5 minutes in almost-boiling water. Skin them.

Lay each sausage on a pastry square, brush the edges with beaten egg or milk, and fold the pastry over. Brush with egg, make two diagonal slashes, bake on a greased tray in a hot oven for 10 to 15 minutes.

See that they don't burn.

Toad-in-the-Hole

Nobody could claim that this is a French dish, but I've given it to many French friends with great success. And it is surprisingly good made with all-meat, well-spiced French sausages of the chipolata size.

Make the Yorkshire pudding mixture of 1 cup flour sifted with a good pinch of salt into a bowl. Form a well in the middle with the back of a wooden spoon and put 2 eggs in it and a little milk from a cup measure. Amalgamate flour and liquid slowly by stirring from the center, and add the rest of the milk.

Put a roasting pan in the oven, with 3 tablespoons of lard in it, or oil, or beef dripping. Be sure to use a clear-flavored fat, not the stale contents of a muddled dripping bowl. The oven should be hot, about 420°F.

Stiffen 1 lb. of sausages, well pricked, in a pan of simmering water for 5 minutes. Watch the pan of fat in the oven to make sure it doesn't burn, take it out when the fat is smoking. Run a layer of Yorkshire pudding mixture over the base of the pan. It should set slightly and make a bed for the stiffened sausages. Pour in the rest of the mixture and return to the hot oven for 30 to 40 minutes.

The pudding should be puffed up and succulent, 90 per cent crisp outside and no unpleasant semi-liquid dough.

See also the grand version of this, *saucisse en brioche,* made from one large sausage (recipe on page 164).

Saucisses aux Pommes

Sausages
Butter
1 lb. eating apples
A little good cider or dry

white wine and some
brandy or, preferably,
Calvados
Cream

Prick the sausages and fry gently in butter, whilst you attend to the apples in another pan.

Slice the cored apples, but don't peel them; fry in butter until they are golden-brown but not frizzled, and arrange them on the serving dish. You can quite well serve the sausages on them at this stage, but the sauce makes an elegant dish.

Pour a ½ cup of cider into the apple pan and let it bubble down for a few moments. Stir in 2 tablespoons Calvados or brandy, and then ½ cup of cream, with the heat turned down. Cook for a few moments very gently and you will have a thick, bland sauce of the Normandy type. Taste and correct the seasoning, before pouring over the sausages and apples.

If you haven't got cider, use dry white wine or *rosé.* Whatever you do, don't use the oversweet gaseous "cyder" sold by English soft-drink merchants—or its equally wretched American counterpart.

Saucisses à la Charcutière

Make a good purée of potatoes, firm but bland, and pile it onto the serving dish in a forked-up cone.

Fry chipolata sausages in butter, and arrange them upright but leaning against the cone of potatoes.

Serve with a *charcutière* sauce (page 45). Or with a *sauce Robert* (page 57), or a well-flavored tomato sauce (page 60).

Onion rings, soaked for an hour in milk, drained and dipped in seasoned flour and deep-fried in oil, make a good accompaniment.

Saucisses -Vin Rouge

Fresh sausages should be lightly fried in butter first.

Dried and smoked small sausages, and the larger *saucissons-cervelas,* go straight into the liquid.

Use 1 cup of red wine, Beaujolais if you can, and see that the sausages bathe in it. Cooking time will vary according to the size of the sausages, between 20 minutes and an hour in a moderate oven once the liquid has returned to simmering point.

Serve with a hot potato salad, made from waxy new potatoes or firm old ones boiled in their skins and then peeled. Mix the dressing whilst the potatoes cook, so that you can toss them in it whilst they are still hot. For 2 lbs. potatoes:

⅜ cup oil
2 scant tablespoons wine
    vinegar
Freshly ground black pep-
    per, salt, 1 clove of gar-
    lic, crushed

1 heaped teaspoon French
    mustard
½ teaspoon brown sugar
Chopped parsley

Don't let the potatoes cook in the dressing, but arrange them whilst still warm on a very hot serving dish. The sausages go in the middle, drained (use the Beaujolais for a casserole), and the dish should be finished with chopped parsley.

This simple and satisfactory dish can be varied by adding 2 tablespoons of raw shallot or scallion, chopped fine, to the potato salad. Or by finishing with chives instead of parsley. Or by using this dressing instead:

¼ lb. fat bacon, fried till crisp, then crushed
1 large onion chopped small, melted in bacon fat and lard
⅓ cup water

⅓ cup wine vinegar
2 teaspoons cornstarch
1 tablespoon brown sugar
2 tablespoons chopped parsley

Stir the water and vinegar into the cornstarch and sugar and cook till thickened. Add the parsley. Toss the potatoes in this, and gently turn whilst the bacon crumbs and the onion are added.

Quiche aux Saucisses et Poireaux

Make a good short-crust pastry with, for instance:

1 cup flour
5 tablespoons butter or butter and lard
A pinch of salt

2 teaspoons confectioners' sugar
And the least possible amount of very cold water to mix

Line a fluted 8-inch flan ring with a removable base. Prick and brush with white of egg. Bake blind, with rice or beans in aluminum foil to stop the pastry rising out of shape, in a moderate oven for 20 minutes.

Fill this with a purée of 1½ lbs. of leeks and, like the spokes of a wheel, lay on top chipolata sausages which you have fried gently in butter for 5 to 10 minutes.

Put back in the oven for the pastry to turn golden-brown. Be sure not to let the *quiche* burn.

NOTE: When making a leek purée, it is simplest to slice the leeks and wash them well, then put them in a thick-bottomed pan with a good lump of butter and a pinch of salt. There will be enough water, even if you drain the washed leeks, to stop them from burning—provided you cook them gently with a lid on the pan. A blender is ideal for reducing them to a purée without overcooking, but patience with a sieve and wooden spoon, or less patience and a "Mouli-légumes," will achieve a good result. Season the purée, and add some cream and 2 egg yolks, though this is not strictly necessary.

This is a very pretty dish and has the added advantage of being a complete meal in one.

Saucisses de Francfort au Chou Rouge

Prepare the red cabbage 1 or 2 days before you intend to eat this dish. It can be reheated several times without loss of flavor (minus the sausages, which should be added last thing), and it even tastes better for maturing slightly.

Any smoked sausages are suitable, cooked separately in hot water for 5 minutes to an hour, according to their size. *Petit salé,* hot, and unsmoked sausages are sometimes accompanied by red cabbage. But, be warned, this is a hefty, cold-day lunch dish.

There are many recipes for red cabbage. But most people prefer it cooked with an equal or lesser quantity of sliced onions and cooking apples, the three layered together and each layer seasoned with brown sugar, salt, and freshly ground black pepper. Finally, ¼ cup of red wine, and the same of wine vinegar, poured over. Cover with a tight-fitting lid and leave in a very slow oven for at least 3 hours. Correct the seasoning just before serving. Arrange on a hot dish with the separately cooked sausages.

Saucisses de Francfort à la Choucroute d'Alsace

Curnonsky gives this recipe, from Colmar. We probably have to use canned *choucroute* in England; nevertheless it is still worth doing. In America, good-quality sauerkraut is also available in plastic bags.

1 onion, chopped (about ¾ cup)
4 tablespoons of goose fat (or duck or lard)
1 lb. *choucroute*
½ cup dry white wine
1 good-sized eating apple, cut into pieces
10 juniper berries, tied in a bit of cloth

2 cups beef stock
1 lb. smoked streaky bacon
2 tablespoons Swiss or Alsatian Kirschwasser
Frankfurter or Strasbourg sausages
A piece of salted pork loin, cut into chops
1 lb. potatoes, boiled

In an enameled cast-iron pot or an earthenware casserole, cook the chopped onion in the goose fat until it is golden. Add the *choucroute,* unwashed if it is fresh from the barrel, or washed very quickly otherwise.

Cook for 5 minutes, stirring with a fork.

Add the white wine, the cut-up apple, and the juniper berries tied in the cloth. Pour on enough of the bouillon to almost cover the *choucroute.*

Put on the lid and cook in a gentle oven for 2 or 3 hours. One hour before serving add the smoked bacon. Half an hour before serving add the Kirsch. Ten minutes before serving add the sausages.

In a separate pot, cook the salted loin chops, simmering them for ½ hour in water, unseasoned, so that they are ready with the *choucroute*.

Heat a big, round serving dish, and arrange the drained *choucroute* on it (having removed the juniper berries), together with the smoked bacon, cut into slices, the sausages and the chops. Serve with potatoes, boiled in their skins, then peeled.

Choucroute Soup

The above recipe can be adapted for soup by cooking ½ lb. of peeled potatoes with the *choucroute* and increasing the stock to 5 cups. Remove the smoked bacon and juniper berries before putting everything else through a sieve or Mouli. Cut the bacon up into small pieces, and the sausages—omit the salted loin chops altogether—and heat through with the soup. Simmer gently for 10 minutes. Just before serving stir in 6 tablespoons (¾ stick) of unsalted butter or cream.

For other soups using salt pork and sausages, see *potée* (pages 173–5).

NOTE: Cumin seeds are often used for flavoring *choucroute* instead of juniper berries.

Saucisses aux Pois Chiches

Soak 1 lb. split green or yellow peas overnight. Next day cook peas and liquid with an onion stuck with 4 cloves, a piece of salt pork or bacon weighing up to ½ lb., a *bouquet garni,* and some salt and pepper. When the peas are cooked, drain them and remove the onion, bacon, etc. Sieve the peas and reheat slowly with some butter—about 2 tablespoons—and a little milk.

Cook the sausages in butter; or simmer them for 5 minutes in hot water if they are the smoked frankfurter type or dried. Put the purée of split peas into a serving dish and arrange the sausages on top.

Saucisses aux Lentilles

Follow the preceding recipe, using lentils which can be cooked exactly like the split peas. The piece of salt pork should be kept for another meal, or else neatly sliced and served with the sausages.

————•◆•————

USING SMALL AND LARGE SAUSAGES

Saucisse en Brioche à la Lyonnaise

Sausage baked in *brioche* dough is a speciality of many high-class *charcuteries* throughout France. For English and American cooks the main problems are the dough itself (the *charcutier* obtains his from the *pâtissier* as a rule) and the timing of the various quite simple procedures. For these reasons I quote the whole of Elizabeth David's recipe from *French Provincial Cooking*: there is no better version, though I would underline the necessity of using a hard-wheat ("all-purpose") flour, not the soft-wheat cake or pastry flour, for a satisfactory result.

"The sausage used in Lyon, where this dish is a renowned speciality, may be one of three kinds; it may be one of the routine cooking sausages, very coarsely cut and interlarded with large cubes of fat; it may be a *cervelas,* a close-textured sausage, very lightly smoked; or it may be a *cervelas truffé,* an unsmoked sausage of coarsely-cut pork generously truffled and spiced. Whichever it is, it will weigh in the region of 12 to 14 oz and be about 1½ inches in diameter, and because the pork for these sausages (as indeed for the majority of fresh or partly cured French sausage) is either brined for a night and a day or has saltpetre added to the mixture before the skins are filled, the colour of the finished sausage is a good red instead of the pinkish-grey characteristic of our own sausages.

"Randall & Aubin, in Brewer Street, Soho, sell a coarsely-cut garlic-flavoured sausage which is not unlike the Lyon sausage, and the Italian shops of Soho supply *cotechino,* the Modena boiling sausage which is also suitable for this dish; and at Harrods' butchery counter there is a special pure pork luncheon sausage, English in character, which is admirable for this dish and for the two which follow, for I see no reason why we should not adapt these splendid French dishes using the ingredients which are available to us here.* And no doubt many readers will be able to persuade their own local butchers to obtain the right casings for these large sausages and to fill them with their own favourite sausage mixture. But it should be borne in mind that if you are going to wrap a sausage in a brioche dough or even a flaky pastry, as for our own sausage rolls, it is really preferable to have a pure meat sausage. If you use a sausage containing the usual English mixture of 35 per cent bread or rusk, it means you are going to eat a rather doughy dish.

"Now for the recipe.

"It must be given in some detail and will take up a good deal of space, but I trust that its rather formidable length will not deter readers from trying it, for in many ways it makes the almost perfect hot first course dish, the majority of the work being done well in advance and the timing of the final cooking such that it

---

* In the United States, French boiling sausage is available at Molinari Brothers, 776 Ninth Avenue, New York City, and at Arsène Tingaud, 1070 Second Avenue, New York City; *cotechino* and other Italian sausages are sold by Manganaro Brothers, 488 Ninth Avenue, New York City, and by Solimeo and Schiraldi, 165 First Avenue, New York City.

can be put in the oven a few moments before your guests are expected and, in half an hour, is ready to emerge, a beautiful, golden roll of brioche enclosing the delicious savoury sausage. The procedure is as follows:

"(1) If the sausage is to be served at lunch, the brioche dough is made the previous night; if for dinner, in the early morning of the same day. It is extremely easy, for this is a simplified brioche dough. First you mix to a paste a scant ½ oz of baker's yeast and 2 tablespoons [4 U.S. tablespoons] of barely tepid milk. In a bowl you then put 6 oz [1½ cups] of plain flour, a half teaspoon of salt, and 1 of sugar. Make a well in the centre. Into this break 2 whole eggs, and add the yeast mixture. Fold the flour over the eggs and yeast and knead all together until the mixture is smooth. Now beat in with your hands 4 oz [8 tablespoons, 1 stick] of the best butter, softened but not melted. Knead again and shape it into a ball. Put it in a clean bowl, a wooden one for preference, in which you have sprinkled some flour. Make a deep crosswise incision across the top of the ball of dough with a knife. Cover it with a clean, folded muslin. Put the bowl in a warm place, such as a heated linen cupboard or near the boiler, or in the plate drawer of the cooker with the oven turned on to a very low temperature. Leave it for 2 hours, by which time it should have risen to at least twice its original volume and will look and feel light and spongy. Break it down, knead it lightly once more into a ball, cover it again, and this time put the bowl in a cool larder and leave it until next day, or until the evening.

"(2) Put your large sausage (the quantity of dough is enough for a 12 to 14 oz sausage) into a pan in which it will lie flat. Cover completely with cold water. Bring very gently to simmering point and thereafter let it cook with the water barely moving, for 45 minutes to an hour. Take it out and put it on a board or dish until it is cool enough to handle. Now remove the skin, very carefully.

"(3) Allowing yourself half an hour the first few times you do this dish (afterwards it will be much quicker) make the final preparations. Very lightly rub a baking sheet with butter. Put your dough on this, sprinkle it with flour, and with your hands spread and pat it out into a rectangular shape on the baking sheet. Turn it over (by this time you can, or should be able to, handle the dough as easily as if it were a piece of material). Put your skinned sausage, still warm, in the centre. Gather up the edges of the dough and, having dipped your fingers in cold water, pinch the edges lightly together, along the top and at the ends, so that the whole thing looks rather like a small bolster. Now dip a pastry brush in cream and paint the whole of the exposed surface with it (cream makes the best glaze for these sorts of dishes—not so shiny as egg and smoother than milk). With the back of a knife lightly mark a few criss-cross lines on the dough. The sausage and its brioche can now be left for 15 to 20 minutes, ready on its baking sheet, before it goes into the centre of a preheated oven at Gas No. 5, 375–80°F. [375–80°F. in U.S.], to bake for 30 minutes. When you take it from the oven, leave the brioche standing for 5 minutes before transferring it, with the aid of a flat fish slice, to a serving dish, and carving it deftly into thickish slices, starting in the middle and working outward. It will be ample for four.

"One should not perhaps expect this dish to come exactly right the first time, except for those accustomed to working with yeast doughs. But although it may sound complicated, after one or two tries it becomes a matter of timing rather than of any special knowledge, and you get a splendid-looking delicious dish with absurdly little trouble. It is mainly a question of assembling all your ingredients and utensils before each of the two main operations–the original mixing of the dough and the final wrapping of the sausage in it. Points to observe carefully are:

"(1) Brioche dough is very much more liquid than bread dough, but if after the initial mixing it is really too soft to handle, it may be because you have added a little too much milk to the yeast, or because the eggs were unusually large, or because you are using a soft flour. A little more flour sprinkled in will put matters right.

"(2) The sausage is to be put into the dough while it is still warm, because if it is left to get quite cold it will separate from the brioche when it is cut; but if it is too hot the fat running from it will make your dough liquid and difficult to handle.

"(3) Be sure to join the edges of the dough well together round the sausage without drawing it too tightly or the sausage will burst through during the baking. This does not detract from the taste of the dish, but rather spoils its appearance.

"(4) It is essential that the sausage be cooked right through to start with; once inside its casing of brioche, it will heat but will scarcely cook any more."

Cassoulet

The tastiest form of baked beans is *cassoulet,* a rich, slowly cooked dish of dried white haricot beans, goose, salt pork, sausages large and small, including the Toulouse sausage (page 127), small squares of pork skin to make the sauce smooth and bland, and bread crumbs to form the crusty golden top. Languedoc is the native home of *cassoulet,* more specifically the small town of Castelnaudary on the Canal du Midi, whose classic version was described by Anatole France as having "a taste, which one finds in the paintings of old Venetian masters, in the amber flesh tints of their women." At Toulouse and Carcassonne cooks add mutton and partridge.

This dish needs careful planning and preparation. It is not cheap. The ideal time to choose for it is when you are able to have a goose: keep the legs to one side, turn them over daily in a mixture of 2 heaped tablespoons of unadulterated salt and a small pinch of saltpeter. Invite your guests and assemble the other ingredients.

Good beans are worth an effort. Most grocers sell dried white haricot beans vaguely described as "foreign." Better quality and a creamier texture are to be found in Soho, where grocers

cassoulet in a cassole and a toupin

import beans from France, varieties known as Soissons and Arpajon from the market-gardening centers near Paris where they were first developed.* Like geese, dried beans are at their best in the autumn; with time they become drier and harder and harder and drier, so beware the grocer with a slow turnover.

The other main requirement is a deep, wide earthenware pot in which all the ingredients are finally amalgamated. Correctly a *cassole* or *toupin,* any earthenware or stoneware casserole will do, provided it is deep and wide.

———→ *Beans* ←———

1 lb. haricot beans or Great Northern white beans
A good-sized piece of pork or bacon skin, cut into squares
A knuckle of pork

1 lb. salt sowbelly
1 large onion stuck with 4 cloves
1 carrot
4 cloves of garlic
Bouquet garni

* In America, Great Northern dried white beans are the best bet.

———➤ *Pork and Goose or Mutton Ragoût* ➤·——

1 lb. boned shoulder of pork

1½–2 lbs. preserved goose (*confits d'oie*, page 331), or duck, or either made up to weight with boned loin or shoulder of mutton

3 large onions, chopped (about 3 cups)

6 cloves of garlic, or according to taste

Bouquet garni, salt and ground black pepper

4 large tomatoes, skinned

2 tablespoons tomato paste

Beef stock

Goose or duck fat or lard

———➤ *Sausages* ➤·——

1 lb. Toulouse sausages (page 127), or *saucisses de campagne* (page 126), or a large 1-lb. boiling sausage of the all-meat *cervelas* type

(page 146), or the pork boiling rings sold in delicatessens or butcher shops

1 lb. *saucisson à l'ail* (page 138)

———➤ *Plus* ➤·——

Plenty of white bread crumbs to form a top crust

Soak the beans overnight. Drain and put them in an earthenware pot with the other ingredients; cover with water. Bring to the boil, and cook in a gentle oven for 1½ hours, or until the beans are tender but not splitting.

Meanwhile prepare the pork and goose ragoût. Put the chopped onions on to sauté to a golden hash in a large frying pan (preferably cast iron). Cut the various meats into eating-sized pieces or joints, and add them to the onions. Turn up the heat a little so that they can brown, without burning. Pour off any surplus fat, then add the tomatoes skinned and chopped into large chunks, and a little stock, about ½ cup, to make enough sauce for the meat to continue cooking in. Flavor with concentrated tomato paste and seasonings, push the *bouquet garni* into the middle. Cover the pan, and keep the contents at a gentle bubble until the beans are ready—about ½ hour.

Add the large *saucisson à l'ail* and the *cervelas* to the beans, so that they have ½ hour's simmering. If you are using sausages, stiffen them in a little goose fat or lard for 10 minutes.

When the beans are cooked, drain off and keep the liquid; remove the onion, carrot, *bouquet garni,* and knuckle bone, and slice the salt pork and knuckle meat. Use the bacon skins, or pork skins, to line the deep earthenware pot you intend to use for the final cooking. Put in half the beans, then the pork and goose ragoût, the sliced meats from the bean-cooking pot, the small and large sausages, and the rest of the beans. Pour over ½ cup of the bean liquid, and finish with a ½-inch layer of bread crumbs dotted with pieces of goose fat or lard.

Cook very slowly, about 320°F., for 1½ hours. The crust will turn a beautiful golden color, and traditionally you should push it down with a spoon three to seven times, so that it can re-form with the aid of another sprinkling of bread crumbs.

The point of this last cooking is to blend all the delicious flavors together gently, without the meat becoming tasteless and stringy. Everything has, after all, already been cooked. If you find that the *cassoulet* is becoming too dry, add a little more of the bean liquid, but don't overdo this.

The quantities can be varied, the essentials are beans, sausages, pork and goose (or goose and mutton, or a small roasting duck). Pork and beans alone are very good (see below, and recipes for Boston baked beans, etc.), but it is the goose or duck that makes the difference.

This is an ideal dish for a winter's Sunday lunch party—it pleases everybody from children to grandparents. The cook should be pleased too, because her guests should not be allowed to eat too much beforehand, and can't eat much afterwards, so her labors are cut to a minimum.

Cassoulet au Beurre de Gascogne

Here is a simple family version of *cassoulet*. An excellent filler on a cold day, which can be prepared after breakfast—if you omit the sausage, or use small ones—and left to look after itself until ½ hour before lunch.

1 lb. haricot beans or Great Northern white beans
Pieces of fresh pork skin
1-lb. piece of *petit salé*, un-

cooked, or brine-pickled sowbelly (page 191)
1 large French sausage of the boiling type, or small smoked sausages

———•← Beurre de Gascogne →•———

8 cloves of garlic
6 tablespoons lard or goose, duck, or chicken fat

4 tablespoons chopped parsley

Soak the beans overnight.

Next day line the casserole with the fresh pork skin, outside down, and put the piece of pork on top. If you use *petit salé*, make sure that the salt is washed off first. Pack in the beans around and on top. Just cover with water, and put on a close-fitting lid. Give it 3 hours in a slow oven, 320°F. Add no salt at this stage.

If you use a large sausage, add it 1 hour before the end of cooking time. If you use small sausages, add them ½ hour before. Taste the *cassoulet* whilst you do this and add salt, pepper, etc. Make the *beurre de Gascogne* by blanching the cloves of garlic in salted boiling water for 5 to 10 minutes. Pound them to a paste, adding the 6 tablespoons of fat and finally the parsley.

Just before serving, strain off the liquid from the beans and pork, taste again, and adjust the seasoning. Mix in the *beurre de Gascogne* at the last moment before serving.

NOTE: If you have no pure fat or dripping, use olive oil or butter.

Potée

BASIC METHOD

Potée is basically a cabbage soup, in the way that *cassoulet* is basically beans and pork. But the addition of other vegetables as well as sausages and pickled meat makes it a complete meal in one pot, again like *cassoulet*. In the southwest of France, this thick soup is called *garbure* and contains, inevitably, *confits d'oie* (page 331). Country housewives use what they have to hand in their own kitchens and attic store, so the ingredients vary; but here is a suggested list and BASIC METHOD:

1 good crisp green cabbage
1 lb. salt sowbelly or streaky bacon in a piece (page 181)
A large piece of pork skin
Salt
6 medium-sized potatoes, peeled
12 new carrots or 4 old ones, cut in pieces

4 small onions, peeled
3 leeks, sliced
A piece of garlic sausage or boiling sausage (*saucisson à l'ail*)
Green beans and peas, if in season
Toulouse or country sausages, or dried or smoked sausages

Cut the cabbage into quarters, plunge it into boiling water to blanch for 10 minutes. Leave it to drain.

Put the pork or bacon and pork skin in a pot and cover with water. Don't add salt. Simmer for ½ hour.

Add the potatoes, carrots, and onions, and any other root vegetables you want to use. Simmer for ½ hour.

Add the garlic sausage, peas and beans—and the smoked or dried sausages if you are using them. Simmer for ½ hour.

Meanwhile slice up the blanched cabbage, stiffen the fresh sausages for 10 minutes in lard or butter, and add them to the *potée* 5 minutes before serving. Remove the piece of salt pork, so that it can be sliced too, then return it to the pot. Taste, and correct seasoning.

One French custom is to add thick slices of wholemeal bread

just before serving the soup, but it is usually best to leave people to do this for themselves in case they are watching their weight. A more popular tradition is the addition of a glass of red or white wine to the last few spoonsful of soup in one's plate—this is known as a *goudale* in the Béarn, where much *garbure* (page 174) is consumed.

Potée (economy recipe)

Use a large piece of pork skin, omit the pork, and stuff some of the larger leaves of the cabbage with half bread crumbs, half ground pork, ham, or bacon, bound with egg. Tie each stuffed leaf into a little package with some tape and add with other green vegetables ½ hour before the end of the cooking time (see above). Remember that even a very small piece of smoked sausage gives a good flavor.

Garbure

Follow the preceding recipe for *potée*, but add some *confits d'oie* (or the remains of roast goose or duck) and a little goose fat, when you put in the garlic sausage.

In deepest winter, instead of green vegetables add ½ lb. of haricot or Great Northern beans, which have been soaked overnight, cooked, and *drained* (see *cassoulet*, page 168). Even a canned red pepper or two makes a difference, or try ½ lb. of chestnuts, shelled and roasted. All these things need to be added ½ hour before the end of cooking time, but don't try them all together—or rather don't use beans and chestnuts together.

Sieve a few pieces of root vegetable, or beans, if you like the liquid itself thickened.

NOTE: Once you have blanched the cabbage, you may find

it more convenient to pack all the ingredients into a huge pot, cover them with fresh water, and leave in a slow oven for 3 hours. But if you have the time, the BASIC METHOD is more popular, most people preferring cabbage to be slightly crisp—*al dente,* like spaghetti or rice—rather than a mush.

See also frankfurter and *choucroute* soup (page 163), and the chapter following on salt pork for *petit salé.* Recipes for making the sausages required are given earlier in this chapter, on pages 127 and 138.

 SALT PORK AND HAMS

Of all *charcuterie* the most easily rewarding to make, from an English or American housewife's point of view, is salt pork and unsmoked ham. Everybody nowadays knows about pâté, but produce a hot, glazed joint of salt pork, or a cold dish of delicate *jambon de Paris*, and you cause a sensation.

This enthusiasm has a long historical tradition. Dumas, in his *Grand Dictionnaire de Cuisine*, tells of the not-so-stupid Emperor Claudius, Robert Graves's Claudius, who walked into the Senate one day crying, "Pères conscrits, dites-moi, je vous prie, est-il possible de vivre sans petit salé?" To which that noble body promptly replied, "Oui, seigneur, plutôt mourir que de se passer de lard." And from then on senators ate large quantities of salt sowbelly and cabbage (*petit salé aux choux*, page 182) to keep alive and flatter Claudius.

Or perhaps they meant it, for the Romans sustained their enthusiasm, beyond their own resources, by imports of ham from Gaul. It was Strabo who early recorded the excellence of French *charcuterie* in his *Geographia*, Book 4, written in the first century A.D.: "Food they [the Gauls] have in very great quantities, along with milk and flesh of all sorts, but particularly the flesh of hogs, both fresh and salted. . . . And their herds of swine are so very large that they supply an abundance . . . of salt-meat, not only to Rome, but to most parts of Italy as well." At the same time Romans in Britain were enjoying their favorite salt pork in another Celtic area: one cremation site of the first century A.D., excavated recently near Winchester, disclosed to the diggers "a tray set with cutlery for a meal, a pig's trotter and a Bath Chap." A vivid but anachronistic description; or were pig's jaws cured *à l'Aquae Sulis* even then?

When I buy kilo bags of *sel marin de Bretagne* from our Trôo grocer, I like to reflect that Strabo's hams were cured in this same gray salt, evaporated nearly two thousand years ago from the same cold Atlantic.

Earlier still, northern meat had to be preserved by burial in pits, or by drying in the wind, because our fitful sun could not sustain a salt industry on Mediterranean lines, where, then as now, huge glistening heaps of white salt dried on low shores, in brilliant light. But with the increased technological skills and achievements of the Iron Age, northern Europeans overcame their salt problem by artificial means. The method they used has left red fertile mounds, easily to be seen around Maldon, in Essex, where excellent sea salt is still produced. Shallow earthenware trays on legs were filled with seawater and fires were lit beneath. The water boiled away leaving a deposit of salt to be scraped off the trays. Naturally there was a high wastage of such friable equipment. New trays were set up on top of the broken pieces, and reduced in their turn to coarse red powder, betraying now, by large, slightly raised circles of red soil in brown ploughed fields, and by lumps of *briquetage* fused with jade-colored vitrifications of sand, the sites of this ancient, essential industry. (The tray's on view in Winchester Museum.)

The problem of salt is still with us (though not, in these days of refrigeration, as a means of preserving meat for winter use). The flavor of sea salt is vastly better than the flavor of refined rock salt. In London continental grocers in Soho stock good salt, and so does Elizabeth David, at 46 Bourne Street, S.W.1, but in smaller towns it may only be available in health-food shops.*

---

* In the U.S. sea salt can be gotten from local fancy-food stores or from the House of Herbs Farms, Salisbury, Connecticut.

saloirs, or brine crocks

Polythene bags of sea salt, which keep well in a dry place, can be brought back from France. Refined rock salt is all right for brine and dry salting, but the flavor of the ham will not be quite so good; all grocers stock refined rock salt. Be careful not to buy free-running table salt, as chemicals are added, to prevent it forming lumps, which make it unsuitable for curing.

The other things needed are easily come by. A large crock, preferably of stoneware, although a plastic bucket will do. A piece of boiled wood which fits right into the crock, to keep the floating pieces of pork below the surface. Household baking soda for cleaning the crock. Saltpeter (to be bought from most druggists) to give the meat an appetizing pink color. Sugar to counteract the hardening effects on the meat of salt and saltpeter. A maximum and minimum thermometer is not essential, but it gives accurate information about the fluctuations of surrounding temperature, which can be deceptive.

As you will see from the brine recipe on page 200, white wine can be used, and flavorings of herbs and spices, but from the actual preserving point of view salt is the only absolute necessity. Brine will keep for several weeks, indefinitely if you strain it off from time to time, clean the crock, and boil up the brine again. In English bacon factories the brine in huge white-tiled curing baths is eternal, perpetually being drained off and added to but never thrown away. A vintage blend, with as many strains as a fine brandy. Details of temperature and length of time in brine are given in the appropriate section on page 193, but any fresh pork recipe is greatly improved in flavor if the joint first spends a clear 12 hours in the crock. This applies even to a delicate truffled loin of pork, or to the famous pork with prunes of Tours.

Smoking is an additional, but not an essential, means of preserving meat which has already spent a few days in brine or else been dried from a hook at a steady temperature of 60°F. (see *saucissons* recipes on pages 141 to 146). It is a difficult process for the amateur to attempt, and obviously a start should be made with small, inexpensive items like sausages. Maintaining a steady smoke is also extremely tricky, sometimes involving sleepless nights on account of visits to the fire. The point of smoking is firstly to remove the moisture from the meat very slowly, like drying, and secondly, unlike drying, to give additional flavor and preservatives. Unless you have an experienced friend to guide you, my advice is to take hams to be smoked at the nearest bacon factory, once you have pickled them in brine.* This applies particularly to hams intended to be eaten raw (the most famous French one is Bayonne ham—in fact cured at Orthez, near Bayonne, although many districts have their own, and one should always inquire in the *charcuterie* for a *jambon cru de la région*).

Living in the country, 3 miles from the nearest butcher, I find that the brine crock has taken many anxieties away. Unexpected visitors can cheerfully be welcomed, and given something

---

* This may prove impossible in some areas of the United States, however.

more interesting than scrambled eggs. After a little initial planning, this is what I have found best to keep in the *saloir:*

1 · A 5-lb. loin of pork (*noisettes,* chops, or a large glazed joint
   —most useful of all cuts).
2 · A boned leg of pork (boiled salt pork, or a *jambon de Paris*),
   and a hock (*jambonneau*).
3 · A 2-lb. piece of sowbelly (fatter end to be used bit by bit
   for improving shin of beef and oxtail stews, the leaner end
   to be simmered in water and served as *petit salé,* page 181).
4 · A shifting population of trotters, ears, tails, pieces of pork
   skin—anything the butcher throws in for a copper or two.

Replace the joints as you use them, and remember that they can spend up to 5 weeks in brine—though this is not really a good idea for small pieces. If you can rely on a dry, airy temperature which will not rise above 60°F., and will stay fairly steady, you can remove the meat from the brine and wrap it tightly in clean linen or cotton and hang it up to dry. Incidentally, there is an excellent chapter on "Pig Curing and By-products," pages 241–63, of *Farmhouse Fare,* published for *The Farmers' Weekly* at $.72.* Many English methods of curing and recipes for brine are given there. If you have room for extensive meat curing beyond the range of the average household, consult Chapters III and IX of *Sausage and Small Goods Production,* by Frank Gerrard, M.Inst.M., M.Inst.R., M.R.S.A., published by Leonard Hill (London) at $2.40. Although it is subtitled "A practical Handbook for all in the Meat Trade," a farmer and his wife for instance, with space and meat supply to hand, could follow some of the methods Mr. Gerrard describes. I would also recommend this book to anyone who is really concerned about the meat products on sale to the public. Apart from the pleasure of reading practical and interesting information, there's the side bonus of discovering what care is taken by manufacturers in achieving their

---

* Americans might also consult the chapter on pig curing in the U.S. Department of Agriculture's Farmers' Bulletin No. 2138, *Slaughtering, Cutting, and Processing Pork.*

twin targets of perfect hygiene and perfect nonentity. No wonder most sausages on sale in England are not worth buying.

Mr. Gerrard also gives this explanation of the different effects of dry-salt curing and brine curing: "When a piece of meat is placed in a strong solution of salt the fluids in the meat begin to flow out and mix with the salt solution. Meanwhile the salt has begun to penetrate the meat and to bring about changes within the meat. These changes slow down the outward flow of fluid from the meat, and finally the flow is reversed. Water as well as salt now flows into the meat from the strong salt solution. The stronger this solution the longer it takes before the reversal of flow takes place. . . .

"If solid salt or solid sugar is used, no action takes place until they have dissolved in the fluid exuding from the meat. Thereafter the changes are similar to those occurring when meat is immersed in strong solutions but occur more slowly, the rate depending upon the speed at which the fluid can exude from the meat."

If you are not used to salting meat, I suggest you begin with dry salting, and make your experiment with a lean piece of sow-belly or spareribs.

DRY-SALT CURE
(*Salaison à Sec*)

Petit Salé

Flavored salt (*sel aromatisé*) is the first requirement.

To every 2½ lbs. salt (enough for 12 lbs. meat in fact):

2 tablespoons saltpeter
2 tablespoons granulated
  sugar
1 teaspoon peppercorns

1 oz. juniper berries
4 bay leaves, crumbled
Thyme leaves from 2
  sprigs, crushed
4 cloves

Mix it all well together. Put about ¾ lb. in the bottom of a stoneware or Pyrex dish.

Take the piece of sowbelly and rub a good handful of salt firmly into the skin side. Turn it over and rub some more into the flesh side, but not so vigorously. Lay it on the layer of salt, flesh-side down, skin-side up, and pack the rest of the salt round the sides and over the top. Put a piece of boiled wood on top (or a scrupulously clean plate) and a light weight.

Leave in a cool, dark place for at least 4 days per inch thickness of meat. You can leave the *petit salé*, on the other hand, in salt for much longer—one handbook recommends 2 months. You will find that the meat juices turn the salt to brine.

Cook the *petit salé* in plenty of plain water, bringing it slowly to the boil, and timing it from then. As sowbelly is never very thick, an hour is the maximum time required; 40 minutes is usually enough. Taste the water, and pour it away after 5 minutes of simmering, if it is too salty. Alternatively, if the meat has been salting for several weeks, soak in tepid water for 2 hours before you start cooking.

Whichever you do, saltiness is easy to remedy, so don't panic. Serve hot with mashed potato, or arranged in slices on top of *choucroute* (page 162). Cold, the way the *charcutier* sells it, it makes a delicious meal with salad.

Petit salé is an excellent accompaniment, in the English style, to roast chicken or turkey. It is often an ingredient of *cassoulet* and cabbage soups and stews, *potée* for instance (page 173).

Petit Salé aux Choux

Here is the good Roman dish, so approved of by the Emperor Claudius.

Choose a crisp green cabbage, cut it in quarters and remove the hard stem part. Whilst the *petit salé* is simmering away, plunge the cabbage into another pan of fast-boiling water, and leave it there for 10 minutes. Drain it well. Pour away the blanching water and remove enough liquid from the *petit salé* pan to give a ¼ inch depth in the cabbage pan. Twenty minutes before the *petit salé* is ready, bring this liquid to the boil and put in the cabbage to cook quickly, with a knob of butter as well.

Cut the *petit salé* in slices and serve on top of the cabbage, which should still be slightly crisp and not a mush.

NOTE: Many recipes tell you to cook the cabbage in with the *petit salé,* but the above method gives a much pleasanter result.

Petit Salé aux Pois Secs

Wintry *petit salé* is delicious with a purée of dried peas, which you should have soaked overnight and cooked in with the meat. When they are done, remove them from the liquid and sieve. Reheat in a separate dish with a good knob of butter and a little meat jelly, if you have some, or a spoonful or two of the *petit salé* liquid.

Serve, too, with purées of other dried vegetables, *aux lentilles,* for instance, or *aux haricots blancs.*

It is a good idea to soak the *petit salé* beforehand, and then cook with just enough liquid to cover it and the dried vegetables. This gives you a thick soup, like the *potées* and *garbures* on pages 173 and 174, in which *petit salé* can also be used.

Petit Salé aux Petits Pois

Serve the *petit salé* on a purée of green peas, which can be old ones, if they are cooked in the French style:

Cook 1 large onion, chopped, in 3 tablespoons of butter until it is golden but not brown. Add the heart of a lettuce, ½ teaspoon of salt, ½ cup of boiling water, and 2 teaspoons of sugar. When it is all boiling away together, pour in 2 or 3 lbs. of shelled peas.

(*If your peas are tender, new ones, omit the water.*) Cover and cook gently. Drain and put through a sieve, correcting the seasoning if necessary.

Serve the *petit salé*, sliced, on top.

Petits Pois au Lard

This is a delicious way of using up, or stretching, a smallish piece of *petit salé* (which is, in effect, a mild green English bacon or *lard*).

Soak the *petit salé* in tepid water for several hours, if it has been in salt longer than 3 or 4 days. Drain and dry it, then cut into small dice. Melt some butter in a large heavy pan and gently fry the dice until they are a golden color. Remove them whilst you make a *roux* with 2 tablespoons of flour. Pour in 1 cup of stock, stirring all the time to avoid lumps. Cook for 2 minutes, then put back the *petit salé*, and add 2 or 3 lbs. of peas, shelled, a chopped onion, and a *bouquet garni*. If your peas are on the hard side, and flavorless, add sugar. Bring the pan back to the boil and after 5 minutes of gentle simmering taste to correct the seasoning. Add plenty of freshly ground black pepper with it and some chopped sage leaves. Simmer until cooked.

Pommes de Terre au Lard

Follow the preceding recipe, only use large potato dice instead of peas. A good glass of wine improves this dish. Naturally you omit the sugar.

Petit Salé aux Poireaux

Cook the *petit salé* (page 181).

Meanwhile prepare a leek purée. Slice the leeks and wash them well. Shake them free of surplus water and put them in a pan with a large knob of butter and a pinch of salt. Put the lid on, and set over a low heat until the butter has melted and a fair amount of water has exuded from the leek slices. Then cook as quickly as you can, and either sieve or purée in an electric blender. Add salt, black pepper, more butter, cream, a dash of sugar, as you think fit. Grated or cream cheese are good additions.

Serve the *petit salé,* sliced, on top of the purée.

Petit Salé aux Pommes

Cook the *petit salé* in the usual way (see recipe, page 181), and serve hot on a dish of apple rings fried in butter, or on a purée of apples.

Petit Salé aux Champignons

Serve the *petit salé,* sliced, on a bed of potato purée, flavored with nutmeg, and surrounded by sautéed mushrooms. Sprinkle with parsley before setting on the table.

Petit Salé aux Marrons

Serve *petit salé* with a purée of chestnuts, or with Brussels sprouts and chestnuts cooked together.

Nick the chestnuts, put them on a baking tray in a hot oven for 8 minutes. Remove a few at a time and shell them. Simmer them in stock until they are soft and purée them or else mix them with cooked Brussels sprouts. Potatoes are unnecessary.

Hochepot

Like *cassoulet* or the thick *potées* and *garbures, hochepot* is one of those delicious all-inclusive dishes in which pork makes a telling appearance. Our Lancashire hotpot is reduced to solo mutton, and the last thing one needs to do to it is to shake (*hocher*) the pot. In northern France the liquid is served as a soup, and the meat afterwards, like the more widely known *pot-au-feu.*

––––•–➤ *Meat* ➤–•––––

1½ lbs. boned ribs of beef
½ lb. mutton, best end of neck chops (weighed without bones)
½ lb. veal, scrag end of middle neck (weighed without bones)

½-lb. piece of *petit salé*
2 pig's ears
Lard
Some all-pork country sausages or pork sausages (pages 126 and 127)

––––•–➤ *Vegetables* ➤–•––––

The crisp heart of a green cabbage, blanched for 10 minutes in boiling water
2 or 3 leeks tied together with 3 stalks of celery
2 or 3 small white turnips, cut up

½ lb. small onions
½ lb. carrots, sliced (about 1¾ cups)
1 large parsnip (½ lb.), cut up
Potatoes, small new ones are the best

––––•–➤ *Seasonings* ➤–•––––

Juniper berries (about 10)
4 cloves

Pepper and salt, and a *bouquet garni*

You will also need a large, deep casserole filled with 2½ or 3 quarts of water.

Put the beef into the cold water, bring it quickly to the boil and skim. Keep it bubbling away whilst you brown the rest of the meat in some lard, except for the *petit salé*, which must be blanched in boiling water for 10 minutes—this could be done with the cabbage.

Keep skimming the big pot, and when the various other meats are browned or blanched, add them to it with the seasonings and the vegetables—except the potatoes.

Bring the pot to the boil again, and reduce the heat so that a simmer is maintained. Cover the pot and leave for 45 minutes. If you have potatoes and sausages, add them a quarter of an hour before the end—in other words, after the pot has simmered for ½ hour. If you do not have new potatoes, cut old ones fairly small.

This soup tends to be fatty, so skim off as much as you can. I usually pour off the liquid into a bowl and let it settle, so that the fat has a chance to rise. Reheat when you have dealt with it, and put some slices of bread in the bottom of the soup tureen.

Whilst the soup is reheating, slice up the meat into nice pieces and arrange on a serving dish with the vegetables, which should have been well drained and (in the case of leeks and celery) cut up. Keep warm in the oven whilst the soup is being drunk, then serve, sprinkled with chopped parsley, on very hot plates.

Quiche Lorraine

Whether you prepare *petit salé* by dry salting or brine cure, you can slice and use it for *quiches* instead of commercial bacon.

Short-crust pastry (1 cup flour, 5 tablespoons combined butter and lard, 2 teaspoons confectioners' sugar, a pinch of salt, water)

¼–⅜ lb. *petit salé,*

washed, sliced, and cut into small pieces

4 egg yolks or 2 whole eggs

1 cup cream (light or heavy)

Grated nutmeg or mace

Freshly ground black pepper, salt

Those shallow, fluted French flan rings are the best to use for *quiches*. They have a removable base that can be pushed gently up to ease out the tart when it is cooked. Grease lightly and line with short-crust pastry. Everybody has their own ideas on avoiding a soggy base—I usually brush the whole pastry lining with white of egg.

Next make the filling. First prepare the *petit salé* in one of two ways—either blanch it for 5 minutes in simmering water or else fry it gently in butter for 5 minutes. Distribute it evenly over the pastry.

Beat the egg yolks, cream, and seasonings together lightly, and pour over the *petit salé.*

Bake in a moderate oven for about 40 minutes. Remember that a *quiche* is really a savory custard tart; it mustn't cook too quickly or it will curdle. Like sweet custard tart, it is best eaten warm, so let it cool down for about 20 minutes before serving.

This recipe can be adjusted in various ways. For instance, when you arrange the *petit salé* on the pastry, add ¼ lb. of Gruyère cheese cut into small dice.

Or as well as the Gruyère, add ¼ lb. of chopped onions (about 1 cup) which have been softened to a golden transparency in some butter. For economy, instead of cream use half milk and half cream—or even all milk. It cannot be denied that flavor and texture both suffer, but the result is quite pleasant.

Or cook in small individual tins or patty pans. More pastry will be required, and a shorter cooking time, according to the size.

Jambons (Hams) par Salaison à Sec

The mildest and most delicious English and American hams are cured the dry-salt way at first, even if some of them later spend a period in brine. Although their names refer to various localities

(Virginian, Kentucky, Suffolk, York), it is no absolute guarantee that that is where they were cured, but only that they were cured in the Virginian, etc., style. This accounts for the puzzling ubiquity of *jambon d'York* all over France. *Jambon de Paris* is another example of this.

The wetter the cure the quicker the salt penetrates the meat, so a dry cure has a gentler, more prolonged effect. With a brine cure sugar is often added to counteract the quick, harsh effects of the salted water, though this was of course out of the question in Cato's day. He described the method used by contemporary northern Italians—or rather, Romans—about 200 B.C., and it is not very different from the method recommended in modern *charcuterie* handbooks, as well as in Bulletin 127 of the British Ministry of Agriculture and Fisheries:

"When you have bought your hams, cut off the hoofs. Take half a peck (10 lbs.) of Roman salt, ground fine, for each. Lay salt over the bottom of the tub; then put in a ham, the skin-side looking downwards. Cover it over with salt. Then put another ham on top, taking care that meat does not touch meat. So deal with them all. When you have got them all snug put salt over them, so that no meat is visible, and make the surface level. When they have been in salt five days take them all out and the salt with them. Then put them in again in reverse order so that those which were before on top are now at the bottom. Cover them over and make them snug in the same way as before. After twelve days, at most, take the hams out, rub off all the salt and hang them up in a draught for two days. On the third day wipe them well over with a sponge and rub them with oil. Hang them for two days in the smoke. Then take them down, rub them well with a mixture of oil and vinegar and hang them up in the meat larder."

Jambon de Campagne

Use flavored salt (*sel aromatisé*), which should be prepared beforehand:

2 lbs. salt	**1 tablespoon cloves**
6 tablespoons saltpeter	**1 tablespoon juniper**
¾ cup sugar	**berries**
1½ oz. peppercorns	**20 bay leaves**
1½ oz. *quatre-épices* (or	**20 sprigs of thyme**
mixed spices)	

Mix it all together.

Prepare the ham from a newly killed pig by removing the thigh bone (leave the knuckle bone, so that you can hang the ham up), and beating it with a wooden mallet so that it exudes any remaining blood and juice. Tie a strong, clean piece of cord round the knuckle bone and hang the ham up in a dark, airy place, with a plate beneath to catch any further liquid which drips out. Leave it for 3 days, but make sure to wipe it with a clean cloth twice a day. Next rub the ham over with the cut side of half a lemon, and then with the flavored salt. Having cleaned your crock with washing soda and boiling water, and then rinsed it with fresh boiling water, put it to drain and dry in a warm place.

Put a layer of the salt in the bottom, then your ham, skin-side down, and pack the rest of the salt round and over it. Make sure that there is some salt in the ham where the thigh bone was; salt should also be forced down the knuckle bone as much as possible. Lay a boiled piece of wood on top and a weight on that, to keep the pork entirely submerged in the brine. Leave the crock in a cool (38°–45°F.), dry place for 10 to 15 days, according to the temperature and humidity of the weather.

If the weather should still be on your side—or you can provide artificially a steady drying temperature between 50° and

60°F., you can wash the ham with a clean nailbrush and tepid water and hang it up for 10 days.

If you are dubious about these conditions—and have no intention of keeping the ham for any length of time anyway— you can proceed straight to the cooking.

If you have embarked on the drying process with confidence, you can either cook the ham after the 10 days, or go on further and smoke it (see page 207). Stored in a close-fitting linen or cotton bag, and hung in a cool dark place, or submerged in a box of cooled wood ash, these hams will keep for months before you need cook or eat them raw.

Cooking instructions for all hams and salted pork, apart from *petit salé*, are given from page 209 on.

———————•••————————

BRINE CURES
(*Salaison par Saumure*)

I can recommend this method as the easiest and most successful of all, from the family cook's point of view. Small joints can be used, and turned into mild, delicate hams and picnic hams without any of the anxieties involved in smoking or dry salting. Even if your *jambonneaux* don't have quite the beautiful conical, pear-shaped form of the *charcutier's*, they will taste quite as good and be a lot cheaper. Boned and rolled shoulder, loin, and leg of pork can be turned into excellent *jambons de Paris*.

In fact, of all the recipes in this book, those in this section are the ones I would most recommend.

Saumure Anglaise pour la Fabrication du Jambon d'York

This English brine produces a good *jambon blanc* (White Ham—another name for *jambon de Paris*). A joint of pork left in it for 2 or 3 days is greatly improved—recipes on page 196.

This is the best one to keep in an all-purpose brine crock.

3 quarts soft or rain
  water
¾ lb. sea salt

¾ lb. granulated or brown
  sugar (about 1½ cups)
4 tablespoons saltpeter

Put all these into a large pan and bring very slowly to the boil, giving them an occasional stir.

Meanwhile cut a small square of clean cotton, linen, or muslin, large enough to hold:

1 level teaspoon juniper
  berries
A small piece of nutmeg
  (ungrated, a good way
  of using up the last frag-
  ments of a nutmeg)

1 bay leaf
3 sprigs of thyme
1 level teaspoon pepper-
  corns
4 cloves

Tie up the cloth so that nothing falls out.

Clean the crock with soda and boiling water. Rinse thoroughly with boiling water, and dry with a clean cloth.

By now the pan of brine should be boiling away. Skim off the murky froth, and take the pan away from the heat. Put in the little bag of spices and herbs and leave to get quite cold in the pan. Pour the brine through a cloth-lined strainer into the crock and put the meat in.

The cooling down takes much longer than you might suppose. You can hurry it up a little by pouring the boiling brine straight into the crock through a cloth-lined strainer, and adding the bag of seasonings then. It should be removed before adding the meat to the quite cold brine.

Put a board on the top, to keep the meat below the surface, and weights (I use a reddish lump of igneous rock; for this purpose stones must not be porous or crumbly).

After 3 days, stir the contents of the crock with a boiled wooden spoon or copper stick. Remove joints required for immediate use as boiled, salt pork (recipe follows), or *fromage de tête* (page 248).

After 6 days, you can remove some of the thinner pieces— sowbelly, for instance, to make *petit salé* (recipe, page 181), or a boned loin to make *jambon blancs;* small hocks, too, for *jambonneaux.*

After 7 days, leg and shoulder of pork should be ready for *jambon blancs,* for immediate use.

Reinforce the brine if you want to cure leg and shoulder for long-keeping hams with 4½ cups of water, boiled up with a scant cup of salt, and 3 oz. of juniper berries added whilst the brine cools. Wait till it is quite cold before adding to the crock.

NOTE: Every time you remove a joint from the brine crock, you remove salt as well. This doesn't matter with a couple of trotters (feet), but with a really large joint the curing power of the brine may be seriously weakened. A concentrated solution of salt and water can be added. This is what many professional meat curers do when their brineometers indicate the necessity. For most of us, preparing food in the uncertain hygiene of a family kitchen, it is prudent to remove the other joints as well as the large one. They can be kept in a cool, dry place for a few hours, until a new lot of brine has been prepared and the crock has been cleaned with boiling soda water and rinsed with boiling water.

Salt Pork, Using Saumure Anglaise

All joints of pork can be salted, from the *parties nobles* (legs and loin), to cheaper joints such as sowbelly, hand (U.S. picnic shoulder) and blade (U.S. Boston butt), trotters, tail, ears, and head. After 12 hours in brine, joints can still be roasted; but if they've been pickled for several days, they should be simmered in a *court-bouillon,* for about 30 minutes to the pound, then skinned, glazed, and put to bake in a moderate oven for a further 20 minutes.

I think there is no better way of cooking pork; the result is tender, full of flavor, and particularly delicious cold.

The two finest pork recipes of all, *enchaud de porc* (boned, truffled loin of pork) and *noisettes de porc aux pruneaux de Tours* (pork *noisettes* with prunes), are improved if the meat spends 12 hours in a *saumure anglaise* first (recipes, pages 235 and 236).

BASIC METHOD

Put the joint of pork in brine, boned or not as you please. Leave it for a minimum of 3 days or a maximum of 30.

When cooking time comes, weigh the joint and tie it into shape if it has been boned. Place it in a large pan, cover with cold water, and bring slowly to the boil. Simmer for 10 minutes and taste the liquid—if it is unpleasantly salty, throw it away and start again. If it is all right, add 2 carrots, cut up, an onion or two stuck with 3 cloves each, peppercorns, and a *bouquet garni.* Allow 30 minutes to the pound cooking time, taken from the start of simmering.

The next and final operation is glazing. Mix up some French mustard, brown sugar, and orange juice (or wine or cider or hard liquor) to a thick but smearable paste. Skin the joint, place it on an ovenproof dish, and cover with the glaze: this is the point for imagination, though I cannot recommend going as far as some Americans do in mixing honey and cherry juice together. Bake in a moderate oven for 20 to 30 minutes. Watch it to see the edges of the fat don't burn, and baste occasionally.

A sauce can be made from the glazing juices; boil down a little of the cooking liquid, add it to the pan juices with some cream or wine, taste frequently, and season.

Serve with plainly boiled potatoes, tossed in butter and chopped parsley or sage, followed by a green salad.

There are many ways of varying this recipe. You can, for instance, omit the glazing, serve with a purée of dried peas (pease pudding, page 183), lentils, or haricot beans.

You can omit the glazing, and serve *à l'anglaise* with buttered young broad beans and a well-made parsley sauce (page 54). Or else leave the joint to cool in the simmering liquid, skin, and press when cold. Toast some white bread crumbs and roll the salt pork in them whilst they are still warm. A pleasant half-way stage between cold pork and ham. Don't use commercially packaged crumbs.

Jambon de Reims en Croûte

An excellent way of using cold, pressed salt pork, given by Curnonsky.

Cut ¼-inch-thick slices, and make (or buy) a large quantity of puff pastry. Roll the pastry out and cut two rectangles for each slice of pork. Brush the edges of one rectangle with beaten egg, score a square lid on the other, and sandwich a slice of meat in between, pressing the edges together to close them. Brush the scored top with beaten egg, and lay on a baking sheet. Complete the other slices of pork *en croûte*, and bake in a hot oven for 20 minutes until the pastry is golden and well risen.

Carefully lift off the scored lids, and pour in some of the delicious port-wine sauce given on page 56, serve the rest separately. Be sure that everything is very hot, sauce, plates, and pork *en croûte*.

Many of the ham recipes given later in this chapter can be adapted for salt pork, so can some of the recipes in the chapter on "Fresh Pork."

UNSMOKED HAMS USING ENGLISH BRINE

Jambon de Paris, or Jambon Blanc

A leg of pork, about 5 lbs.
Court-bouillon, including:
  2 carrots, sliced (about
    1½ cups)
  2 onions, each stuck with
    3 cloves

Bouquet garni
Salt, pepper, *quatre-épices*
Odd scraps of pig's skin,
  bones, a pig's trotter
  (foot)

Bone the leg and leave it in brine at least 10 days, at most 30. Assemble the ingredients for a *court-bouillon,* but don't put them into the cooking pot.

Roll the leg of pork into as even a shape as possible and tie it at frequent intervals to keep it tidy. Wrap it firmly in a cloth and tie again. Weigh it.

Put the bundle into a large pan, cover generously with cold water, and bring slowly to the boil. Simmer for 10 minutes, and taste the water. If it is very salty indeed, throw it away and start again. When you are happy on this score add the ingredients for the *court-bouillon.*

For small hams of this type, 20 minutes per pound, plus 20 minutes, is quite time enough. Reckon from the start of simmering.

Let the ham cool in its liquid, then leave it—still wrapped up—overnight under a weight.

A fine piece of boned loin makes a good *jambon de Paris.*

Jambon à l'Américaine

Smithfield hams come from a small village in Virginia and have nothing to do with Smithfield Market in London. They are famous for their mild, sweet cure. This is the kind of ham to serve with pickled peaches (page 54) or spiced apples (page 39) or pineapple, and here is a simplified method:

A leg of pork weighing 5 lbs. or over, boned

1 lb. white sea salt (Tidman's or Maldon salt, not *gros sel*)

⅜ lb. saltpeter

½ lb. granulated sugar

English brine (page 191)

Mix together the salt, sugar, and salpeter, and rub the boned leg with it. Pay particular attention to the part of the leg which is not covered by the skin. Leave the meat in the salt.

Next day do the same thing all over again, and the 2 days following. Four days of dry cure in all.

Scrape off any salt that is still clinging, and put the leg into English brine for 6 or 7 days. String it firmly into a neat tubular shape.

If you have a good drying place (cool, airy, the temperature between 50° and 60°F., without violent fluctuations, no direct sunlight), squeeze the ham of as much moisture as possible and hang it up, in a boiled string bag, for 20 days.

If you can't be sure of drying the ham properly, let it hang for several days only.

Cook like a *jambon de Paris* (page 196).

(This ham can be smoked, but only to give it a light golden color.)

Jambon d'York

A leg of pork, at least 5 lbs., not boned

1 lb. white sea salt

7 oz. granulated sugar (barely ¾ cup)

4 tablespoons saltpeter

English brine (page 191)

Mix salt, sugar, and saltpeter together and rub the leg of pork well with it, push the mixture down the bone as far as possible. Leave the meat in the salt overnight, then rub it all over again.

Scrape off surplus salt, when the ham has been in the mixture a total of 24 hours, and put it into a crock of English brine for a fortnight.

At the end of this time, remove it from the brine, squeeze out as much moisture as possible with the aid of a clean board and hang the leg up to dry in an airy place (temperature between 50° and 60°F.) for several days.

(This ham can be smoked after drying, over oak, or beech chips, or over branches of juniper and rosemary.)

Cook in the same way as *jambon de Paris* (page 196).

Jambonneau (*Picnic Ham or Shoulder*)

This pretty little rounded cone, nicely bread-crumbed, with a stalk of white bone sticking out, is one of the most charming sights in the *charcuterie*. Here's a way of making one:

Buy a forehock and salt it in an English brine (page 191) for 8 days.

jambonneaux

Put it into a large pan with a *bouquet garni,* a large onion stuck with 5 cloves, 2 medium carrots, sliced (about 1½ cups), and a level teaspoon of saltpeter (to give it an extra-rosy color). Cover with water. Bring to the boil and simmer very gently for 2 hours.

Let it cool in the cooking liquid for 1 hour.

Remove it onto a large dish, skin and pat it into the best shape you can manage. Push down the meat at the point of the cone to expose a small piece of bone—you should aim at a large pear shape—and trim off any uneven bits.

Toast plenty of white bread crumbs on a baking tray in the oven, and whilst they are still warm roll the *jambonneau* firmly over them until it is completely covered.

Leave overnight, and eat within 2 days—this is not a keeping ham.

Épaule Roulée (*Rolled Picnic Shoulder*)

Buy a whole picnic shoulder and bone it. Use bits of meat from the fleshier part to pad out the thinner part and roll the joint up, after sprinkling it with pepper and spices. Tie firmly and leave in brine 12 days.

Hang up to dry in a cool, airy place (60°F.), away from direct sunlight or humidity. It will be ready after 4 days.

(This ham can be smoked after drying.)

This is an especially good ham for *le jambon de Reims en croûte* (page 195).

Saumure Italienne

Alcohol makes an excellent preservative, so it is not surprising to find it used for curing pork, along with the processes of salting, drying, and smoking. In Scotland, beer is used to make a rich sweet brine (page 201); and at the other end of Europe, the Italians use their plentiful dry white wine, particularly in the northern plain around Modena. There the hams are cut squat and thick, and spend a month to 5 weeks in a brine of this type:

6½ cups soft water or rain   2 lbs. white sea salt
  water   ⅛ cup bicarbonate of soda
4 tablespoons saltpeter   6½ cups dry white wine
                               1 oz. whole spices

Put the water, saltpeter, sea salt, and bicarbonate into a large pan and bring to the boil, giving an occasional stir. As it bubbles, add the wine and spices, and take off the heat immediately, so that the brine does not boil again once the wine has been added. Leave it to get quite cold, then strain through muslin or a double thickness of cheesecloth into the scrupulously clean crock.

A rolled picnic shoulder, prepared in the same way as for the previous recipe, is a good joint to cure in this brine. Give it a fortnight (10–12 days, if the weather is hot) in the brine, then hang from a hook in a cool, airy place, where the temperature is between 50° and 60°F., for 4 to 6 days. Cook in the usual way —see *jambon de Paris* (page 196), and serve with a white wine sauce (page 43).

A leg of pork would give you a Modena-type ham; 4 weeks in brine, 4 days to dry, then store in olive (or pure vegetable) oil—not unlike a Mediterranean *confit de porc,* substituting the local form of fat for lard.

(Both shoulder and leg can alternatively be smoked, rather than preserved in oil, for eating raw. Again I would repeat my warning not to rely on the safety of home smoking unless you can do it under the care of an expert.)

Saumure Écossaise

5 cups of good strong beer
1 lb. sea salt
½ lb. rock salt (*gros sel*) or block salt
A small piece of *salprunella*, crushed, or 1 level teaspoon saltpeter

½ lb. soft, dark-brown sugar (1¼ cups)
1 teaspoon freshly ground black pepper
1 teaspoon freshly ground allspice

Bring all these ingredients to the boil in a large pan and let them cool overnight. Strain carefully.

Rub the ham with ¼ cup dark-brown sugar and 2 heaped tablespoons saltpeter, and leave it overnight.

Next day rub the ham over again with the ¼ cup brown sugar and 2 heaped tablespoons saltpeter, put it into a deep dish, and pour the beer brine over it. Leave to cure for a month, but every day turn the ham over and rub the brine well in, particularly down the bone.

(This farmhouse cure was intended for hams which would be spending some time up the big kitchen chimney being smoked —but without this, you will get a delicious result.)

SMOKED HAM
(*Jambon Fumé*)

Smoking involves three major problems—space, advanced standards of hygiene, and expertise. Smoking, that is to say, for preservation over a fair period of time. A smoky *flavor* can be induced by small apparatus of the Abu Smoking Box type (available at Habitat Ltd., 77 Fulham Road, London S.W.3*); but

---

* Available in the U.S. at Hammacher Schlemmer, 145 East Fifty-seventh Street, New York City.

this is only suitable for small objects like sausages, in any case.

From an English point of view, the main purpose of smoking hams would be to produce a *jambon cru* of the Bayonne type, which is either not widely available in our country, or very expensive. The best solution for most people would be to make arrangements with the nearest bacon factory for smoking,* and then get down to the actual pickling process at home.

If, however, you want to experiment with smoking, you might consult pp. 35–8 of *Sausages and Small Goods Production,* by Frank Gerrard, or pages 30–43 of the U.S. Department of Agriculture's Farmers' Bulletin No. 2138, *Slaughtering, Cutting, and Processing Pork.* Less easily obtainable are French handbooks on *charcuterie,* which deal more fully with smoking on the farm-house scale, as this is still widely carried on in country districts. The most useful, I find, is *La Charcuterie à la Campagne,* by Henriette Babet-Charton, published by La Maison Rustique, 26 rue Jacob, Paris vi^e. She suggests three ways of smoking, firstly by hanging the pieces above the mouth of the bread oven, secondly by suspending them from an iron bar placed high up across a wide farmhouse chimney, and thirdly by building a special smoke box which can be fixed against the chimney breast when required; the illustrations give an idea of the last two methods.

Many French houses still have a bread oven in the large fireplace, like English farms. The idea is to hang the joints and sausages, once cured, above the opening so that the smoke from the fire inside the oven billows up and around them in a gentle steady waft. This system ensures that the temperature of the smoke never rises above 90°F., at which point the fat begins to melt, and the hams are spoilt. By burning green branches you ensure plenty of smoke—for extra flavor burn juniper, pine, sage, bay, and heather. In the past, Breton hams were smoked in fires of seaweed. Beat the fire down to keep it smoldering, not burning in flames. The first day, smoke the hams for ½ hour, then take them down and rub them whilst they are still warm with

* This may prove quite difficult or impossible in some areas of the U.S.

pepper, spices, thyme, crumbled bay leaves, which will cling to the softened fat. Leave them to cool and dry for 48 hours. Then smoke them for 1 hour. Leave them again for 48 hours, and smoke again for 1 hour. This should be enough for a light flavor.

If you have a wide old-fashioned chimney, which you are not using to cook in as many French farmers' wives do, you can either stretch wire between two hooks high up, or else make use of a permanently fixed iron bar. The fire will be more subject to draughts caused by household comings and goings, and will therefore need more attention. The best plan is to confine the smoking to a couple of hours every day, over a longish period, when you can be sure of attending to the fire without too many interruptions. In the bacon factory, a series of smoking rooms are supplied from a furnace room for so long each day, and the whole business is carefully controlled; but don't be discouraged, after all factory curing is a newcomer against the long history of smoked meat. Allow at least 3 weeks for fireplace smoking.

If you are handy, the best method of all is to fit up a fireplace with a smoking box, fitted onto the wall above the fire.

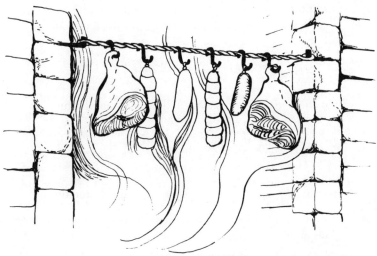

French farmhouse meat smoking

The first requirement is a sheet of metal across the whole chimney, with a piece of bent piping going through it and through the wall up into the smoking box. Another piece of bent piping goes out of the top of the box and back into the chimney. Leave the meat in the box for 8 days, and smoke for 2 hours every day.

Weight loss is a good indication of whether a ham is properly smoked. It should lose about a quarter, which means that an 8-lb. ham will end up at 6 lbs., more or less. Then there is the strong smoky aroma, and the beautiful deep golden-brown color that we all know from Christmas hams and sides of bacon.

The next problem is storage. French country hams and sausages are kept in deep boxes of wood ash, prunings from the vineyard perhaps, or the ashes of a beech. Lay a sifted layer in the bottom of the box, arrange hams and sausages wrapped tightly in strong clean canvas or thick cotton, then sift more ashes over the top. You can repeat the process until everything is tidily layered away. Naturally the box must be kept in a clean, dry place, preferably raised up off the floor.

Looking romantically back into the mists of agriculture, most people see the farmer's kitchen decorated with head-banging hams, suspended from heavy iron hooks at the far end of the room, away from the heat of the fire, but still dry and contented. And if you have a large kitchen, this is an excellent solution to the storage problem. Although it may be gratifying to glance occasionally at a golden ham, it is really much safer to sew it into a canvas, linen or calico covering, and limewash it three times. But if you can rely on the steady, dry temperature produced, for instance, by a solid-fuel stove, hams can be stored without wrapping. Remember that the temperature should not rise above 60°F., nor go down below 32°F. No sunlight. Have you ever noticed that cheese and ham rooms are always north-facing? Do not rely on a cellar (dark it is true, but often humid), or an attic (dark also, but subject to rapid fluctuations of temperature and stuffiness). An inadequately dried piece of meat soon grows mold, so watch for the slightest sign of moisture.

Another point is this: home-cured hams are much stronger

and saltier than the mild, sweet cures of commercial ham and bacon, which can be stored in low temperatures, and will in any case not be stored for very long. William Cobbett's provident cottager required his great side of bacon to last for many months; it had to, it was the only major source of protein for the whole family during winter months. Nowadays we can lay on the salt with a lighter hand, but not so lightly as the factory with its rapid cures by injections of brine. Home-cured hams therefore will require long overnight soaking, if they are to be cooked.

But there are, notably, three hams of international reputation that nobody would think of boiling. These are the Parma, Westphalia, and Bayonne hams, bought at great expense (like smoked salmon) to be served in thin, thin slices with curls of unsalted butter, *and no bread,* or fresh, ripe figs or melon. In France, Bayonne ham (cured really at Orthez, about 40 miles away) is more widely on sale in *charcuteries* than Parma or Westphalia hams; and there will often be local *jambons de campagne* too— of coarser, heartier flavor, but much cheaper, and closely approximating to the kind of result you can achieve by home-curing and home or local bacon-factory smoking.

Jambon de Campagne Fumé

1 fine leg of pork
13 cups water
2 lbs. salt
1½ tablespoons granulated sugar
1 teaspoon saltpeter
1 scant teaspoon whole cloves
2 level teaspoons peppercorns
4 bay leaves
3 sprigs of thyme

Bring the water to the boil, and add the salt when it bubbles hard. Draw it off the fire, stirring in the herbs and spices. When the brine is absolutely cold, strain it and whisk in the saltpeter and sugar.

Lay the leg of pork, skin-side down, in the stoneware crock and pour the brine over it. (If you are curing two legs, lay them flesh to flesh, not skin to skin.)

After 3 days take the leg out (using kitchen tongs, not your hands), and press it firmly with a boiled piece of wood. This is necessary to squeeze out any blood which still remains and would spoil the finished ham. Put the ham back in the brine for another 3 days, then fortify with some more brine (2 cups water brought to the boil with 3 heaped tablespoons salt, take it off the fire and add ¾ oz. crushed juniper berries; let it cool and strain into the brine crock).

Leave the ham another week, before taking it out and drying it well for 10 days, on a board, in a cool, airy larder.

Smoke it in the chimney—or take it to the bacon factory.

(If you do not smoke the ham, and still want to keep it for a while, scrape it well when you take it out of the brine crock and dry it off. Then rub all the part uncovered by skin with some brandy or other hard liquor.)

NOTE: Before you start to slice your *jambon de campagne*, and send out invitations to the feast, make sure that it is sweet and wholesome. It should smell good, and when you stick a larding needle or metal knitting needle down the bone, it should come out as clean and fresh as when it went in, with slight overtones of smoky ham.

Filet de Porc Fumé (*Smoked Loin of Pork*)

4- to 5-lb. piece of pork loin (loin end)	¼ cup brown sugar
	3 tablespoons saltpeter
12½ cups water	*Bouquet garni*
1¼ lbs. salt	½ teaspoon peppercorns

Bring the water, salt, sugar, and saltpeter to the boil. Take off the fire, add the *bouquet* and peppercorns, leave to cool.

Put the fillet of pork into a stoneware brine crock—the tall jars are best for this joint—and strain the cold brine over it. Put a clean board on top, lightly weighted with a clean stone, to keep the meat below the surface. Don't disturb it for 8 or 9 days.

Hang it up to dry in a cool, airy place, suspended in a boiled string bag, for 4 days.

Smoke it for 24 to 30 hours.

This ham can be eaten raw, in thin slices, like the more conventional leg hams.

Alternatively you can simmer it for 2½ hours, once boiling point has been reached. Serve it with *choucroute* (page 162), lightly cooked buttered cabbage, or a purée of dried vegetables.

NOTE: This is a good recipe to try if you want to practice your smoking technique. It's a short program of curing, so you don't build up hope for weeks, only to find that you have a large moldy flop on your hands.

Jambon de Bayonne

Here is a simplified version of the process, to be attempted after the hay harvest in a dry summer:

1 leg of pork

———➤ *Dry Salting* ➤———

2 lbs. salt

2 tablespoons saltpeter

½ lb. granulated sugar (1 cup)

———➤ *Brine* ➤———

6 cups red wine

6 cups soft or rain water

3 tablespoons saltpeter

1 lb. white block salt

¾ lb. sea salt

6 sprigs rosemary

½ cup olive oil

If you have a ham from a newly killed pig, you will have to beat it with a piece of clean wood—one of those old-fashioned butter pats are excellent for this. This brings out a certain amount of blood, and also smooths out the wrinkles in the skin. Thread a piece of strong string through the knuckle so that you can suspend the ham over a dish, in a dry and airy place, for 3 to 5 days—according to the temperature. You will find that a pinkish liquid runs out, mop it off twice a day at least.

If you are buying the leg straight from the butcher, tell him what you want it for. You will probably not have to go through the above performance.

The next step is to remove the bone, which is not too difficult provided you have a small, very sharp knife and plenty of elbow room.

Mix the dry-salting ingredients well together. Don't overlook this stage, as the brine has no sugar in it at all and a certain amount is needed to counteract the hardening effect of the salt and saltpeter. Rub the mixture well into the ham, particularly into the hollow left by the bone and other areas of exposed flesh. Pat the ham into a nice shape after this vigorous operation and leave it overnight, whilst you make the brine and leave it to cool down.

The brine is made in the usual way, by boiling all the brine ingredients together *except the oil.* After a moment's bubbling, remove the pot from the fire, strain it directly into the clean, empty crock, and pour in the oil. Stir everything round and leave it to get quite cold.

Next day take the ham out of the dry-salt mixture and put it in the brine. Weight with a board and stone.

Leave it for 12 days, making sure that the crock inhabits a steady dry temperature, never exceeding 60°F.

Drain the ham, hang it up for 48 hours whilst you go searching for newly dried hay, and suitable wood for the smoking fire.

Wrap the ham up in plenty of hay, holding it in place with string, and put it to smoke until it is deep golden-brown.

COOKING HAM AND SALT PORK

Once again I would repeat the warning—with home-cured ham particularly, make absolutely sure that it is still good before you cook it. It should smell unsuspicious and appetizing—push a larding or metal knitting needle right into the middle of the ham, it should come out clean and sweet.

SOAKING

The point of soaking is to remove excess salt, and to restore moisture to the dried-out tissues.

It follows therefore that salt pork and very lightly cured hams (*jambons de Paris,* page 196) need no soaking.

On the other hand home-cured hams, which have been subjected to a prolonged curing followed by smoking, need to be left in water overnight.

With commercial hams, follow the instructions provided with them. Otherwise make inquiries from the supplier. For mild cures 4 to 6 hours of soaking may well be enough.

Very large hams need longer than small hams cured in the same way.

But don't worry. You will have a further chance to rectify saltiness in the cooking process.

COOKING UTENSILS

Borrow or buy a ham boiler.

If this is impossible, try and find a pot large enough to hold the ham with *plenty of water.* In the case of a large ham, a washing copper is a good solution. This also enables you to suspend the ham, by a strong, clean cord, so that the more quickly cooked knuckle end is out of the water.

COOKING

Weigh the salt pork or soaked ham. Calculate the cooking time.

For salt pork and smaller hams, up to 4 lbs., reckon 30 minutes to the pound, plus an extra 30 minutes. But watch the joint—the last 30 minutes may be unnecessary: if so, take the pot to the side of the stove and leave the joint in the liquid to keep hot. Or glaze it in the oven.

For hams of 5 lbs. and over, up to 10 lbs., 20 minutes per pound, plus 20 minutes.

For hams of 10 lbs. and over, the period of time gets progressively less. This diagram from Bulletin 127 of the British Ministry of Agriculture and Fisheries' *Home Curing of Bacon and Hams* gives you the answer.

Draw a vertical line from the pounds to the diagonal, and a horizontal line from the point where they intersect to the hours' scale. In other words a ham just over 16 lbs. needs 4 hours cooking time.

Put the joint or ham into the pot, cover with plenty of cold water, and bring slowly to the boil. Count your cooking time from now, and keep the water at a simmer. After 10 minutes or quarter of an hour, taste the water. If it is unpleasantly salty,

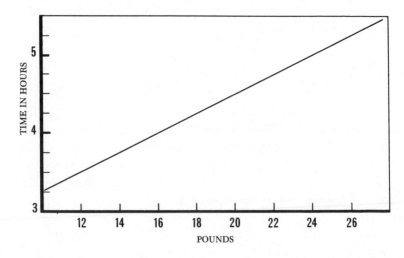

throw it away and start again, reckoning the cooking time from the second boiling point, *less 10 minutes or quarter of an hour.*

———·•◆•·———

FINISHING—COLD HAM

When the ham is cooked, leave it to cool for an hour or two in the liquid. Then remove it, and take off the skin. Toast plenty of white bread crumbs and press them into the fat of the ham whilst both are still warm.

(If the ham was cooked boneless, let it cool for an hour in the liquid, remove the skin, and press the ham, either with a board and weight, or with a weight into an appropriately shaped mold. Remove string afterwards, and cloth, if it was cooked in a cloth.)

Leave the ham to set in a cool place for 12 hours. This makes it much easier to carve.

———·•◆•·———

FINISHING—HOT HAM

The simplest and most attractive way to finish a hot ham is to glaze it.

Remove the ham from the cooking liquid ½ hour before the end of cooking time. Peel off the skin, and smear the ham with, for instance, a mixture of brown sugar and French mustard, or brown sugar and mustard powder, moistened with a little of the cooking liquor.

Put it in a moderate oven for the rest of the cooking time.

There are endless variations and complications on this theme. Some of them are given later on in this chapter. You can invent more for yourself, remembering that the most successful glazes combine sweetness and spiciness. One attractive finish is achieved by scoring the fat of the ham in a lattice pattern, studding the intersections with cloves, and then smearing the glaze on gently. Be careful not to score right through the fat to the lean.

The juices from the glazing can be turned into the sauce, with a little extra liquid from the boiling operation, or cream, or a wine like Madeira, Marsala, port, sherry, etc.

CARVING

The essential requirement is a very sharp knife, preferably one with a long, thin blade.

Remember that there are right and left hams, if your ham has been cooked on the bone. If the ham is boneless and pressed, you will carve it straight down, so right and left are of no consequence. The knuckle must lie toward the carver—to his left for a right-hand ham, and to his right for a left-hand ham. Cut each slice from alternate sides, as thinly as possible with an even, smooth movement of the knife—this prevents a ridgy appearance.

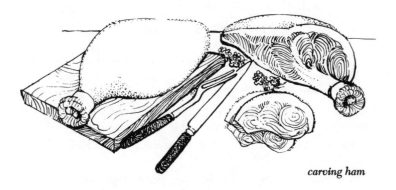

carving ham

Jambon à l'Anglaise (or en Chausson)

Three-quarters cook the ham, leave it to cool for an hour in its own liquid, then peel off the skin.

Meanwhile make a large quantity of short-crust pastry (a

12-lb. ham needs 3 lbs. flour, 1½ lbs. butter or butter and lard, mixed with as little very cold water and salt to season as possible). Roll out the pastry and put the ham, rounded, or right-side down in the middle. Gather up the pastry and seal it together.

Grease the baking tray with lard and turn the ham over on to it, so that the sealed side is underneath. Brush with beaten egg and decorate with leaves, flowers, or abstract shapes of pastry. Brush the decorations with beaten egg, and make a small hole at the highest point of the ham—this allows steam to escape during the cooking, and a glass of Madeira or other suitable wine to be poured in at the end.

Bake in a moderately hot oven for three quarters to one hour. Pour in the small glass of Madeira (up to 3 oz.) and serve. Everything can be eaten—except the bone.

———— *Variations* ————

Make sauces of increasing luxury and complication (Madeira sauce, port sauce, Périgueux sauce, wine and cream sauces, pages 52–7), and pour a few spoonfuls into the steam vent, serving the rest separately.

Line the pastry with a suitable forcemeat—preferably containing truffles; or at least mushrooms, chopped and fried in butter with finely chopped onions, and a final addition of white bread crumbs. Very homely, but good—make the pastry of flour and water. Don't eat the crust, it's a juice conserver only.

Jambon Persillé de Bourgogne

This is the famous and beautiful Eastertide dish of Burgundy. The major requirements are plenty of white wine, the ham, plenty of parsley, and one of those old-fashioned bedroom washbowls. I use a leg of pork cured in the York or American style, or a 3-lb. piece of gammon. It goes into a ham boiler with plenty of cold water, which is slowly brought to the boil to draw out excess salt. Pour off the water if it is very salty and start again. When the water is once more at the boil, simmer the ham very gently for 45 minutes.

Remove from the water and cut the meat off the bone in sizable chunks. Put them into a pan with a large knuckle of veal, chopped into pieces; 2 calves' feet, boned, and tied together; a few sprigs of chervil and tarragon tied together with a bay leaf, 2 sprigs of thyme, and 2 sprigs of parsley; 8 peppercorns tied into a little bag. Cover with dry white wine and bring to a gentle boil. Skim off fat as it rises, and leave the ham to cook very thoroughly, as it will need to be mashed and flaked with a fork.

However before you do this, attend to the jelly. Pour off the cooking liquid through a strainer lined with a piece of clean cotton sheeting or a double thickness of cheesecloth. Taste it to make sure it is not too salty. Add 2 tablespoons of white wine vinegar, and leave it to set a little.

Meanwhile crush the ham into a bowl.

Before the jelly sets altogether, stir in plenty of chopped parsley—at least 8 tablespoons—and pour over the ham. Leave to set overnight in a cold place. Turn out the *jambon persillé,* and serve. When it is cut, it will display a beautifully marbled green-and-pink appearance. If you like, you can keep back some of the parsley jelly, remelt it gently next day and pour over the ham in an even green layer.

Jambon au Madère

Cook the ham in a bouillon for three quarters of its cooking time—reckon 20 minutes to the pound, plus 20 minutes, from the time it reaches simmering point. See page 210.

Skin the ham and transfer it to a closer-fitting pot. Pour over 2 cups of Madeira, put on the lid, and cook in a moderate

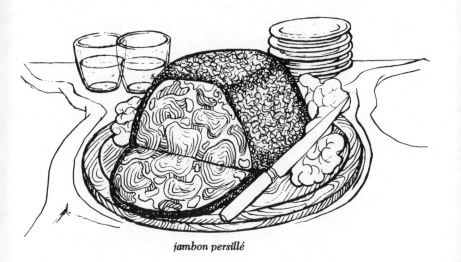

jambon persillé

oven for 50 minutes or the rest of the cooking time—whichever is the longer.

Transfer the ham again to a shallow dish, sprinkle it with confectioners' sugar, or a brown sugar, spices and French mustard glaze, and put it to melt in a hot oven. See that it doesn't burn but turns to a succulent golden sheen.

Meanwhile deal with the sauce. Taste the braising liquid—add some stock or Madeira, reduce it or leave it alone, according to your judgment. Thicken it by adding a little knob of *beurre manié* (2 tablespoons flour kneaded into 1 tablespoon butter).

———•— *Variations and Accompaniments* —•———

(1) Use another fortified wine—Marsala, port, sherry, or any heavy wine instead of Madeira.

(2) Serve with a cream sauce made by reducing the braising liquid and adding 1 cup of heavy cream. Surround the glazed ham with little piles of vegetables cooked in butter (new carrots, tiny onions, mushrooms, young peas, young green beans). This is *jambon à la crème*.

(3) Serve *jambon à la crème* with a purée of spinach or spinach and sorrel instead of the little piles of vegetables. Get the spinach as dry as possible and flavor the purée with a little sugar, salt, pepper, cheese, cream as you think fit—spinach varies so much that you have to use your discretion. If you do grow sorrel, add a few leaves for their sharp, spring flavor.

(4) Belgian chicory (*witloof* or *endive de Bruxelles*), blanched for 15 minutes in boiling water, then braised in butter in the oven, makes a good accompaniment to *jambon au madère*.

(5) Most popular of all, *jambon au madère*, or *à la crème*, served with young green peas and new potatoes in the early summer.

Saupiquet de Jambon

Saupiquet—not to be confused with *salpicon*, a dice of vegetables or meat or both, bound with thick sauce—was the name of a medieval sauce made of wine thickened with bread. Nowadays it means a piquant but delicate cream sauce. I find that Elizabeth David's version, *saupiquet des Amognes* (from her *French Provincial Cooking*), is the most successful with its hint of juniper and bland sharpness.

She recommends it with slices of uncooked ham or gammon, soaked for ½ hour, then fried in butter. Or else with slices of cooked ham, arranged on a plate and covered with the sauce, then put to heat through in the oven. I serve it with a whole boiled ham at Christmastime—the time for extravagance.

Whichever version you choose, make sure that the serving dishes, the sauceboat, and the plates are very hot. Cream sauces soon lose their charm on tepid china.

1 cup beef or veal stock, heated	3 tablespoons flour
	4 shallots
3 tablespoons butter	½ cup wine vinegar

3 crushed juniper berries

½ cup white wine

1 cup (½ pint) heavy cream

Extra butter

Chop the shallots almost to a hash; put them with the juniper berries and wine vinegar into a little pan. Boil away the vinegar until the pan is practically dry.

Melt the butter in another pan, make a *roux* with the flour, and cook until it turns pale coffee color. Pour in the heated stock carefully, stir all the time until the sauce thickens. Add the white wine and the shallots. Simmer gently for ½ hour at the side of the stove. If this is impracticable, a double boiler or a basin set over a pan of just-boiling water works very well. This long, gentle cooking contributes everything to the smooth maturing of the sauce.

Near the time of serving, sieve the sauce into a clean pan or basin, add the cream and season. Finish with a small knob of butter and reheat without boiling. Stand the pan in another pan of hot water while you deal finally with the ham.

Jambon au Foin

Hay and ham suggest hay boxes and folk dancing, but in fact combine excellently, the hay being used to give the ham a scent of coumarin, the substance (hydroxycinnamiclactone, to be precise) which occurs in sweet vernal grass and makes newly mown hay so fragrant (it is also found in tonka beans, from Guyana or Grenada, with which snuff is perfumed). The French farmer's wife beds the ham in sweet, newly dried hay, covering the ham and hay with water. I follow Eliza Acton's method, wrapping the ham and covering with one part white wine and two parts water. The ham is then simmered until cooked. Let the ham cool in the liquor. Serve with unsalted or lightly salted butter and new bread with a good crust; and white wine or cider.

HOT RECIPES USING COOKED HAM

Saupiquet des Amognes

The best way, and the most delicious, of reheating cooked ham. Lay the slices in an ovenproof dish, pour over the *saupiquet* sauce (page 57). Ten minutes in a gentle oven and it is ready to serve.

Omelette au Jambon

For one person, chop ⅛ lb. cooked ham into small dice, and fry gently in an 8-inch omelette pan with a little butter. When the ham's well heated through and turning golden, pour on 2 lightly beaten eggs, seasoned with some pepper and a pinch of salt.

As the eggs cook, draw up the solid parts to one end of the pan, so that the liquid runs down and cooks in its turn. But be careful not to overcook. When they are served, omelettes should still be liquid inside, though firm on the outside and lightly browned. Sprinkle with chopped parsley, and rush it to table on a very hot plate.

Soufflé au Jambon

½ lb. lean cooked ham
2 tablespoons butter
2 tablespoons flour
A generous ½ cup milk or
  light cream

3 eggs, yolks and whites
  separated
Salt, pepper

Grind the ham twice and pound to a smooth mass in a mortar. Make a very thick white sauce with the butter, flour, and milk or cream, cooking until it comes away from the side of the pan. Use a wooden spoon for stirring. Add the ham and season well.

If you have an electric blender, grind the ham once or chop it roughly. Put it in the blender jar with the thick white sauce and whirl at top speed. Reheat in the pan, but not to boiling point. The egg yolks should now be added, one by one.

Beat the egg whites until they are stiff, fold lightly into the pan mixture with a metal spoon, and pour into a soufflé dish with an oiled greaseproof paper collar.

Bake in a moderate oven for 25 minutes. Serve immediately —remember to remove the paper collar—to seated guests.

This soufflé can be cooked in small individual soufflé dishes. They will only take about 10 minutes to cook, and the oven should be hotter than for a large soufflé.

Quiche au Jambon

Follow the recipe for *quiche Lorraine* (page 187), using ham instead of *petit salé*.

It is, in brief, a flan ring lined with short-crust pastry, filled with a layer of chopped ham and 1 cup of cream beaten up with 3 eggs, and seasoned. Bake for 30 to 40 minutes in a moderate oven. Serve warm—not hot, and not cold, but warm. Or cook as *petites quiches* in small tins.

Diced Gruyère cheese can also be added with the ham.

Croque-Monsieur

This delightfully named hot sandwich, can be served as an hors d'oeuvre.

Choose good bread: *pain au lait, pain de mie,* or *pain brioché.* Cut thin slices, butter them, and make them into sandwiches with a layer of Gruyère cheese and a layer of lean ham on top. Cut into elegant triangles, and fry in half butter, half oil, until they are golden-brown on both sides.

—— → *Variation* → ——

Fry slices of bread on one side only, butter the unfried side, lay thick slices of ham on top and cover with a paste made of grated Gruyère cheese, French mustard, and heavy cream—enough to make the mixture spread. Grill gently until gold and bubbly—serve on very hot plates.

Jambon au Sauce Moutarde, or *au Gratin*

Arrange the ham in not-too-thin slices on an ovenproof serving dish, and cover with the following sauce:

4 tablespoons French mustard

2 tablespoons grated cheese, Gruyère or mild Cheddar

4–5 tablespoons heavy cream

Mix these three ingredients together and add to some rich *béchamel* sauce, made from 2 tablespoons each of butter and flour, and 1 cup of milk or ½ cup each of milk and light cream. Season.

Pour over the ham, top with grated cheese, and brown under the grill or in a hot oven.

More elaborately, you can cook ½ cup of heated white wine into the butter-and-flour *roux,* when making the *béchamel* sauce, before adding the milk.

Croquettes de Jambon

Like ham cornets, this dish can be homely or grand, according
to inclination and resources. Piled in a pyramid on a very white
cloth and silver dish, accompanied by a fine Madeira sauce,
they made a popular appearance at nineteenth-century banquets;
sprinkled with parsley on an earthenware dish, with a friendly
bowl of tomato sauce, they are not out of place in the nursery.
Here is a basic recipe, to which you can add Madeira, truffles,
and so on, or which you can leave alone:

4 tablespoons (½ stick) butter	Butter
4 tablespoons flour	2 egg yolks
2 cups good milk	Salt, pepper, and mace or nutmeg
½ lb. ham	Egg and bread crumbs to finish
¼ lb. mushrooms	

Make a *béchamel* sauce with the butter, flour, and milk. Do
not season it, but leave on the side of the stove (or over a low
heat) to reduce by half—you should end up with 1 cup of very
thick sauce. This operation should not be rushed, nor side-
stepped by halving the amount of milk.

Chop the mushrooms and cook them in a little butter. Grind
the ham twice and add it to the mushrooms.

Add the ham mixture to the *béchamel* sauce, when it has
reduced to the right amount, and sieve. If you have an electric
blender, now is the time to use it.

Reheat to just under boiling point, and add the egg yolks,
beating them in well for 2 or 3 minutes.

Pour the mixture into a buttered 1-inch-deep dish to cool.

When you want to serve the *croquettes*, cut the mixture
into even pieces, roll them lightly in flour; then in egg; then
in bread crumbs; and fry quickly to golden-brown in boiling
oil. A salad or "French-fry" basket helps.

If you are feeling fanciful, and have nothing better to do, cut the mixture into shapes—crescents, triangles, circles, rings, and so on. Serve with Madeira sauce (page 52) or tomato sauce (page 60).

Timbales de Jambon

For timbales, you need small soufflé dishes, or dariole molds. Grind ½ lb. of ham twice—do not use all lean ham, but a normal amount of fat as well. Mix it with a scant ½ cup of heavy cream, in the blender, to a smooth consistency. Season with salt, pepper, and French mustard.

Butter the molds and line them with the ham mixture, break an egg into each one and set them in a shallow pan of hot water. Put them into a moderately hot oven until the eggs are cooked but not hard—about 20 minutes.

Sprinkle with a little parsley and serve with triangles of hot, thin toast.

You can turn the timbales out onto circles of fried bread or toast; or a bed of spinach purée, and serve with a Mornay sauce (page 53) as *timbales florentines*.

Endives au Gratin

Have as many heads of chicory as slices of ham. Blanch the chicory for 15 minutes in boiling salted water. Drain well, wrap each one in a slice of ham, and lay side by side in a buttered au gratin dish. Pour over enough Mornay sauce (page 53) to cover (try and use a dish which just holds the chicory, as they should not be swamped in liquid), sprinkle with grated cheese, and brown in the oven, slowly for 20 minutes and then fast for 10.

Jambon Persillé au Gratin

Prepare a stiff, well-flavored potato purée. Do not stint on the butter. Stir in plenty of chopped parsley and turn out onto a buttered plate to cool. You will need about a scant ½ cup of potato purée for each slice of ham, which should be rolled round the potato and laid in a buttered dish close to its neighbor. Pour over Mornay sauce (page 53) or cream sauce (page 42), sprinkle grated cheese (preferably Parmesan) over the top, and bake in a moderate oven for 45 minutes. Brown under the grill or turn the oven up.

This is a simple dish but not to be despised provided the potato purée and sauce are made with care and discrimination.

Vol-au-Vent (Croûstade) au Jambon

Smallish amounts of leftover ham can be attractively stretched with *vol-au-vent* cases or *croûstades*.

Make a *salpicon* of ham, by dicing it and mixing with a little rich *béchamel* sauce and chopped sautéed mushrooms.

This mixture can be as simple as you like, or as luxurious (*béchamel* sauce made with butter, flour, and light cream; chopped truffles; or a brown sauce flavored with Madeira).

—— *Make either* ——

One large *vol-au-vent* case of puff pastry, or several small ones. Roll out the pastry, not too thinly. Cut out a large circle, and mark a smaller one inside that does not go right through the pastry. Brush with beaten egg and bake in a hot oven. Remove the inner circle, which will form a lid, put in the hot ham *salpicon*, lay the lid on top, and serve.

——— *Or* ———

Fry some soft bread rolls in deep fat until they are crisp and golden. Let them cool a little, then scoop out the inside after cutting out a lid. Put them into the oven to reheat and dry. Fill them with the hot *salpicon*, put the lids on top, and serve.

Ham and Fruit

The use of pineapple and peaches with ham is American. The French are used to the more subtle combinations of orange, prunes, and apple with pork and ham. Their juice, or the alcoholic liquors made from it, can be used in the glaze and the sauce. Lightly fried orange and apple rings or prunes simmered in white wine make good accompaniments.

See the recipes in the "Fresh Pork Cookery" chapter, beginning on page 227.

———————

RECIPES USING COLD COOKED HAM

Jambon en Cornets

Take some large thin slices of ham and form them into a cone shape—like the improvised bags in old-fashioned grocer's shops. Use swizzle sticks to hold them in shape, or some aspic or Madeira jelly which is on the verge of setting.

Fill the cornets with a *salpicon* of diced vegetables, or vegetables and chicken bound with mayonnaise. Olives, capers, anchovies, red peppers can be used for additional spice. Cream cheese whipped with cream and a little aspic jelly, with walnuts folded in, make the cornets into a more substantial luncheon dish.

Or you can pipe into the cornets, with a forcing bag, some of the mixture kept aside from next day's . . .

Ham Mousse

½ lb. cooked ham, with no fat
½ cup thick white sauce (page 42)
¾ cup aspic or Madeira.

jelly, semi-liquid but cool
1 cup heavy cream, whipped
2 egg whites
Salt, cayenne pepper

Grind the ham twice. Whirl it in the electric blender with the white sauce. If you have no blender, pound the ham alone in a mortar.

Put the ham mixture into a bowl, stir in the aspic jelly, and then the whipped cream. Season well.

Beat the egg whites until they are very stiff. Add the ham mixture when it is almost set, folding it in carefully with a metal spoon.

Tie a lightly oiled collar of greaseproof paper or aluminum foil round the soufflé dish and pile in the mixture lightly. It should come well above the edge of the dish, so that when it is firmly set and the collar removed it has the appearance of a soufflé hot from the oven, and well risen.

Leave in a refrigerator to set, and serve chilled.

NOTE: Chicken, or chicken and tongue, or ham and tongue can be used instead of all ham.

Ham or Cold Salt Pork with Swedish Mayonnaise

Cut the meat into slices, arrange on a dish, and serve with green salad, boiled new potatoes tossed in butter and chopped parsley, and a bowl of the mayonnaise and apple purée sauce given on page 63.

This is an unusual and always popular sauce to serve with cold ham and pork.

Ham with Orange and Chicory Salad

Arrange some sliced ham on a dish, and serve with the following salad:

3 large oranges, peeled and sliced into rounds
3 heads of chicory, sliced
½ large mild onion, cut into rings

Vinaigrette sauce (page 65)
Chopped parsley

Cut the orange slices in quarters, mix with the chicory, and turn in the dressing. Top with onion rings and a sprinkling of chopped parsley.

Black olives can be added as well.

•⊶ FRESH PORK COOKERY ⊷•

The most obvious, visible difference in the French cooking of fresh pork—apart, of course, from the elegant butchery—is the lack of crackling. In the *charcuterie*, the *porc rôti* will be a neat boneless cylinder, pale pink from its night in brine, studded with an occasional clove of garlic, and sold by the succulent slice.

The outer layer of fat and skin will have been used in pâtés, sausages, and *crépinettes*. If the *charcutier* is the butcher as well, you will see nicely cut oblongs of white fat barding the lean roasts of beef. If you want to buy a fillet of beef for roasting, you can also buy fat to cut into larding strips. The skin, *la couenne*, is available too, for additional flavor and texture in beef casseroles. As you can see from the recipe on page 330, crackling is not unknown in France, but it is served quite separately from roast pork.

The finest roasting joint of all is the loin, usually divided into two on account of its length. The leg end is known as the *filet* or *longe*, and the smaller end as the *carré*. When the *filet* is cut into chops it becomes escalopes or the small, round *noisettes*. When the *carré* is cut into chops, it becomes *côtes* and the smaller *côtelettes*.

The leg, together with the loin, are the *parties nobles* of the pig, but the leg is most usually turned into ham. The French for both is *jambon* (though *gigot* is often used for a fresh roasting leg), and the adjective *frais* to designate an uncured leg is often omitted. Be careful of this when using a French cookery book, or an English one derived from French sources. Read the recipe very carefully before visiting the butcher, and decide which is most likely—fresh leg of pork, gammon, or cooked ham.

The cheaper joints of pork benefit even more than leg and loin from being salted in brine before they are cooked. Boned picnic shoulder or shoulder arm of pork (*épaule désossée*), for instance, British spareribs—shoulder or blade end in U.S.— (*échine*), and British bladebone—American shoulder butt or Boston butt—(*palette*), and the often-despised sowbelly (*poitrine*) gain in flavor and tenderness for 3 days in *saumure anglaise* (page 191). They can then be stewed or braised to advantage, or simmered in water and finally glazed. Try combining sowbelly of pork, salted or not, with shin of beef in the casserole on page 239; the pork supplies a bland smoothness which greatly improves the flavor and texture of the sauce.

The extremities of the pig can also be eaten fresh, but they have been dealt with in a separate chapter, beginning on page 248.

————— • • • —————

ROASTING

Unlike beef or lamb, there is nothing to be gained by undercooking pork. Indeed it is neither desirable nor safe to do so. Pork should be well and gently cooked, whatever the cut and whatever the method of cooking used.

Prepare a joint of pork for roasting by boning, salting, marinading, or seasoning. Then weigh it, and reckon 30 minutes cooking time for joints up to and including 4 lbs. Add 20 minutes a pound for each pound over. Put the joint on a rack in the roasting pan, and set it in a low oven, 325°F. There is no need to add fat or water. Test the joint near the end of the cooking time with a larding or knitting needle. The liquid which oozes out should be colorless. If it is pink the joint is not ready.

Make a sauce from the pan juices after pouring off excess fat, according to taste and recipe.

Longe (Carré, Gigot) de Porc Truffée

Truffles are the finest flavoring of all for pork. Even a ¾-oz. can makes a remarkable difference to a 4-lb. joint. If you want to eat the pork cold, follow the pot-roasted version of this recipe on page 235.

Open the can of truffles, cut them into small pieces, and reserve the juice. Bone the joint (which will taste even better after 24 hours in brine, page 191). Make incisions in the fat and put pieces of truffle in. Save some for the bone cavity. Roll and tie the joint. Cook the joint according to the basic roasting method. Make the sauce by pouring a scant ¾ cup of white wine into the pan juices—remember to strain off the excess fat first into a separate basin, it will be deliciously truffle-flavored. When it has thickened a little add the truffle liquid from the can and cook the sauce very gently, with barely a bubble, for 5 minutes.

Do not obscure the delicate flavor of this dish by hearty accompaniments and garnishes. Some plainly boiled new potatoes, tossed in butter and parsley, are all that is required. Follow with a green salad.

Longe de Porc aux Pistaches

Follow the preceding recipe, but stud the pork with blanched pistachio nuts.

Longe de Porc Rôtie

Stud the pork with slivers of garlic. Serve plainly garnished with watercress or with *sauce Robert,* or *sauce piquante, sauce diable,* or *sauce à la charcutière.*

Longe de Porc à la Normande

Baste and make the sauce with good cider. Serve with unsweetened apple purée made with eating apples.

Or salt the pork and serve with a cream *sauce normande* (page 47).

Longe de Porc Clamart

Roast pork served with the Clamart or St.-Germain garnish of young green peas and artichoke hearts, finished in butter. One of the best combinations with pork or ham.

Porc Rôti à la Bourgeoise

An hour before the pork is cooked, add small new carrots and tiny onions to the roasting pan. Turn them over from time to time so that they glaze. Serve the vegetables round the meat, garnish with parsley.

If small new potatoes are cooked in the pan as well, you have pork *à la bonne femme.*

Porc Rôti à la Berrichonne

Shell and simmer 1 lb. chestnuts for 20 minutes, blanch 1 lb. of small onions, and add them with a few rolls of bacon to the pork 45 minutes before the end of cooking time.

An attractive way of serving chestnuts with pork or ham is to cook them to a purée, flavor with pan juices from the pork or crumbs of crisply fried bacon, and serve it in small *barquettes* or *tartelettes* of short pastry, baked blind.

Porc Rôti aux Herbes

Sage is not often associated with pork in France, but if you grow it or can get some fresh, here is a way of combining it with pork in the French style (don't use dried sage).

Make incisions in the joint of pork and insert small sprigs or leaves of sage. Mix 2 tablespoons of salt, 2 tablespoons of thyme, and ½ bay leaf, crumbled, and rub this over the fat and boned sides of the joint. Leave overnight. Rub the seasoned salt in again next morning, before tying up the joint for roasting.

In Provence plenty of crushed garlic, bread crumbs, and some olive oil are mixed together into a paste and this is spread over the joint 45 minutes before the end of cooking time. It forms an appetizing golden crust.

Porc Rôti aux Choux Rouges

In northern France pork is accompanied by red cabbage, *choucroute*, and purées of dried vegetables, all cooked separately from the meat but served round it on the same dish. A sprinkling of green herbs lightens the appearance.

This is a heavy way of serving pork. Like *petit salé aux choux* (page 182), *potée* (page 173), *garbure* (page 174), *hochepot* (page 186), and *cassoulet* (page 168), it is most wisely eaten in cold weather at midday.

Carré de Porc au Fenouil

This recipe was given to me by Mme Champy, the owner of the Tabac at Trôo. Fennel grows wild on the cliff there, but it is easily cultivated in the garden, see page 28.

Rub the pork over with salt and fennel leaves. Put a branch or two of fennel in a dish and leave the joint on it overnight.

Next day insert some slivers of garlic into the fat of the pork, and roast in the usual way.

Skim excess fat off the pan juices, and make the sauce by adding white or *rosé* wine to them and reducing. Serve with potatoes sautéed in lard, flavored with a sprig of fennel, and serve them with a sprinkling of chopped fennel.

Glazed Roast Pork

In the absence of crackling, glazing is the logical extension of basting when applied to roast pork. It involves a combination of spiciness (French mustard, cloves, or ground spices) and sweetness (orange, in juice or marmalade form, red-currant jelly, brown sugar) which not only mingle their flavors harmoniously with the pork, but also provide it with an irresistible coat of gleaming golden-brown. The pan juices are enriched, making a variety of sauces possible beyond the conventional range. The glaze can be the consistency of heavy cream or a virtual paste (*pommade*), which extends its use to grilled chops.

Porc Rôti à l'Orange

Insert some slivers of garlic into a roasting joint of pork, and 2 or 3 small sprigs of rosemary. Don't overdo either herb, orange must be the predominating flavor.

Roast the pork as described on page 228, but ½ hour before the end of cooking time, skin the joint and glaze it with a mixture of:

1½ tablespoons French mustard	The juice of 1 orange
2 tablespoons Oxford-type orange marmalade	2 teaspoons brown sugar

Skim excess fat off the pan juices at the end, and make a sauce by adding to them white wine, orange juice, and Madeira or Marsala or a little Curaçao, so that you have a piquant, not-too-sweet sauce.

Cut 2 oranges into thin slices, heat them through carefully in the sauce, and serve round the joint of pork. The sauce is finally poured over the joint. The lightest sprinkling of parsley makes an attractive finish.

Porc Rôti aux Pommes

Glaze the pork with a mixture of French mustard, melted red-currant jelly, and a little brown sugar and ground cloves.

Serve with apple rings, peeled, cored, and fried lightly in butter; or cored eating apples baked in the roasting pan beneath the rack.

NOTE: If you would like a crustier glaze, incorporate bread crumbs in the mixture.

BRAISING, POT-ROASTING, AND STEWING

The first two methods amount to much the same thing in the case of pork, as the meat is moist enough to require very little additional liquid. What moisture there is is conserved by covering the pot with a tight-fitting lid, which means that it is a good method for cheaper joints of pork. If you tell the butcher that you wish to braise a joint *en casserole,* he will probably give you a piece of *échine* (shoulder or blade end) or the loin end of pork.

Here is a typical way of pot-roasting very popular in small French villages, where not everybody has an oven:

Choose a heavy cast-iron pan, melt some lard or butter and oil in it, and brown the neatly tied joint of pork all over, including the two ends. Warm some *eau-de-vie, marc,* brandy, or vodka in a small pan, set it alight, and pour over the browned pork.

Add a *mirepoix* of carrots and onions, some crushed garlic, and about ½ cup of *rosé* wine. Grind salt and pepper over, put on the lid, and turn the heat down low enough to keep the liquid gently bubbling. Allow ½ hour to the pound.

Turn the meat over from time to time. Add new potatoes for the last ½ hour.

Taste the sauce and adjust the flavor and seasoning as you like. Skim off the fat. The French like their *jus* or gravy to be concentrated and well-flavored—this means that there can't be a vast quantity of it, just a spoonful or two for each person.

Some farmers say that if the pork is accompanied by a hash of onions, sautéed in butter and flamed in brandy, it will keep you sober through a day's hard drinking. Recommended for market-day breakfast.

Use a cast-iron pot which has been enameled if you can— otherwise the sauce turns a disconcerting blackish color, due to the wine. It tastes all right, but the appearance may put people off.

Carré (Échine) de Porc en Gelée à la Vendômoise

Follow the method described above, but omit the *mirepoix* and add the bones. Increase the quantity of liquid to 2½ cups, by adding 2 cups of water or stock. Let the pork cool in the liquid, scrape off the fat and keep it for frying potatoes, or bread on another occasion, and serve the pork sliced, surrounded by chopped jelly.

The pork can be seasoned in many of the ways suggested earlier in this chapter. I think of it stuffed with long purplish-black *trompettes des morts* funghi from the woods near Trôo, and served at the midday *Vendange* picnic.

Enchaud de Porc à la Périgourdine

This southwestern version of our Vendômois pork is one of the
two best recipes for pork that I know. The other one is *noisettes
de porc aux pruneaux de Tours* (page 236).

Buy a really good piece of loin of pork about 5 lbs. in
weight. Ask the butcher to bone it for you and remove the skin.

Leave the joint in brine, *saumure anglaise* (page 191), for
24 hours. This is where I depart from Elizabeth David, who
gives the recipe in her *French Provincial Cooking*.

Next day drain the pork well and dry it with a clean cloth.
Lay it out, boned side up, on a board and season with pepper,
and the truffles from a small can cut into pieces, and a few slivers
of garlic. Salt, too, if the pork did not soak in brine.

Roll the meat together and tie at frequent intervals with fine
string. Put the joint into a deep dish, surround it with the bones
and pieces of skin. Let it cook uncovered for ½ hour in a low
oven, 330°F. The fat will turn pale gold. Pour in ½ cup of white
wine and 2 cups of water, or 2½ cups clear, hot meat stock, together with the juice from the canned truffles. Cover with the
lid or a double sheet of aluminum foil, and leave the meat for
2 to 2½ hours, to cook, at the same temperature.

Remove the bones, skin, etc., and leave the meat to cool
in the liquid. Next day remove the fat and treasure it for spreading on bread. Serve the pork in slices surrounded with its jelly,
chopped. This dish smells wonderful, tastes wonderful—and
looks wonderful, the pale-pink meat contrasting with the black
nuggets of truffle and the creamy white fat.

Gigot de Porc en Sanglier

If a leg of pork is soaked for 2 to 4 days, depending on the
temperature, in the cooked marinade given on page 67, it can
then be braised and served as a passable imitation of wild

boar. It is perhaps more usual to treat legs of mutton *en chevreuil,* like venison, but with pork it works just as well.

After the 4 days of soaking, brown the pork in lard then remove it to a heavy, lidded pan whilst you make the sauce.

Stir 2 heaped tablespoons of flour into the lard in which the pork browned, and add the strained marinade gradually so that no lumps form. Dilute the sauce with hot stock until it is the consistency of light cream. Pour it over the leg of pork and put the lid on the pan.

Cook in a low oven for 2 to 3 hours, according to the weight of the pork.

The sauce will need to be reduced, after you have skimmed off the fat. Taste it continuously, and season until you are satisfied.

Chops and small cuts like *noisettes,* escalopes, and the pork undercut known, in England and the United States, as tenderloin can be braised too. One of the best pork recipes ever invented gives a good idea of the BASIC METHOD.

Noisettes de Porc aux Pruneaux de Tours

This bland combination of pork, prunes, cream, and the white wine of Vouvray embodies what Henry James described as "the good-humored and succulent Touraine." The wine is made—as the best white wines are—from grapes which are almost rotting on the vines. One local vigneron says: "They piss in your hand." The first time I made this dish I couldn't afford the Vouvray, so I improved on the very ordinary white wine in the larder by using Christmas prunes, which had been steeping in a mixture of half *marc,* a crude *eau-de-vie,* and half syrup. Delicious, if unorthodox.

1 lb. large Californian
prunes (unless you can
find Touraine ones)
½ bottle (1½ cups) white
Vouvray (drink the
other half with the dish)
Salt, pepper, a little flour

2 *noisettes* per person
About 2 tablespoons butter
1 tablespoon red-currant
jelly
1 cup heavy cream
Dash of lemon juice

Put the prunes to soak overnight in the Vouvray. Next day pour off about ¼ cup of the liquid, and put the rest of it with the prunes into a slow oven to cook. Three quarters of an hour is enough, but in fact you can leave them there for up to 1½ hours provided they simmer slowly enough. Cover them so that the juice does not evaporate.

Season and flour the *noisettes*. Cook them gently in the butter on each side, making sure that the butter doesn't go brown. Add the ¼ cup of steeping juice and leave the pork to cook for 40 minutes with a lid on the pan.

Pour on the juice from cooking the prunes. Cook for 3 minutes, then remove the pork to a large flat serving dish and arrange the prunes around the *noisettes* whilst the sauce in the frying pan boils down to a thinnish syrup. Add the red-currant jelly. Then the cream, bit by bit, stirring it in well so that after each addition it is properly amalgamated. Because English and American cream don't have that slightly sour tang of French cream, I add a dash of lemon at the end before pouring the sauce over the *noisettes* and prunes. Leave in the oven for 5 minutes. Serve this dish on its own.

Côtes de Porc à la Vosgienne

Here is another recipe for pork and plums, this time the pretty little yellow *Mirabelles* (greengages) which grow in gardens all over France, not just in the Vosges, where this dish is supposed to have originated:

1 large onion	1 lb. *Mirabelle* plums or
6 tablespoons (¾ stick)	other firm, ripe plums
butter	Sugar
4 pork chops, cut thick	1–2 tablespoons white wine
1 cup white wine	vinegar
	1 beef bouillon cube

Chop the onion, fry it gently in the butter, and when it is half cooked add the chops to color slightly on both sides. This is an operation demanding care as the butter must not catch or the delicate flavor will be lost. Add ⅓ cup of the wine to the pan, put the lid on, and simmer until the chops are cooked.

Meanwhile cook the plums in just enough water to stop them catching. Don't let them overcook, so that they collapse into a mush. As English or American plums will not be so naturally sweet as French ones, add a very little sugar.

Arrange the chops and plums on a dish and make a sauce with the pan juices, the rest of the white wine, the vinegar, and the bouillon cube, which should be crumbled first, then added bit by bit as required.

NOTE: This method can be adapted in many ways, using different herbs and spices. The small amount of sauce has a fresh flavor which makes a change from the more meditated piquant sauces that have been quietly maturing on the side of the stove for hours.

Stewed Pork (Ragoût de Porc)

The fattiness of pork means that it needs careful attention when stewed, to make sure that all excess fat is removed both at the beginning and end of the cooking.

Pork tails and bones are successful cooked in this way, also shoulder and sowbelly, although in the latter case the best result is achieved by stewing it with shin of beef.

This is the method: cut 2–3 lbs. of meat into regular pieces and roll them in seasoned flour.

Melt a little lard in a heavy frying pan and brown some sliced onions. Add the meat and brown on all sides. Pour off the fat, then sprinkle in a teaspoonful of sugar, which will caramelize and help to give the sauce a good color.

Heat ½ cup of *rosé* wine and add it to the meat and onions. Whilst it is bubbling away, heat 1 cup of good stock, then add that. Depending on the quantity of meat you may require more or less liquid; the pork should be hardly covered.

Season with salt, pepper, crushed juniper berries, thyme, sage, garlic—whichever you prefer—cover the pot, and simmer until the meat is tender and dropping off the bones.

Strain off all the sauce into an upright glass jar—I use a 5-cup tumbler from a pub sale—so that the fat can rise and be skimmed. Check the seasoning, reduce the sauce if necessary, and pour over the meat, which you have arranged in a clean dish. Serve with a light dressing of parsley and boiled potatoes.

Jarret de Boeuf en Daube

Use equal quantities of shin of beef and sowbelly.

To 1 lb. of each use 2 large onions. Follow the method given in the preceding recipe, substituting red wine for the *rosé*. Season with more pepper than you would use for pork. Serve with boiled rice or potatoes.

NOTE: Like all stews, these are better made one day and heated through the next. The long wait overnight in the wine sauce acts as a marinade in maturing and tenderizing the meat. Remember to heat through thoroughly by bringing to the boil, then simmering for ½ hour, or longer if the stew was only half-cooked the previous day.

FRYING AND GRILLING

These methods involve the small cuts of pork and are virtually interchangeable according to your circumstances. If you have really good pork chops, grill them. If you are in the least bit dubious, fry or braise them (see pages 233–9). Either method should be applied gently—unlike fillet steak, pork chops will take about 20 minutes under the grill or in the sauté pan.

Filets Mignons de Porc Sautés

Buy a tenderloin, the undercut of bacon and butcher pigs, which looks like a pallid, miniature fillet of beef, and cut it across, slightly at an angle, into slices about ½ inch thick.

Beat them out gently, season, dip them in egg, then roll in bread crumbs and fry gently in butter for about 4 minutes on each side.

Serve garnished with watercress and lightly fried apple rings. Pour over a little sauce made from the pan juices by stirring in some white wine and stock. There should not be a lot of sauce.

NOTE: Tenderloin can be cooked in a great variety of ways. Use it for *porc aux pruneaux de Tours* (page 236), but reduce the cooking time for the meat.

Wrap it in bards of hard fat back and roast it for ½ hour.

Split it not quite in two lengthways, flatten, stuff, and roll it up; roast for 45 minutes.

Keep the garnishings and accompaniments light—young green peas, very small new potatoes, or onions or carrots. Don't overburden a delicate cut.

Côtes de Porc Sautées à la Gasconne

This is a good dish for *amateurs* of garlic and olives, from *Larousse Gastronomique*. Don't be frightened of the quantity of garlic.

Buy thick pork chops. Two hours before you intend to cook them, pique each one with a sliver of garlic, sprinkle with thyme and bay leaf, crumbled, and salt, pepper, oil, and lemon juice. Leave them to marinade.

Meanwhile prepare the olives and garlic. You require 6 of each per chop. Pit the olives, peel the cloves of garlic. Get ready two small pans of water, bring them to the boil, and plunge the garlic in one, the olives in the other. Leave them for 2 minutes at a galloping boil, remove, and drain. Chop the garlic roughly.

Now attend to the chops. Fry them quickly on both sides in duck or goose fat or butter. Three minutes on each side is enough. Add the chopped garlic, turn it over in the fat, and leave to cook with the chops slowly, with a lid on the pan. This will take from ½ hour to ¾, depending on the quality of the chops. Arrange the cooked chops on a mound of mashed potatoes, with the olives, and put them into a low oven while you attend to the sauce. This is made by pouring white wine and some concentrated beef stock into the cooking pan, and reducing them. Pour the sauce over the chops, without straining, bits of garlic and all. Sprinkle with chopped marjoram or parsley.

Côtes de Porc à la Bayonnaise

Larousse Gastronomique also gives this recipe, which is particularly good if you can find edible *cèpes* (*boletus, bolet comestible, cèpe de Bordeaux*).

Marinade the chops as in the preceding recipe.

Meanwhile prepare some small new potatoes; and the *cèpes*, which you do by slicing them across and removing the yellow spongy under-layer, as well as any small forms of animal life.

Fry the potatoes gently in lard for 5 minutes, and the *cèpes* in a little oil. Give the chops a brisk 5 minutes in lard, on each side, then put them with the vegetables to cook together in a lidded earthenware dish. Simmer in a low oven for 45 minutes. Sprinkle with chopped parsley.

Côtes de Porc à la Charcutière

Make the *charcutière* sauce the previous day (page 45), but don't put in the gherkins until just before serving.

Follow the preceding recipe, but reheat the sauce in the grill pan, add the gherkins and herbs, and serve in a separate sauceboat.

(All the piquant sauces are delicious with pork chops. And *sauce bercy*, see page 43.)

Côtes de Porc Vallée d'Auge

Score thick chops lightly on each side. Spread one side with a mixture of chopped shallots and chopped parsley. Dot with melted butter and grill. Turn the chops carefully over, spread the other side with shallots and parsley and butter, and grill.

Heat ½ cup or a little more cider or dry white wine in a small pan whilst the grilling goes on. Transfer the chops to a serving dish and pour the hot cider or wine into the grill pan. Bring to the boil over a strong heat on top of the stove and let it reduce to a good sauce. Stir in all the little bits and juice from the chops.

If you have any Calvados or applejack, add some to the cider or wine. Pour over the chops, and serve with mashed potatoes and a green salad. (Elizabeth David's recipe.)

Côtes de Porc Avesnoise

A delicious way of serving pork chops from Avesnes-sur-Helpe in the very north of France. The method can be adapted for use with other glazing mixtures (see pages 191 and 232); but this French rarebit style is the best of all.

Grate a quantity of Gruyère or Emmenthal cheese (2 oz. [about ½ cup grated] is enough for 3 chops), mix it to a thick paste with half-and-half French mustard and cream. It should spread but not run.

Grill the chops on both sides as in the recipe for *côtes de porc au vin blanc*. When they are done, spread one side of each chop with the Gruyère paste and set under the grill. The mixture will melt, bubble, and turn gold.

One of the most appetizing ways of serving pork, the smell is irresistible and draws the whole family into the kitchen.

Côtes de Porc au Vin Blanc

After a long day's work or excursion, grilled pork chops are everybody's solution to the evening meal. With a little fore-thought, you can improve on everybody else's solution and enjoy a much better meal.

Season the chops. Put previously cooked potatoes into a pan with milk, to heat through for mashing.

Grill the chops fast for 1 minute, then lower the heat and give them 9 minutes. Turn over, and repeat with 1 minute fast and 9 minutes slow.

Deal with the potatoes, adding plenty of butter and nutmeg or mace; arrange the chops round them and put the dish into the oven whilst you make the sauce.

Take the rack out of the grill pan, pour in some white or *rosé* wine, bubble it all together on top of the stove. Taste and season. Be sure to scrape in all the little brown bits. Pour over the chops and serve. Have French mustard on the table.

(Watercress always makes a good appearance with pork.)

Côtes de Porc Ambassadrice

4 pork chops	4 large mushroom caps
Salt, pepper	4 slices truffle (optional)
About 6 tablespoons (¾	A scant ½ cup Madeira
stick) butter	Meat glaze or concentrated
4 chicken livers	beef stock

Sauté the seasoned chops in the butter gently, until they are cooked. Arrange them in an ovenproof serving dish and keep them warm. Sauté the chicken livers next, arrange them on top of the chops, then the mushroom caps and put them on top again. If you are using truffles, they should be put on last of all.

Swill the frying pan round with the Madeira, scraping all the delicious bits that have stuck to the pan into the juice. Add some meat glaze or concentrated stock to make a little sauce. Correct the seasoning, then pour over the chops and garnish with a light sprinkling of parsley.

(In earlier times, the dish would have included cocks' combs and kidneys, for the full *ambassadrice* garnish.)

OTHER SUGGESTIONS FOR SERVING PORK CHOPS

À *la ratatouille.* A stew of onions, peppers, *courgettes* (zucchini), aubergines (eggplants), and tomatoes.

Provençale. A thick purée of tomatoes, well spiced, and finished with strips of red blanched or canned pimientos, and pitted, blanched black olives.

Aux haricots verts. Green sliced beans, finished with chopped almonds fried in butter.

Aux marrons. Chestnut purée, or cooked chestnuts and Brussels sprouts in Mornay sauce (page 53).

Aux poireaux. Leek purée. Cook the sliced leeks in a little butter. Whirl them in the electric blender (or sieve), adding fresh cream, salt, pepper, and a good pinch of sugar. Serve the chops on top.

Aux champignons. Surrounded by mushrooms sautéed in butter, tiny glazed onions, and diced sautéed bacon. Flavor with thyme.

Soubise. Sauce recipe given on page 59.

À l'orange. See page 232, or *sauce bigarade* (page 43).

With small pats of some of the butters given on page 44.

───── ·•◆•· ─────

SUCKLING PIG
(*Cochon de Lait*)

Suckling pig is killed, as its name suggests, when it is from 2 to 6 weeks old. It makes a good festival dish either hot, or cold in a galantine. One of the special delights of roast suckling pig, in France, England, and the United States alike, is the beautiful crackling. To this end it should be basted with olive oil so that the skin becomes *croquante*.

Cochon de Lait Rôti

First make a light herb-and-vegetable stuffing—this is a good one:

2 large onions, chopped (about 2 cups)
4 stalks celery, chopped (about 2 cups)
⅜ lb. (12 tablespoons, 1½ sticks) butter
Grated rind and juice of 1 lemon plus juice of another
Plenty of chopped parsley

2 sprigs of thyme
3 cups bread crumbs
Salt, pepper
2 large eggs, beaten

A 12- to 14-lb. suckling pig
Olive oil

½ cup white wine
½ cup good stock

Simmer the onion and celery in ¼ lb. (1 stick) of the butter very gently for 15 minutes. They should not brown at all but melt to a golden transparency. Put the contents of the pan into a bowl, add the remaining 4 tablespoons (½ stick) of butter, the grated rind and juice of 1 lemon, the herbs, bread crumbs, and beaten eggs. Taste and season. Add the juice of the second lemon if necessary; you need a good tang.

Stuff the pig and sew it up with "heavy-duty" white thread. Make 3 or 4 scorings on either side of the backbone, at an angle, like arrow heads, and brush the pig over with olive oil. Set it on its side on a rack in a large roasting pan and cook in a moderate oven for 2½ hours, turning over at half-time. Be careful of the crackling as you do this. Some recipes suggest brushing the crackling with heavy cream 20 minutes before the end of cooking time, but this should not be necessary.

To make the accompanying sauce, pour the liquid from the roasting pan into a tall heavy glass jar. This makes it easy to skim or siphon off the fat. Return the gravy to the stove, adding ½ cup of white wine and the same of good stock. Boil it down a little, tasting and correcting the seasoning.

No vegetables are necessary apart from plain boiled potatoes, finished in butter and parsley, and watercress. Some people like an unsweetened purée of eating apples.

NOTE: Many cookery-book writers are anxious that the suckling pig should be presented on the table with an American mortician's skill. "Truss the legs and tail in a lifelike position, a small red apple in mouth and cranberries in the eye sockets." "Try and preserve as nearly as possible the animal's original shape and form." But do not overemphasize these effects, few people have the robust constitutions required to look a small creature in its cranberry eye.

Galantine de Cochon de Lait

A sensational dish for a large party, but not one that will keep, on account of the jelly.

⅜ lb. lean veal

A little over ½ lb. hard
fat back

2¼ cups bread crumbs,
soaked in a little milk

A small can of truffles (1-
to 2-oz. can)

2 large eggs plus 1 addi-
tional egg yolk

¼ lb. ham

A 12- to 14-lb. suckling pig

½ lemon

———— *Braising* ————

Carrots, onions, veal
knuckle bone, garlic,
bouquet garni, salt and
pepper, 2 or 3 cloves

2 cups white wine

2 cups beef stock

Grind the veal and ⅜ lb. of the hard fat back, plus any trimmings from the suckling pig. Squeeze the soaked bread, mix it with the meat, and add the truffles and the eggs. If you want to make a particularly spendid *farce,* add slivers of almonds and pistachio nuts (blanched).

Cut the ham and the remaining fat back into matchsticks.

Line the cavity of the pig with stuffing, then a layer of ham and fat back. Stuffing again, then the ham, etc. Finish with the stuffing. Sew the pig up with "heavy-duty" white thread. Truss the front and back legs together, rub all over with the cut side of ½ lemon and tie or sew into a cloth.

Chop the carrots and onions into large dice, and put with all the other braising ingredients into a large pan. Lay the suckling pig on top and cover over, either with a lid or a double layer of aluminum foil.

Bring to the boil and simmer gently for 4 hours (3 may be enough for a very small pig). Leave the pig to cool in the pan, and don't unwrap until it is cold. Melt the braising liquid, strain, skim, reduce, and season. Clarify if necessary (page 41). Brush a layer of jelly over the pig when it is almost set and serve the rest, chopped, around it.

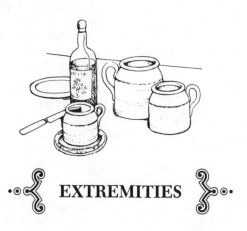

•○⚡ EXTREMITIES ⚡○•

THE HEAD

Pig's head, like the other extremities, is sold cheaply in England and the U.S. It makes an excellent brawn, or headcheese (*fromage de tête, hure*), or galantine, if suitable attention is paid to its preparation. Anyone can grill a steak or chop, but the cheaper cuts require careful and sophisticated cooking. This does not mean that the methods are difficult or tortuous, but they do require judgment and care over detail. Lack of proper care, above the statutory requirements of hygiene, and insensitivity to flavor make many manufactured meat dishes in England and America uneatable. This commercial debasement of brawn, black puddings, meat pies, and sausages has misled people into feeling that only the expensive parts of a pig are worth eating.

There is little difference between *fromage de tête* and *hure* and *galantine de porc*. *Fromage* is a mixture of the meat set in jelly, *hure* is a mixture of the meat enveloped in the skin of the head, galantine is a mixture of the meat with hardly any internal jelly, but a coating of jelly round the outside.

Fromage de Tête

½ pig's head
1 trotter (foot)

3 tablespoons wine vinegar
Water to cover

2 onions
2 carrots
2 leeks
2 cloves garlic
2 bay leaves
2 sprigs parsley
2 sprigs thyme
8 peppercorns

1½ cups white wine
Lemon juice to taste
Quatre-épices or a mixture
  of allspice, cloves, and
  nutmeg
Toasted bread crumbs,
  parsley

Half a pig's head makes enough for the average family; but try to acquire the whole brain for a separate dish. Ask the butcher to chop the head into two or three bits, so that it will fit easily into a pan.

Deal with the brain immediately (see page 248).

Put the pig's head and trotter into the brine tub (page 191), if you have one ready. This makes a great improvement in the flavor of the brawn (headcheese). Even 24 hours makes a difference; if you leave them there for 2 or 3 days you will need to bring them to the boil in a pan of cold water to draw off excessive salt before you start the proper cooking.

You can cook several feet at once with the head, to be eaten on another occasion. If you do this, bind them up tightly in cheesecloth so that they keep their shape. Reckon 5 hours' cooking time.

Once you've drawn off the salt and thrown away the scummy water, add all the other ingredients to the meat in the pan, except the wine, lemon juice, spices, bread crumbs, and parsley. See that the new water really does cover all the meat. Bring slowly to the boil, and wedge the lid on tightly. Use aluminum foil, and a weight (I have a lump of red rock for this) to keep the lid down.

Simmer as gently as you can for 4 to 8 hours. The length of time will depend on your success in keeping the simmer down to a bare bubble. The slower and steadier the better. Do this on a low heat, or in a low oven. The meat is cooked when it drops easily off the bone.

No salt yet. Wait until you've drained off the liquid, put 2 cups of it into a clean pan with the white wine, and boil it down to 2 cups again. Then taste, and season with salt and lemon juice if you think it needs further sharpening. The point of this operation is to make a well-flavored jelly. Remember that cold food loses flavor, so allow for this. The secret is to keep tasting the liquid as it reduces.

Meanwhile pick out the meat from the solid remains. Throw the bones and vegetables away. Keep the tongue whole, chop the rest of the meat into smallish dice. There's no short cut to this. Whatever you do, don't put the meat through the grinder or you'll end up with a nasty jellied mush. Season the meat with the spices. Don't overdo it.

Add the meat to the pan of reduced *bouillon*, simmer very slowly for 20 minutes. Taste again and put the pan in the larder to cool down. Keep tasting as it cools and correct the seasoning. Just before it sets, put a layer of chopped meat in the loaf pan, add the tongue whole along the middle, and then add the rest of the chopped meat. Spoon off some of the liquid if you think there's too much of it.

When the *fromage* has set, unmold it and cover with home-toasted bread crumbs, not the yellow commercial ones. Put a few slices of white bread in the oven to dry to a pale brown. Crush them between sheets of greaseproof paper (or in a pestle and mortar), then press them gently onto the *fromage* when they are nearly cold. Surround with parsley, and put the dish in the refrigerator to chill.

———— *Variations* ————

The *court-bouillon* can be flavored with whatever you have to hand: turnip, celery, onion studded with cloves, orange and lemon rind, a few crushed juniper berries or allspice berries and nutmeg if you are unable to buy the French *charcuterie* spice-blend *quatre-épices*. You could line the mold with slices of hard-boiled eggs (don't cover with toasted bread crumbs at the end), put them in layers with the chopped meat in which you have included the tongue chopped, or use the eggs whole as for a veal-ham-and-egg pie.

Serve with—French mustard (to my mind essential with most pork dishes, particularly the smooth, gelatinous ones), hard-boiled eggs, green salad dressed with 4 tablespoons of raw chopped mild onions or scallions and 4 tablespoons of chopped parsley as well as oil and vinegar and seasonings. Mashed potato is a standard accompaniment to *charcuterie*—slimmers might prefer thin toast, or wholewheat or rye bread.

Hure

Here you are dealing with the whole head. If you are feeling adventurous and have sharp knives, you might like to bone it before cooking. Or perhaps you have a skillful butcher who would do it for you. Then you could proceed to a *tête de cochon farcie*, or a simulated boar's head (given by Alexis Soyer in *The Modern Housewife or Ménagère*, 1850, and quoted in André Simon's *Concise Encyclopaedia of Gastronomy*).

But first an easier way.

Remove the ears and tongue, but leave the head whole. Put everything into the brine tub, if you have one ready, for 3 days (page 191). Assemble the ingredients for a *court-bouillon,* similar to the one described in the preceding recipe, vegetables, wine vinegar, wine (in this case to be included from the beginning); and find a pan large enough to take the head comfortably. An old boiling fowl makes a useful addition, but it is not necessary. It is no good whatever using a young roaster, because it has little flavor compared with the good strong taste of a mature hen. The point of using the whole head is to end up with a large area of skin (*couenne*) in which to envelop the cooked meats. Wrap it up tightly in a cheesecloth or napkin, and place it in the pan with the boiling fowl if you decide to use one. The ears and tongue can then be fitted into the spaces with the vegetables. Add plenty of water to cover the ingredients, and set the pot to boil. Keep at a gentle simmer for between 5 and 8 hours, removing the tongue after 2.

Remove the head, unwrap it, and let it cool down a little so that you can handle it. Keep the strained liquid boiling away gently. Take the bones out of the head, and the meat as well. Lay the skin outside down on a clean piece of cloth, and cut the meat into strips and dice, including the chicken, but excluding the tongue. Season well with spices. You can augment the meat with homemade sausage meat.

Arrange your meats as elegantly as possible in the skin, with the tongue in the middle; fold the skin completely round the chopped meats so that you end up with a sausage-like pudding which can be tied up firmly in the cloth. Simmer this for an hour in the liquid. Remove and squeeze gently to get rid of the juice. Unwrap. You can either ease the *hure* gently into a mold, or leave it under a weight to cool. If you do put it into a mold, put a piece of wood on top and a weight. Finish with toasted bread crumbs.

———•► *Variation* ◄•———

A delicious and elegant variation is *hure à la pistache*. You follow the preceding recipe until you get to the meat-chopping stage, then you chop the tongue too. Arrange the chopped meats as before, but this time include whole pistachio nuts. Their pale-green-and-lavender beauty adds a sensational effect when you slice the marbled *hure;* their texture and flavor go well with the bland meat. Serve simply with salad, as the delicate flavor must not be drowned.

Serve with—the accompaniments suggested for *fromage de tête*, except in the case of *hure à la pistache*, which is a dish on its own.

Tête de Porc Farcie

If you feel like boning the head before you start cooking (or you can persuade your butcher to do so), try this recipe. Should you come to disaster and pierce the skin, you could always lay your largest piece of it out flat on a cloth and roll everything up as for *hure*.

1 pig's head

————• *Court-bouillon* •————

1 calf's foot (2 trotters, or feet, would do instead)	3 cloves of garlic
	3½ cups white wine
3 onions stuck with cloves	Salt and pepper to taste
4 carrots cut in rounds	Extra water to cover

Set all this to boil whilst you make the stuffing.

————• *Stuffing (Farce)* •————

Tongue from the head, sliced	½ lb. ground veal if possible
Homemade sausage meat (according to the size of the cavity), page 115	Parsley

Stuff the head, sew up the neck. Tie it up in a cloth, and add it to the pan of *court-bouillon* with the bones. Simmer very gently for at least 5 hours.

Remove from the liquid, which you leave to boil down for the jelly; leave it to cool a little, then unwrap. Push carefully but firmly into a mold, filling the gaps with the reduced liquid. I find that it is necessary to use a board and weight.

Galantine

Ingredients for *court-bouillon* as in the previous recipe	1 pig's head
	A few parings of truffles or whole truffles

Cut the meat off the head and chop it into thin slices. Chop the tongue and ears too. Leave for 24 hours, with 6 tablespoons of salt, freshly ground pepper, and the spices you prefer, in an earthenware dish in a cool place.

Next day tie the meat up in a cheesecloth, and simmer it for at least 5 hours very gently in the *court-bouillon*, to which you have added the bones. Do not salt the *bouillon* for the first 2 hours, then taste and see if it requires it.

Take the meat out, and let it cool a very little. Leave the liquid to reduce on a hard flame, but do not let it get too salty. Unwrap the meat and pack it into the mold very tightly leaving no gaps. Should you be able to afford the truffles, mix them in at this stage. Put a board and weight on top to keep everything pressed down; leave to get cold.

In the autumn instead of truffles you could substitute the black mushroom called "horn of plenty" (*craterellus cornucopioides*), as they often do in France for the pâtés eaten during the grape-picking and harvest supper afterwards. Then they are mixed in with the raw meat and baked with it, but 5 hours of simmering with the galantine would be far too much. I just simmer them in 2 tablespoons of water at the very end of the cooking time, and mix them with the meat when everything is ready to go into the mold.

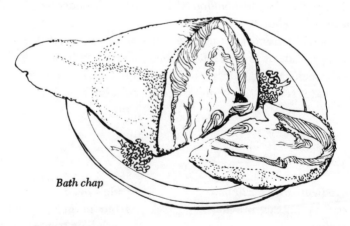

Bath chap

Whilst the galantine is setting, attend to the liquid. Strain it off and leave to jelly. A certain amount of scum separates itself, and you may find that the jelly is clear, once you have removed the opaque layers. If it needs clarifying, turn to page 41.

Here is the recipe for the English Bath chap, made from the jowl of the pig (*bajoue*). I have never seen anything similar in the *charcuterie*, but it is worthy of a place there.

Bath Chap

Court-bouillon as for the two preceding recipes

Half the lower jaw of the pig
Bread crumbs to finish

Ask the butcher to cut off the jaw as for a Bath chap. I usually cook it in with the rest of the head, wrapped up tightly in a cloth so that it doesn't lose its shape. It must be salted in brine for 2 to 3 days first, however (see page 191).

Simmer gently for 4 hours. Unwrap it and carefully remove the bones. Mold the jaw into a nice Bath-chap shape, and leave it to cool with a weight on top. When it's quite cold, cover with toasted bread crumbs and cut the end of the snout off, as it upsets some people. Chill.

———•— *Variations* —•———

You can alter the flavor of the *court-bouillon* as suggested for the other recipes, but I don't think this makes as much difference to the chap as it does to *fromage* or *hure*.

Serve—chilled and sliced thinly, with the usual accompaniments: hard-boiled eggs, green salad, mashed potato, French mustard, perhaps pickled walnuts, capers, or gherkins.

PIG'S EARS
(Oreilles de Porc)

Pig's ears are one of the most appetizing delicacies in the *charcuterie,* lying swathed in jelly on their white tray. Expensive too, you will find. In England your butcher will very likely give them to you free. In the U.S., I am told, they can be purchased easily and cheaply in the South and can be found in supermarkets and pork butchers in many of the large cities. If you buy a whole head, to use in the various ways suggested, ask if you could have some extra pairs of ears as well; then you will have the makings of a separate dish for the whole family. Clean the ears well, and see that the hair is properly singed off; you need not soak them in the brine tub, but here again the flavor is greatly improved if they are pickled for 2 or 3 days.

NOTE: The whole of the pig's ear can be eaten. The cartilage has an agreeably contrasting bite which goes well with the blandness of the meat.

Oreilles de Porc Grillées Sainte-Ménéhould

Pig's ears, cleaned and pickled	Melted butter
Court-bouillon (wine unnecessary)	Bread crumbs to finish

Simmer the pig's ears very gently for 2 to 3 hours. Watch that the delicious gelatinous covering does not fall off the cartilage—take the ears out before this happens. Put them to cool under a weight.

About ½ hour before you are ready to eat, cut the ears in half lengthways, dip them in melted butter, then in white bread crumbs. Grill them gently until the coating is crisp or put them in a hot oven. It is this method of finishing that is known as Sainte-Ménéhould, the name of a small town in the Marne famous for its pork products. In earlier days the pigs wandered in the surrounding wooded plateau of the Argonne, eating themselves to a pitch of succulence in ideal conditions.

—— *Variations* ——

Serve them hot from the *court-bouillon*, accompanied by a vinaigrette sauce: 2 tablespoons wine vinegar, mustard, sugar, salt, pepper mixed well together—then beat in slowly 10 tablespoons of oil, and add chopped onions, parsley, garlic, shallots, capers, or gherkins to taste.

Cool the ears, cut in strips, dip in batter, and fry.

Cool the ears, cut in strips, dip in beaten egg, then bread crumbs, and fry.

Oreilles de Porc au Diable

When the cooked ears have cooled down, cut them in half lengthways. Brush them with French mustard, dip in melted butter and bread crumbs, then grill. You can equally well put them in a brisk oven, if this is more convenient, but don't let them go beyond the point of crispness. Charred ears are not attractive. Serve with *sauce diable* (page 49) or any other piquant sauce.

Oreilles de Porc aux Lentilles

This is a favorite French way of serving pig's ears. You can cook them separately, and serve with the lentil purée; or you can cook everything together.

Pig's ears
1 lb. lentils, soaked overnight and drained
2 medium carrots, diced
(about 1½ cups)
2 medium onions, chopped
(about 1½ cups)

1 large onion stuck with 4
cloves
Bouquet garni, salt, pepper
4 tablespoons (½ stick)
butter

Take a large pan that will hold everything comfortably. Sauté the chopped onion in the butter first, then add the rest of the ingredients and cover with water. Bring to the boil and simmer until everything is done. This takes a good hour.

To serve, cut the ears lengthways in two or three strips and lay on the drained vegetables.

Oreilles de Porc Braisées

A grander recipe for devotees.

1 lb. of diced vegetables:
onions, carrots, celery
¼ lb. diced bacon fat
4 pig's ears
½ cup white wine or Ma-
deira
2½ cups beef stock,
heated

1 large onion, chopped
(about 1 cup)
¼ lb. mushrooms, sliced
(about 1¼ cups)
¼ lb. mushrooms, chopped
(about 1 cup)
¼ lb. (1 stick) butter
6 tablespoons flour
Paprika

Butter a fireproof dish, lay in the vegetables and bacon fat.

Put the pig's ears, well cleaned, on top. Pour over the wine or Madeira, bring to the boil, and simmer for 2 minutes. Pour over the heated stock, bring to the boil, cover the dish, and transfer to a moderate oven for a good hour.

When the ears are nearly cooked, set about making the sauce

and, first of all, the garnish: fry the chopped onion in 4 table-spoons (½ stick) of the butter until it is pale gold, add the sliced mushrooms and cook them for 2 or 3 minutes. Keep warm.

For the sauce, melt the remaining 4 tablespoons of butter in a small pan, cook the ¼ lb. of chopped mushrooms in it until the juice runs. Sprinkle on the flour and cook gently for 2 minutes. Add bit by bit enough of the braising liquid to make a smooth sauce the consistency of thick cream. Season.

Arrange the ears, cut in half lengthways, and the sautéed onions and sliced mushrooms on an ovenproof serving dish. Pour over the sauce, sprinkle with paprika, and brown in a hot oven or under the grill.

———◆•◆———

BRAINS
(*Cervelles de Porc*)

In France, brains for sale lie on a white tray, ringed with parsley, and neatly finished with a high-price ticket. In England, they lurk messily on a sodden piece of greaseproof paper in a corner, and the price is much lower. In the United States, one is more apt to find them frozen, at least in regular butcher shops.

So do not be put off by their appearance. An hour in salted water and the membrane holding the blood vessels is quite easy to remove. Simmer them in salted milk or a light stock for 15 to 20 minutes, remove with a perforated spoon, and leave to cool on a meat dish with a strainer tray. Once prepared, you can do many things with them.

Here are five recipes from which you can develop further ones of your own:

Cervelles de Porc à la Sauce Béchamel

Simmer the brains in milk, and use it to make the sauce. Melt a good 2 tablespoons of butter in a pan, stir in 2 heaped table-spoons of flour. Add the simmering milk bit by bit until you have a smooth white sauce. Use extra milk if necessary. Season well and pour over the brains. Sprinkle with chopped parsley and surround with triangles of fried bread or toast. This is a very bland dish, excellent for children or invalids, or for a late supper.

Cervelles de Porc au Beurre Noir

Slice the cooled brains and sauté to golden-brown in some butter. Remove to a serving dish to keep warm, while you make the *beurre noir*. Melt 6 tablespoons (¾ stick) butter in a pan, cook to golden-brown (not black, as the name suggests), and pour over the brains. Quickly swill the pan round with 2 tablespoons of white wine vinegar and pour this in its turn over the brains. Garnish with chopped parsley and serve with baked bread (or toast, if you have a helping hand to make it while you are dealing with the *beurre noir*).

Cervelles de Porc en Matelote

If you want to make a good substantial main dish out of several sets of brains, this is a splendid way of doing it.

The secret of all good *matelotes*—whether of eel, fish, or brains—is to cook the sauce slowly for at least an hour before adding the main ingredient. Red-wine sauces improve with long, gentle cooking; you can quite well prepare them the previous day, and reheat when required for the final preparation of the dish.

Sauté an assortment of diced vegetables (½–¾ lb.) in 6 tablespoons (¾ stick) butter—choose leeks, carrots, onions, celery. Pour on 2½ cups of red wine (or half red wine, half stock) and simmer for at least an hour, covered. Remove the lid and boil hard until the liquid has reduced to about 1 cup. Strain into

a clean saucepan and thicken with *beurre manié*—2 heaped
tablespoons of flour kneaded into 2 level tablespoons of butter—
added in little knobs to the hot sauce gradually until it thickens
to the consistency of heavy cream. Stir all the time and keep just
below the boil.

Sauté some tiny pickling onions and button mushrooms in
butter. Arrange them on a serving dish with the sliced, prepared
brains. Strain the *matelote* sauce over them and leave in a low
oven for 10 minutes. Chopped parsley makes a good finish, and
toast a good accompaniment.

Bouchées à la Reine

The *reine* was Maria Leszczńska, gourmet queen of Louis XV,
and although her *bouchées* are correctly filled with morsels of
chicken in a cream sauce, brains as well as sweetbreads are often
used in French homes instead of, or as well as, the chicken. As
most of the preparations can be done well in advance, *bouchées
à la reine* make a good starting course for a dinner party.

Use 1 lb. puff pastry to make a number of small *vol-au-vent*
cases or one large one. Store them in an air-tight tin, if you are
making them well in advance of consumption.

3 pairs of pig's brains, prepared
¼ to ½ lb. mushrooms,
  sliced (1¼ to 2½ cups)
1 cup *béchamel* sauce
  (page 42)

½ cup heavy cream
Optional extra: small
  amount of cooked
  chicken or sweetbreads
Salt, pepper, lemon juice

Heat the *béchamel* sauce, add the mushrooms, and cook
slowly for at least 20 minutes, add the brains, and other meat, if
you are using cooked chicken and sweetbreads, diced, and the
cream. Keep the pan over a low flame until the brains are heated

262 · THE ART OF CHARCUTERIE

through, and set the *vol-au-vent* cases on an ovenproof serving dish in a hot oven. Season the mixture in the pan with salt, pepper, and a dash of lemon juice, fill the cases and serve very hot.

Brains and pastry are an excellent combination—try them baked in puff pastry like apple dumplings (*cervelles en chausson*), or as a filling with cream sauce for a short-pastry *barquettes* and *tartelettes,* which have been baked blind in advance—capers and small strips of lemon peel or anchovy on top give a sharp contrast.

Soufflé de Cervelles

In the case of pig's brains, you will need two pairs. Prepare them in the usual way and put them through a sieve when they are cooked. Make the quantity up to a good cup with some cream and some *velouté* sauce (page 61). Melt a good 2 tablespoons of butter in a pan, add 2 heaped tablespoons of flour, and cook for a few moments. Add ½ cup of milk and stir until the mixture is thick and comes away from the side of the pan. Mix in the cup of brain purée. Season well. Bring the mixture up to the boil, and remove from the heat. Beat 3 egg whites to a stiff foam. Then add the 3 yolks one at a time to the pan, beating them well in. Finally fold the beaten whites in gently and lightly. Pour the mixture into a soufflé dish, buttered, and collared with greaseproof paper to contain the rising soufflé. Cook in a moderate oven for 20 minutes, remove the greaseproof paper quickly (for this reason it is prudent to have tied the string with a bow rather than a knot), and bring it straight to the table.

If you wish to make this delicious soufflé into a more showy affair, add 3 oz. grated Parmesan cheese and a tiny can of truffles cut into thin strips just before you add the egg yolks, and bake the soufflé in tiny soufflé dishes or ramekins. They only take about 10 minutes in a medium to hot oven. The name of this soufflé (*soufflé de cervelles à la chanoinesse*) is a reminder of the very high standard of convent cooking in the past. Vows of holy poverty did not exclude truffles, it seems.

———•◆•———

THE TONGUE
(*Langue de Porc*)

Any recipe for beef tongue can be adapted for pig's tongues. Similarly salting, even for one day, is a great improvement to the flavor and quite practical. When you bring the tongues home, rub them over with a good handful of *gros sel* (bay salt, Tidman's sea salt, or Maldon salt) and a pinch of saltpeter and leave them to rest in a dish with the remaining salt. Before you go to bed, turn them over. Next day they are ready to be braised or poached. But first, here is a recipe which does not demand prior salting and which makes a delicious standby for feeding unexpected visitors.

Langue de Porc en Rillettes (*Potted Pig's Tongue*)

You need the tongue, the 2 cheeks, and the neck, plus 2 lbs. of all fat, or very fat, pork.

Scald the tongue, remove the skin and cartilage. Skin and bone the neck. Chop all the meat, but keep the fat separately.

Take a heavy iron pan, heat the chopped fat pork in it until the melted lard runs out. Pour it off into a basin, and add the lean pork. Cover, and cook for 4 hours.

Season well with salt, pepper, and *quatre-épices*. Pound in a mortar or whirl in the electric blender with some of the melted fat poured off in the beginning. The best texture is obtained by pounding the meat for a while, then transferring it to a sieve over a bowl and tearing it apart with two forks, until all is reduced to a mass of fine fibers.

Sterilize some small stoneware pots—in Touraine special

brown-glazed thick mugs are traditional—pile in the *rillettes,* leave them to cool, and cover with a ½-inch layer of melted lard. When this has set firm, cover with aluminum foil. *Rillettes* will keep in a cool place for several weeks without benefit of refrigerator or deep freeze.

See other kinds of *rillettes* (page 334).

Braised Tongue (Langue de Porc Braisée)

It sometimes seems to me that the most important thing about braising is the pan, and attention should be paid to this before you start cooking. The success of braising depends on the small amount of liquid used and the slowness of the cooking. It follows that the pan must be thick, the lid air-tight, to avoid burning. If you aren't too sure about the lid of your pan, make a flour-and-water paste to secure it. The French, who developed the art of braising to a pitch of excellence, have a special *braisière* or *daubière,* a rectangular or oval vessel with a deep, well-fitting lid—see the many "en daube" recipes to be found in French cookery books. When the philosopher Jean-Jacques Rousseau perfected his recipe for braised beef, *daube à la Montigny-en-Vexin,* he would have used an iron or earthenware pot buried in hot ashes, with a flat lid to hold hot charcoal. Nowadays the *braisière* is more conveniently produced in tinned copper or enameled cast iron (see page 19) as well as fireproof porcelain or glass. And unless you are feeling experimental on bonfire night, make use of a slow oven rather than red-hot ashes and charcoal.

If you have a suitable metal pan, all the cooking from first to last can be done in it. Otherwise you must prepare the *mirepoix* and sauce in a heavy frying pan, then transfer everything to the braising pot.

First remove your tongues from the salt, wash and plunge into boiling water for 5 minutes. This enables you to remove the skin and small bits of cartilage and bone.

Dice ½ lb. lean slices of bacon.

Chop, roughly, 1 onion, 2 leeks, 1 carrot.

Fry the bacon gently in 2 tablespoons of butter; when it turns transparent add the chopped vegetables, and more butter if it seems necessary.

When the onion has turned transparent in its turn, and golden, season with salt, pepper, a clove of crushed garlic, 1 sprig of thyme and 2 of parsley.

Continue frying until the vegetables and bacon are nicely browned. Stir in 4 level tablespoons of flour, cook until it takes on a pale-brown color. Then add gradually, stirring all the time, ½ cup of red wine and 1 cup of stock. Bring to the boil, add a bay leaf.

If you are not using a metal braising pan, this is the moment to transfer the *mirepoix* and liquid from the frying pan to whatever dish you intend to use.

Lay the pig's tongues (enough to weigh between 2 and 3 lbs.) on top of the vegetables, cover the pot closely, and put into a low oven for 2 to 3 hours to simmer gently.

When the tongues are cooked, remove them. Pour the sauce through a sieve into a clean pan, skin, taste, reduce by boiling hard. Keep tasting.

Meanwhile arrange the cooked tongues nicely on a serving dish, surround with mashed potatoes, put into the oven to keep warm. Flavor the reduced sauce with tomato purée, for instance, or Madeira or sherry—pour some over the tongues, put the rest into the sauceboat, and pass separately.

Langues de Porc Pochées

Wash the salt off the tongues. Plunge them for 5 minutes into fast-boiling water so that the skin and small pieces of cartilage can be removed.

Unsalted tongues should soak for 3 hours in cold water, before skinning and trimming as above.

Put the tongues into a pan, cover with light stock, and

bring slowly to the boil. Add a *bouquet garni*. They will need about 2 hours of gentle simmering.

A bland parsley sauce is the traditional accompaniment to this mild dish. For a contrast, try any sauce made with wine, mushrooms, tomato, or piquant ingredients. In some parts of France *choucroute* (page 162) is served with it.

Langue de Porc Garnie

The time taken to poach or braise tongues leaves the cook free to prepare an attractive garnish, which will be arranged round the tongues on a large serving dish at the last moment.

For a family lunch on a cold day, buttered *pasta* or buttered rice are ideal—plenty of butter, and an accompanying tomato sauce. More elegantly, for a dinner party, surround the tongues with braised chestnuts, fried mushrooms, tiny glazed onions and small sausages, and a final scattering of chopped parsley. Madeira- or sherry-flavored sauce.

Here are two excellent ways of using up—or stretching—cooked tongue. It doesn't matter whether the tongue has been braised or poached.

Langue de Porc, Sauce Diable

Cut cold cooked tongue into slices about ¼ inch thick. Spread them lightly on both sides with French mustard, dip in melted butter and bread crumbs. Lay them on the rack of the boiler pan, dribble melted butter over, and brown them on both sides under a gentle heat. Serve with *sauce diable* (page 49) on a bed of mashed potato.

Langue de Porc, Sauce Duxelle

Slice cold cooked tongue thinly. Cut an equal number of ham slices to the same shape and arrange on a flat oven dish in a circle, alternating with the slices of tongue. Butter the dish first. Cover with a *duxelle* sauce (page 49), to which some of the liquid from cooking the tongues can be added. Scatter an even layer of bread crumbs over the top, dot with tiny pieces of butter, and brown under the grill or in a hot oven.

Langue de Porc à l'Écarlate

In England we are normally accustomed to pickled ox tongue of a deep and wonderful red. Pig's tongues can be pickled in the same way. In France this is known as scarlet tongue—*langue* (*de boeuf,* or *de porc*) *à l'écarlate*—and the addition of sugar to the brine, as well as spices and herbs, results in a much more subtle, less angry flavor.

Soak the tongues in cold water whilst you make the brine.

Put 15 cups of water into a large pan. Stir in 1½ lbs. of *gros sel* (unrefined salt, or sea salt, see page 34), 1 lb. dark-brown sugar, and ¼ cup saltpeter. Season according to inclination with a bay leaf, whole peppercorns, and crushed juniper berries. Bring to the boil, gallop for 5 minutes, and set aside to cool—this takes several hours.

When the brine is nearly cold, remove the tongues from the cold water and plunge them into fast-boiling water for 5 minutes, so that they can be skinned and trimmed. Prick them all over with a larding or darning needle. Lay them in a plastic bucket or bowl (or a stoneware salting jar, if you have one) and strain the cold brine over. You will need to weight the tongues down with a scrubbed piece of wood, as they must be entirely submerged. Cover the whole thing over with a clean cloth to keep the dust out and leave for 5 days in a cool, dry place.

To cook the tongues, put them in a roomy pan and cover with cold water. Bring slowly to the boil and simmer for 2 hours. Taste the water after ½ hour's simmering; if it is unpleasantly salty, pour most of it away and add fresh hot water to cover. This should not be necessary, but if you have had to leave the tongues in brine for longer than 5 days, it is as well to know what to do.

When the tongues are cooked, leave to cool under a light weight. Serve with green salad and potatoes, mashed, boiled, or baked in their jackets.

Langues de Porc à la Mode de Troyes

Troyes is an old town on the Seine in northern Burgundy, worth visiting for its viciously flamboyant rood screen in the church of St. Mary Magdalene—and for its *charcuterie* (see *andouillettes de Troyes,* page 286). Tongues treated in the Troyes manner make a very pretty cold dish for a buffet supper.

Follow the preceding recipe for *langue de porc à l'écarlate,* but only pickle the tongues for 3 days.

When the tongues are quite cooled under a light weight, stuff them into lengths of intestine and tie at each end to make a sausage-*cum*-cracker shape. Plunge the encased tongues for a moment into a pan of fast-boiling water, which will make the intestine cling to the shape of the tongue. Cross-garter with thick string, brush either with caramel (not to be confused with sugar burnt black and tarry) or cochineal (be light-handed and discreet). Leave for 2 or 3 hours, then remove the string and you will find the *langue de porc* attractively patterned.

To make the caramel, boil 16 tablespoons of sugar and 6 of water in a pan, without stirring. Watch it. Remove from the heat when the color is deep golden-brown.

Langue de Porc Fumée

If you are interested in smoking meat (see page 207), you could make a start with pig's tongues. Like sausages, they are not very expensive, so if the first experiments are a disaster you will not be seriously out of pocket.

Soak, clean, and pickle the tongue as for *langue à l'écarlate* on page 267, but remove it from the brine after 48 hours. Stuff into a piece of intestine, tie at both ends, and hang in a fresh draught of air for 2 hours. Plunge into fast-boiling water for a moment, so that the intestine clings to the shape of the tongue. Smoke for 3 days.

Provided you hang the tongue in a cool, dry place, with a steady temperature of not more than 60°F., it will keep for several weeks. When the tongue is required for cooking, put it in a roomy pan and cover well with plenty of cold water. Add an onion stuck with 5 cloves, a carrot, a clove of garlic, 8 whole peppercorns, and a *bouquet garni*. Bring to the boil slowly and simmer gently for 2 to 3 hours. Test it with a metal skewer after 2 hours—if it goes in easily, the tongue is cooked. Eat it hot or cold.

PIG'S TROTTERS, OR FEET
(Pieds de Porc)

I once commented on the limited variety of prepared and cooked pork on sale in England to an executive in a large pork factory. He recalled that in the early days of this century the Managing Director always had pig's trotters to start his important dinner parties, but that nowadays the housewife was ashamed to be seen coming out of the butcher's shop with a packet of trotters and tail. The French housewife has to pay the equivalent of 9s ($1.08 U.S.) for half a pig's foot, cooked it is true, but still a high price. There is usually a tray of them in most *charcuteries,* bread-crumbed (*pieds panés*), waiting to be taken home and grilled for an hors d'oeuvre. As one is lucky enough to buy them so cheaply in England,* I usually serve them in various ways for a main luncheon dish, accompanied by mashed potato. They have often spent 48 hours in brine, but this is not essential, though it certainly improves their flavor.

BASIC METHOD

4 pig's trotters (feet)
2 carrots, sliced (about 1½ cups)
2 onions, stuck with 3 cloves each
2 leeks, sliced
2 stalks of celery, sliced (about ¾ cup)

Bouquet garni (parsley, thyme, bay)
Some good bits of pork skin (*couenne*)
½ cup white wine
¼ cup white wine vinegar

Singe, scrape, and salt the trotters.

If you intend to bread-crumb and grill the feet eventually, or if you intend to stuff them, you must tie the trotters one on each side of a small flat piece of wood about 2 inches wide and 8 inches long. Do this by bandaging them closely and firmly, so that they cannot lose their shape in the cooking.

(If you are going to serve feet straight from the cooking pot, with a vinaigrette or piquant sauce, you need not tie them up. But on the whole, I think it is worth the initial trouble. At least you are saved the final business of separating bits of trotter from bits of vegetable just before the meal, when there are better uses for your time.)

Bandaged or unbandaged, fit the feet into a roomy pot. Add the rest of the ingredients and cover with plenty of water. Bring to the boil, cover tightly, and simmer for 6 hours. This

---

* Pig's feet are equally inexpensive in the U.S., I am told.

is an ideal recipe for solid-fuel cookers—leave the pot overnight on the simmering plate at the side.

Now you can deal with the trotters in many ways.

Pieds de Porc Vinaigrette

Untie the trotters, remove the bones but preserve the foot
shape, and lay them on a bed of mashed potato. Serve with a
cold vinaigrette sauce (page 65), with additions to suit the
family tastes—chopped raw shallot, parsley, chives, capers,
chopped pickled gherkin or sweet-sour cucumber, chopped
pickled walnuts, chopped fresh tarragon.

Pig's Trotters (Feet) with Onion Sauce

Put 4 heaped tablespoons of chopped mild onion or shallot
into a small pan, together with ⅝ cup of wine vinegar, 8 crushed
juniper berries, and 6 crushed peppercorns. Put over a good
heat and cook until the vinegar has nearly evaporated. Add 1
cup of liquor from the trotters. Simmer gently for 15 minutes.
Fork 2 tablespoons of flour into 2 bare tablespoons of butter
(*beurre manié,* see page 44) until they are well amalgamated;
drop little bits into the simmering sauce, stirring gently until
it is slightly thickened. Do not strain this sauce.

Pieds de Porc Panés

These are the crumbed trotters, all ready for grilling, that you
can buy from the *charcuterie* in France. Like most recipes for

272 · THE ART OF CHARCUTERIE

pig's feet, you can do the preparatory boiling one day and the finishing the next.

Follow the BASIC METHOD given on page 270, and unwrap the trotters when they are cool enough to handle. Cut them in half, making sure that the bones fall evenly. When they are quite cold, brush with melted butter and roll in toasted bread crumbs (cornflake crumbs are heretical, but satisfactory—the point is that the crumbs must be crisp). You can now leave them until next day. All they will need is a gentle grilling to warm them through and crisp up the outside.

Serve a vinaigrette or piquant sauce, or *sauce Ste.-Ménéhould* (page 58).

Pieds de Porc à la Sainte-Ménéhould

The most famous of all the French ways of cooking pig's ears and pig's trotters (feet), the Sainte-Ménéhould method, gives a crisp texture to gelatinous meat, which has been boiled, by rolling it in bread crumbs, then grilling, baking, or frying—a method similar to that of the preceding recipe. But in Sainte-Ménéhould itself, in the Argonne where pigs once ran in the huge woods of the plateau (scene of much of the Verdun fighting in the First World War), pig's trotters with a difference can be bought for reheating. Spiced with *quatre-épices* and rolled, like *pieds panés*, in bread crumbs, they have been cooked for so long—48 hours— that they can be eaten bones and all. This gives three textures— crisp, gelatinous, and the hard-soft biscuit of the edible bones. An extremely delicious combination. They are served in local hotels quite dry, without sauces, and you eat them with French mustard.

One *charcutier's* wife told me that it is the addition of a certain vegetable that causes the bones to soften, as well as the prolonged slow cooking. Local skeptics tartly hint at "produits chimiques."

Pieds de Porc Farcis

4 pig's trotters (feet)
Ingredients for the *bouil-*
lon as in BASIC METHOD
(page 270)
½ lb. pork, ground
½ lb. veal (or chicken),
ground

1 onion, finely chopped
(about ¾ cup)
1 clove garlic, crushed
4 tablespoons parsley,
chopped
2 egg yolks
Salt and pepper

Follow the BASIC METHOD of preparing the trotters. While they are cooking, make the stuffing with the pork, veal, onion, garlic, parsley, and egg yolks. Season with salt and pepper.

After 5 hours' simmering, take the pot off the stove and let it cool down. Remove the feet when they are not too hot to · handle comfortably—do not let them get cold, as it will be difficult to remove the bones then. Slit them carefully lengthways, and take out the bones. This is a neat-fingered operation which demands time and patience.

Stuff the trotters with the *farce* you've prepared, sew them up, wrap them in cheesecloth, and simmer them for another hour in the *bouillon*. You can eat them hot; or cold, sliced like a *saucisson*.

Pieds de Porc Truffés (*or Farcis, if you can't afford truffles*)

Ingredients as in preceding recipe plus a tiny can of truffles and some pig's caul (*crépine*).

Follow the BASIC METHOD, until the feet are cooked (5 hours) and cool enough to handle. Make a stuffing as in the preceding recipe. Run the caul under the hot tap (this makes it easy and supple to handle), and cut it into 5-inch squares. On each square lay a piece or two of truffle or truffle peeling, then a layer of cooked trotter, a layer of stuffing, a layer of cooked trotter, a layer of stuffing. Wrap the caul round these layers to make a cutlet-shaped parcel. Fry gently in butter or lard until golden-brown, or grill. Don't ruin their delicate flavor with a sauce.

PIG'S TAILS
(Queues de Porc)

If you live in a pig-producing county, Wiltshire for instance, you often see a pile of pig's tails in the butcher's window.* Like the other extremities, they are cheap and delicious. In France, the *charcutier* uses them in his various brawns (headcheeses)— I have rarely seen them offered for sale as a separate item. But on French farms, when the pig is killed, its tail is well scalded and put into the brine tub for several days.

BASIC METHOD

(If you have brine ready prepared [page 191], immerse 4 pig's tails for 2 to 3 days.)

To cook, put the pig's tails into a large pot with 2 onions, each stuck with 4 cloves, 1 carrot, sliced, and 2 leeks, sliced, 8 whole peppercorns, a *bouquet garni,* and plenty of water to cover. Simmer for 1½ to 2 hours. They are done when the meat separates fairly easily from the bones—though there is always some pleasurable picking to be done at table, as the small vertebrae are complicated compared with trotter (foot) bones.

Cut the tails into lengths and serve on a bed of mashed potato, with a sprinkling of chopped parsley. The onion sauce given on page 59 goes well with this dish or else a sauce made from the reduced and thickened boiling liquid. (Keep any remaining liquid for soup.)

---

* This is a rare sight in most of the United States, though; however, many butchers do have (albeit out of sight or in some corner of a showcase) or are willing to get pig's tails.

Queues de Porc aux Lentilles

Soak 1 lb. lentils overnight. A good hour before the pig's tails are likely to be cooked, stew 2 large onions, chopped (about 2 cups), in 6 tablespoons (¾ stick) butter. When they are golden and soft, add the soaked, drained lentils and cover with water. Season and simmer for an hour. Serve the pig's tails on top of the lentils.

Queues de Porc Grillées

When the pig's tails are cooked, remove them from the pot, cut them up, and press under a light weight until they are cold. This can be done the day before they are required.

Half an hour before the meal, brush the pieces with melted butter and roll them firmly in toasted bread crumbs. Grill gently.

Serve with mashed potatoes and a piquant sauce or French mustard.

Queues de Porc Braisées

Dice an onion, a carrot, 2 stalks of celery, and ¼ lb. streaky bacon. Sweat them in 6 tablespoons (¾ stick) of butter in a heavy pan until they begin to brown. Add 2 tablespoons of flour and stir till it is cooked in with the fat—about 2 minutes. Gradually pour in ½ cup of red wine and 1 cup of stock, until you have a smooth sauce. Lay the pig's tails on top of the vegetables, cover the pan tightly, and simmer for 2 hours. Make a sauce by adding Madeira—or vermouth—to the strained liquid, and serve the tails cut into short lengths, surrounded by buttered rice.

An attractive arrangement of vegetables—say, glazed onions, mushrooms, peas, or stuffed tomatoes—round the braised tails turns them into a dish for a special occasion.

Gelée de Cochon

Last of all, a recipe using the extremities—ears, trotters, and tail, to make a clear soup or a jellied cold consommé.

A mixture of ears, tail, trotters (feet), and pork bones
¾ cup white wine
1 large onion, chopped (about 1 cup)
1 bay leaf

2 cloves of garlic, crushed
A good pinch of *quatre-épices* or a mixture of spices
The juice of 1 lemon
Meat extract

Scald, scrape, and singe ears, tail, and trotters.

Put all the ingredients into a large pan, except for the lemon juice and meat extract. Barely cover with water and *add no salt.* Bring to the boil.

When the pot is bubbling hard, skim off any gray, bitty-looking froth as it rises. This helps to keep the jelly clear. Reduce the heat, cover the pan, and simmer gently for 6 hours. This can be done either on top of the stove or in the oven.

Strain off the liquid, through muslin or a double thickness of cheesecloth, into a clean pan, and reduce it over a hard flame until you have about 2½ cups left. Season with salt, lemon juice, and a little meat extract to improve color and flavor, though the latter may not be necessary.

It can now be served hot (an excellent soup for people who are dieting), or left to cool into a jelly. To serve as cold consommé, break the jelly up with a fork and pile lightly into wide glasses. Chill.

In fact, this recipe gives you a sort of aspic jelly. Slightly un-orthodox, perhaps, but quite delicious enough to make an hors d'oeuvre or luncheon dish such as *oeufs en gelée.*

For this you will need as many ramekins, or small soufflé dishes, and as many eggs as you have visitors. Also a slice or two of ham, some flat-leaf parsley or stuffed olives—anything edible and decorative, to embellish the simple ingredients.

First of all, poach the eggs, trim them neatly so that they will fit into the ramekins, and keep them in cold water until they are wanted.

Melt the jelly till it just runs, and set a thin layer of it in the bottom of the ramekins. Lay the parsley or olives on top, then another thin layer of jelly to hold them in place. The egg goes in next, with more jelly to fill up the surrounding gaps. Last of all the ham, and some jelly to hold it in place. Put the ramekins in a cool place or in the refrigerator until they are set and ready to be turned out.

You can further improve the jelly by the addition of some sherry or port or Madeira, according to taste.

You will see from this that the *gelée de cochon* has many possible uses in the preparation of cold food—*chaudfroid* of chicken and game for instance (see page 48), or a cold ham mousse (see page 225).

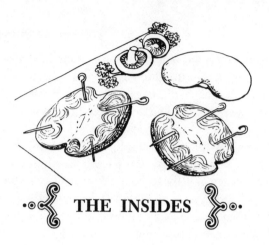

•⚬{ THE INSIDES }⚬•

*"Sowse us therefore, in the Powdering-
Tub of thy Mercy, that we may be Tripes fit for the
Heavenly Table."*

THE INTESTINES OR TRIPES

A favorite series for misericords and manuscript illumination in the Middle Ages was the Labors of the Months. In both France and England, October is often given to the grape harvest, and November to the acorn harvest or the annual pig-killing (*le sacrifice du porc*). The pigs had fattened on acorns, Christmas was coming, the weather was cool and dry. The men sharpened their knives, and excited children soon ran—as they had done since Neolithic times and as they did in country villages until quite recently—to the terrible dying squeal of the pigs. It wasn't horrified sympathy that drew them, but the thought of bladder balloons.

On many French farms still, to my own knowledge in the Vendômois, pig-killing day is a festival. Of course with modern feeding methods and the butcher's cold room in the village, there is not the great pressure of excitement, the heady feeling of survival and winter stores laid by. Neither is it a set annual occasion any more; another pig is killed whenever the last one is practically finished. Only a jar or two left of *rillettes* and *rillons*, a few smoked sausages in the coolest darkness of the cave cellar, no more succulent morsels of *confit du porc* to be speared by an exploratory fork as the lard is slowly melted in the great pots.

So one convenient morning early, either a part-time free-lance *charcutier* or one of the men from the nearest *charcuterie* arrives at the farm. The pig is killed, scalded, scraped free of its fine silky hair, drained of its blood, and finally hung up on a tough sort of coat hanger hooked onto a ladder against a shed, head down, back to the wall, still warm. The man makes a circular slit round the anus and cuts right down the center of the body to the snout, keeping the two sides apart with a wooden stick. Gradually the insides spill out—they mustn't be split or burst by mistake—and the bladder is emptied, washed inside and out, and blown up. If the children don't get it, it's put to one side until the fat is all melted down together and the farmer's wife is presented with her bladder of lard.

Next comes the disentangling of the caul (*crépinette, toilette*) or peritoneum, which encloses the guts in its fatty veil. This is treasured for *pieds farcis* and *crépinettes* (see pages 273 and 117). Then the mesentery (*fraise*), a frilly membrane which holds the intestines in position, has to be removed. This is used for lard making, or most deliciously eaten on its own (see page 289). The intestines and stomach are put into a large basket, whilst the pluck and windpipe are pulled away and laid on the trestle table with the bladder and extra bits of fat that have come away.

Charcuterie handbooks now instruct you to "take the basket of intestines to the nearest river or stream where they can be washed in plenty of water." Lucky the farmer's wife who has a bath, because this process is heavy and boring. You start with the stomach and large intestine (*gros boyau*, consisting of the rectum and colon), cleaning, scraping, outside and inside, removing the inner mucous lining. The small intestine (*le menu*) is trickier—it needs a small piece of wood to turn it inside out. Divide it into lengths first, it's much easier, then scrape and wash it until it's transparent. If you have taps, you can fit the lengths on like hose pipes to wash them thoroughly. Knot one end of each piece of small intestine, in preparation for sausage making, then leave everything covered with salt until you need it.

It is easy to see why more and more people in France prefer to patronize the *charcutier*. On the other hand, it is much cheaper to rear your own pig and have your own *charcuterie*. You also have the comfortable knowledge that the pig has been well fed. "Everything's raised on powder these days," the country house-wives grumble. "Chickens, pork, all collapse to mush when you cook them. Even the peasants use powder"—but not for the pigs they eat themselves. That's the story you hear. Perhaps it it true. But I am sure that those medieval pigs hanging headless on misericords, or strung up by their feet, were fairly tough by today's standards. Though this is probably a matter of improved breeding, rather than improved modern feeding stuffs.

TRIPE OR CHITTERLING SAUSAGES
(Andouilles, Andouillettes)

Andouilles are large, invariably salted and smoked, sold in slices by weight, like salami, and eaten cold. *Andouillettes* are smaller, the size of a large sausage or a little bigger, occasionally smoked or salted, and eaten hot after a gentle grilling.*

If the *charcutier* orders his *andouilles* from Vire in Normandy, the capital of the *andouille,* they will be hanging up among the other *saucissons secs.* They are easily distinguishable on account of their black skins and their mottled grayish-brown section, with the pieces of tripe looking like the fossilized coral in Frosterley marble, or else graded by size and drawn into

---

* *Andouille,* which sounds unusual, is in fact most appropriately derived from a Late Latin adjective, *inductibilis,* "that may be drawn over something." When you come to the method of filling the skins, you will understand how nice the derivation is. In Palsgrave's *Lesclaircissement de la langue françoise* (1530) he gives "Chyterlyng, Endoile" a good halfway name between *inductibilis* and *andouille.*

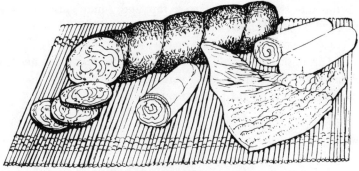

andouille, andouillettes, and tripe

each other, so that the slices look like regular growth rings across a tree stump. If the *charcutier* makes his own, they may well be a lot smaller, about the size of a man's clenched fist and about as knobbly. Their skins are probably a more succulent and wrinkled black, and when you go near to choose one your mouth waters with their sharp smell of a white-wine marinade.

Andouillettes are about the same size as *boudin blanc,* but craggier with the pieces of tripe. Some *charcutiers,* however, mold them into squared prisms cut off into exactly similar lengths, and pile them up quite architecturally into a pyramid. Or they may be wrapped up, each one, in a roll of greaseproof paper. It may be pure coincidence, but the nicest *andouillettes* we've ever eaten belonged to the more rugged, tied-at-each-end school, and we bought them in the Dordogne at Montignac, after an unusually solitary hour in Lascaux Cave. They were fried too quickly over a picnic stove from Woolworth's, but no other *andouillettes* have ever tasted so good.

Andouilles and *andouillettes* are quite easy to make at home; the most difficult part is acquiring the large intestine and belly of the pig. Chain (supermarket) butchers are no help in this, you need to find a butcher who chooses his own meat at the local slaughterhouse. Pig factories are sometimes obliging. If you have to clean the tripes yourself, the bath is the best place because, as well as having plenty of room, you can fix the ends of the intestines over the cold tap and run plenty of water through. When it comes to the manufacture, a relay of unsqueamish helpers with neat fingers is an advantage.

The basic mixture is the same for both *andouilles* and *andouillettes,* apart from local variations. It's the size that distinguishes them as far as the home cook is concerned.

BASIC METHOD

| Large intestine and belly of the pig (or part) | Fat bacon (⅓ of above weight) |

——◆ *Bouillon* ◆——

Half-and-half milk and water to cover	3 medium carrots
2 or 3 onions stuck with 4 cloves each	Salt, pepper
	A *bouquet garni*
	Spices

(If the intestines, etc., have not been cleaned, soak in cold water for 24 hours in a cool place. Overnight only in warm, humid weather. Then clean and scrape them. Simmer for an hour in water.)

Set aside enough intestine for the casings—thinner pieces for *andouillettes,* fatter for *andouilles*—and cut them into suitable lengths. Sprinkle with salt and store in the refrigerator or the coolest part of the larder.

Slice up, with scissors or a sharp knife, the rest of the intestine and the belly, into strips ⅛ to ½ inch wide and a little shorter than your lengths of casing. Put them in a bowl and sprinkle with plenty of salt, freshly ground black pepper, and a mixture of spices such as *quatre-épices* (page 32). Remember that *andouillettes* and *andouilles* need a strong spice contrast to the slightly rubbery smoothness of the tripe filling. Let the strips macerate in the seasonings for 24 hours, in a cool, dry place.

Next day, cut the fat bacon into pieces about the width and length of the tripe pieces. If you refrigerate the fat first, this job becomes quite easy. Divide the tripe and bacon strips into bundles and tie each one, at one end, with a length of "heavy-duty" white thread.

Wash the salt off the casings, and draw the bundles in, by means of the "heavy-duty" thread (this is where the neat-figured are at a premium). Cut away the thread and tie the *andouilles* or *andouillettes* at each end.

(If this process appalls you, you can, more simply, chop the tripe and bacon fat rather than slice it into regular lengths. If you have a sausage-making attachment to an electric mixer, you can treat the mixture like sausage meat and fill the skins that way—but use the very large-holed plate as the final result should not be too smooth or solid in texture.)

If the knobbliness of your *andouilles* and *andouillettes* seems excessively exaggerated, roll them backward and forward with the palm of your hand on a smooth surface (formica or marble slab).

—•— Cooking Andouillettes —•—

Prick them with a darning needle and arrange evenly in a large saucepan. Cover with milk and water in equal quantities, add the other *bouillon* ingredients, and bring to the boil. Simmer gently for 3 hours. Leave them to cool down in the liquid until tepid, then lay them side by side closely in a shallow dish and put a lightly weighted board on top. This gives a handsome squared-off appearance, which is not strictly necessary but gratifying. In France they are often glazed with a mixture of lard and veal fat in equal quantities, or—when the weather gets warmer—with one fifth mutton fat and four fifths veal fat.

Now they can be fried, or else slashed across in three or four places and grilled. Serve them on their own, as a starting course, with French mustard; or with mashed potato as a main luncheon dish. Well-spiced *andouillettes* are a great treat and worth the trouble of making.

——•—*Cooking Andouilles* —•——

The *andouillettes* cooking program can be followed entirely
—or when the *andouilles* have quite cooled under a light weight,
they can be sliced and served as part of an hors d'oeuvre.
It is better to salt or salt and smoke them first. Four days in
brine (page 191) is a great improver, 2 days in brine and 3 days
smoking is better still. Smoking produces a wrinkly, brownish-
black exterior, which is most appetizing.

Substitute white wine for milk in the *bouillon* step.

Although, as I have said above, *andouilles* can be eaten hot
like *andouillettes,* they are at their best salted, smoked, and
smelling of white wine, and served cold in thin slices.

Although *andouilles* are served like *saucissons secs,* they are
not when domestically produced a keeping sausage. When salted
and smoked they keep good longer than *andouillettes,* which
should be eaten within 2 days of manufacture, but it is wise to
eat them within the week.

Andouilles de Campagne

Follow the BASIC METHOD. Salt for 4 days in brine (page 191)
before hanging up in a cool, airy place to dry out thoroughly.
Poach for 3 hours in the milk-and-water *bouillon,* cool, and
grill.

Andouillettes Fines de Porc

A delectable recipe from *Larousse Gastronomique.*

Mudgeon, mesentery
  (*fraise*), cut in squares
Half its weight in lean
  bacon, cut in squares

Enough meat stock to
  cover
An onion stuck with cloves

Enough intestines to con-
tain the meat, soaking in
cold water

Thyme, parsley, and bay
leaf
Salt and pepper

Put everything, except the intestine skins, into a large pan and bring it slowly to the boil. Keep well covered and simmer gently for 1½ to 2 hours.

Pour off the liquid, chop the meat coarsely, and mix in ¼ lb. mushrooms that have been lightly fried in butter with chopped onions and parsley. Do not let the onion brown. Add ¼ cup of well-flavored meat stock and 6 raw egg yolks.

As with all sausage-making when chopped or ground meats are used, your task is virtually impossible without an electric mixer with a sausage-making attachment. If you don't have such a thing, it will be a good deal quicker to take your mixture in to the butcher's shop and ask them to put it into skins than to laboriously push it down yourself.

Assuming that you have filled the skins one way or another, you should tie them every 5 inches, prick each *andouillette* several times with a needle, and poach in a milk-and-water *bouillon* as described in the BASIC METHOD. Drain, press, glaze, and grill as described.

Andouillettes de Nancy (*Lorraine*)

Nancy, like Troyes, Tours, and Strasbourg, is famous for its *andouillettes*. There are several variants, but this is the most exotic of the recipes.

2 lbs. calf's mesentery
  (*fraise*)
2 lbs. all-fat pork (*panne*)
As many truffles as you can
  afford, up to 6 oz.

A good ½ cup Madeira
Salt, freshly ground black
  pepper, spices according
  to taste

Soak the mesentery well in plenty of cold water for at least 2 hours. Then blanch it in boiling, salted water for another 2 hours. Whilst it is draining and cooling down, chop the fat pork (excluding the rind, *couenne*) into fairly small pieces. Do not grind. Mix it in a large bowl with the wine and truffles and seasonings. Then chop the mesentery into small strips—much smaller than the BASIC METHOD, more like shreds. Add this to the bowl, and stir everything together well. Cover and leave in a cool place for 24 hours.

Wash the intestine skins well, and fill them with the mixture. Tie every 5 inches, finish as in the BASIC METHOD. You can salt these (3 days in brine), but they are much nicer eaten fresh. Don't smoke them, as this would be too much for the delicate flavor of truffles and Madeira.

Andouillettes de Troyes (Aube District of Champagne)

2 lbs. calf's udder—young heifer, not old cow (*tétine*)	1 heaped tablespoon chopped parsley
2 lbs. calf's mudgeon, mesentery (*fraise*)	6 tablespoons (¾ stick) butter
½ lb. mushrooms, sliced	½ cup white wine
About ½ cup chopped scallions or shallots	4 egg yolks
	Salt, freshly ground black pepper, ground nutmeg

Soak both udder and mudgeon well in plenty of cold water for 2 hours. Blanch them in boiling, salted water for an hour. Cut them into small strips. Sauté mushrooms, scallions or shallots, and parsley in the butter until the onions are golden *but not browned*. Add pepper, nutmeg, and wine. Bubble for a moment, salt well, and put into a big bowl. Add the meat and bind with the egg yolks. Fill the skins, simmer in half white wine and half water *bouillon* for 45 minutes—in other words, follow the BASIC METHOD, apart from the cooking time.

Omelette à l'Andouillette

Andouillettes are expensive in the *charcuterie*—this is an excellent way of stretching them with the more economical addition of eggs. Or if you have an *andouillette* or two left from a previous meal, this is the best way to use them up. The amount of *andouillette* can be less, but here are the usual quantities of ingredients for four people:

2 *andouillettes*, cooked or uncooked	8 eggs
Butter for greasing the pan	Salt, pepper, chopped parsley

If the *andouillettes* are uncooked, fry them in lard or butter first. Skin the *andouillettes* and crumble the inside. Grease the omelette pan—a large one—and put the pieces of *andouillettes* in to heat through thoroughly. Beat the eggs, season with salt, a very little pepper because the *andouillettes* will be spicy, and parsley, pour over the pieces in the omelette pan, and finish as for an ordinary omelette. Keep the inside a little runny. Serve on a hot dish, with hot plates, red wine, bread, and butter.

Andouilles de Vire

The old granite town of Vire, in the Normandy Department of Calvados, has been rebuilt with rather cheerless efficiency after its wartime desolation. Almost every other shop sign in this crossroads town proclaims the famous *andouilles;* but they are good all the same, and here is one of the many recipes.

2 lbs. large intestine, stomach, and mesentery, *or* 2 lbs. calf's mesentery	Salt, freshly ground black pepper
A good ½ cup white wine	1 small red pepper (*piment doux*)
2 teaspoons mustard powder	Length of large intestine for the *andouille* skin

Clean the meat, leave it to soak in cold water for 24 hours. Then wash in hot water, drain, and dry thoroughly. Cut the meat into strips the length of the *andouilles* and about ½ inch wide—the strips from the mesentery will be shorter, as they should be cut straight across the frill rather than lengthways.

Mix the white wine, mustard, salt and pepper, and the red pepper, freed of its seeds and stalk and crushed to a pulp. This can all be done in the jar of an electric blender.

Marinade the strips in the white-wine–and–pepper liquid for 2 days, covered. Then insert them into the skin(s) and tie both ends. Now you should smoke them for 3 days (see page 202), then simmer them for 3 hours in a white-wine–and–water *bouillon* (equal parts of each). Some recipes suggest leaving the *andouilles* in brine for 2 days before the smoking—see brine recipe, page 191.

Alternatively you can omit the salting and smoking processes and proceed with the cooking. They won't be exactly *andouilles de Vire,* but they will be good.

CHITTERLINGS

Here is the English way of dealing with the large intestine of the pig. The unforgettable name is of unknown derivation, but appears in the thirteenth century in dog-Latin form in a description of women washing "chitterlingis" down by the waterside. Which brings us right up to modern French handbooks, "take the stomach and intestines to the nearest stream or river."

In the West Country you often see these opaque white plaited objects in the windows of pork butcher shops. They have been all prepared and are ready to be grilled. If you can get some suitable intestine for skins, you can make *andouillettes de Nancy* and *de Troyes* with these chitterlings. Naturally you omit the first cooking, the preparatory blanching in boiling water.

But supposing you are starting from scratch, this is what

you do. Use the stomach and large intestine, which should be freed of its fat. Separate them, and clean the intestine thoroughly by turning it inside out with the aid of a piece of wood. There you will find a mucous skin which must be got rid of—the same thing applies to the stomach. Wash thoroughly in cold water, leave to soak in freshly drawn salted water until you need them. Simmer in a milk-and-water *bouillon,* half and half, seasoned with salt, pepper, spices, an onion stuck with cloves, carrots, spices, and a *bouquet garni,* for about 2 hours, or until they are cooked. Let them cool in the liquid; then drain and dry before grilling. It is usual, in Wiltshire at any rate, to plait the intestines after their soak in cold, salted water. They certainly look more attractive.

Serve with mashed potatoes and an oil–and–lemon-juice vinaigrette sauce.

MESENTERY, FRILL, OR CROW
(*Fraise*)

The mesentery is a fatty membrane, "a pellycle or a skyn the whiche doth tye the guttes together." It's a beautiful frilly object like a creamy ruff, but you won't see it offered for sale, as a general rule, in England, the United States, or France. *Charcutiers* incorporate it into their *andouilles* and *andouillettes* (pages 280–8), English pig factories use it exclusively in the making of lard (page 327).

We did once buy some in a seaside *charcuterie* at Préfailles near Pornic, south of Nantes. These attractive, crisply browned morsels, like paper frills, were sold under the name of *grillons.* They didn't at all resemble the *grillons* or *grattons,* which remain when all the fatty parts of the pig have been melted down for lard (*saindoux*)—these are usually a soft hash, like poor-quality *rillettes* (page 334).

BASIC METHOD

Soak the mesentery in cold water, salted, for 2 hours, after it has been cleaned under a cold running tap. If you ask your butcher to order you some from the slaughterhouse, specify a certain quantity (bearing in mind that it shrinks in cooking, but that it is also very rich and to be eaten in small quantities) or you will end up, as I did the first time, with a plastic bucketful.

Drain, dry, and cut into 6-inch lengths.

——— *Either* ———

Put 2 tablespoons of lard into a heavy frying pan, set on the stove, and when it is smoking put the bits of mesentery in to fry until they are crisp and browned at the edges. Eat hot or cold; with mashed potatoes if hot, and a lemon-juice–and–oil vinaigrette.

——— *Or* ———

Poach for 2 hours in a milk-and-water *bouillon,* with the usual seasonings. Alternatively, in a white *bouillon,* which is 5 cups of water very slightly thickened with flour, and seasoned in the usual way plus a dash of wine vinegar.

When it is cooked, serve with mashed potatoes, and a lemon-juice–and–oil vinaigrette, sharped with chopped gherkins, capers, and chopped raw onion.

Or else, cut the pieces in half, drain them well, and fry them in foaming butter as they are, *or* dipped in batter, *or* egg–and–bread-crumbed.

———•—•—•———

TRIPE RECIPES

In France, large towns will have their own *triperies,* where cooked tripe as well as offal is sold. It is, of course, calf's tripe, but in small towns and villages the *charcutier* sells it regularly in jellied hunks, starred with brilliant rounds of carrot. It is an excellent thing to warm through for a cold day's picnic, particularly if you can improve it with tomatoes stewed in a little wine or Normandy cider with a spoonful or two of Calvados as well. There is no denying that tripe is best cooked in large quantities for a long, slow time, which is why most French house-wives like to buy it ready prepared. Ideally, too, it should go to the oven in the beautiful honey-golden *tripières* that can sometimes be bought in large kitchenware shops in France. They are bulbous round pots, with two small handles or lugs and a small round opening in the top, with a well-fitting lid which should be fastened securely onto the pot with a flour-and-water paste so that none of the juice evaporates.

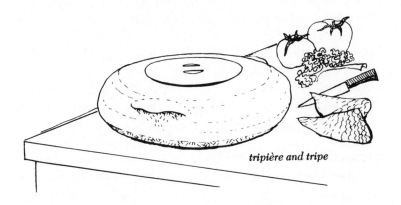

tripière and tripe

As a hard-up student in Florence, I alternated my daily diet of eggs cooked in oil in the oven with *trippa alla fiorentina*—a delicious confection of tripe, tomatoes, and Parmesan cheese. But I must confess that for a deep midday sense of internal peace, there is nothing to beat *tripes à la mode de Caen*, eaten in a small restaurant in Caen, with good Normandy cider to bear it company and a glass of Calvados, a *trou Normand*, to follow. Tripes fit, indeed, for the Heavenly Table.

Many English people have been put off tripe by the insipid flavor of tripe and onions in the Lancashire style. Tripe needs to be raised from its visceral connections with a more seasoned form of preparation, and I make no excuse for including the Italian, or rather Florentine, manner of preparing tripe. If you have to convert a reluctant family, start with *trippa alla fiorentina;* if you have a number of friends who like tripe, cook *tripes à la mode de Caen* in vast quantity and invite them all. *Tripe à la lyonnaise,* a slightly unorthodox version, is for the true *amateur.* First the classic:

Tripes à la Mode de Caen

NOTE: Ask your butcher to try and get you calf's tripe. I doubt you'll be successful, but it's worth asking. The one usually on sale is ox tripe. Include 1 lb. of mesentery, if possible.

3 lbs. tripe, cut in squares, if it's already blanched

2 calf's feet, 1 cow heel, *or* 4 pig's trotters, chopped into pieces by the butcher

4 leeks, halved lengthways

3 carrots, quartered lengthways

5 large onions, stuck with 2 cloves each

2 cloves garlic

2 stalks celery

Bouquet garni: bay leaf, thyme, parsley, all tied together

Salt, freshly ground black pepper, cayenne (or a dash of Tabasco)

Enough dry cider (not a sweet, cheap, commercially ruined cider) or dry white wine to cover

A scant ½ cup of Calvados preferably, otherwise brandy

¼ lb. pig's skin (*couenne*)

Tripe has usually been cleaned, washed, and blanched, whether you buy it in France or England or the U.S. But if it hasn't been prepared, you must scrape it under a cold running tap and blanch it for ½ hour in boiling water. Drain and dry it thoroughly.

Do not omit the feet, calf's, pig's, or cow heel. They are absolutely essential for a gelatinous smoothness. The butcher will split and divide them into pieces.

Find a large, thick pot with a good lid. Lay the pig's skin, cut in strips, on the bottom; next a mixed layer of tripe, feet, and vegetables, put the *bouquet garni* in the center and some salt pork if you have it to hand (unessential but pleasant), then the rest of the meat and vegetables. Season with salt, freshly ground black pepper, cayenne (or a dash of Tabasco sauce).

Pour in dry cider or wine to the height of the ingredients, and the Calvados or brandy. Do not be tempted to use the sweet, gaseous liquid sometimes sold as cider—as a green cook I once did so, and the results were too horrible to describe. If you cannot afford the alcohol, switch quickly to the Italian style of cooking tripe, described on page 294.

Make a slightly tacky flour-and-water dough. Put a ring of it round the edge of the pot, slap the lid on, and bend the dough up over it. If you aren't used to doing this, allow yourself plenty of time and plenty of dough.

Put the pot into a slow oven (310°–320°F.), and go out for the day or go to bed. Anyway leave it alone for 10 hours— a grueling test of will power.

Next day, assuming you have left it to cook all night, remove the lid with the aid of a knife. Take out the vegetables and bones and *bouquet garni,* and pour off the sauce into a clean pan. You will have to skim off the fat first of all, then taste it. If the flavor leaves something to be desired, boil the sauce down hard and reach for the pepper mill. Some cooks add a knob of *beurre manié* (2 tablespoons of flour kneaded into 2 tablespoons of butter), which slightly thickens the sauce, but the feet and skin should give enough thick smoothness without the addition of flour.

Bring the sauce to the boil again when you have poured it back onto the tripe, let it bubble gently for 10 minutes. Serve very hot with a good sprinkling of parsley, and have well-heated soup plates. You will also need plenty of crusty bread, cut very thick, to mop up the sauce; cider or white wine to drink; and if possible a glass of Calvados or brandy afterwards. This is a great aid to digestion, and should certainly not be overlooked if you intend to eat anything else afterwards.

Tripes à la Lyonnaise

A more lively version of tripe and onions.

Equal weight of tripe and
  onions
Water to cover the tripe
An extra onion stuck with
  4 cloves
Carrots
Celery

Leeks
Bouquet garni
Pepper and salt
1 egg, beaten
Bread crumbs
Butter

Buy your tripe ready blanched; if not, you will have to scald it, scrape it, and soak it for 3 hours in cold water with a dash of vinegar. Then blanch it for a good ½ hour in boiling, salted water.

Cook it for 2 hours in the water flavored with vegetables, seasoning, and herbs. Peel and slice the onions (except the onion stuck with cloves, which is used in the *bouillon*), and sauté them gently in the butter until they are cooked and golden. Keep them warm. Do not cook the onions until the tripe is ready and drained. Cut the tripe into squares, dip them in the beaten egg, then in the bread crumbs, and fry in butter until they are crisp. This can be done in the butter left from frying the onions. Put the tripe pieces on top of the onions, swill the buttery pan round with some wine vinegar and pour it over the tripe. Sprinkle the top with chopped parsley and serve the dish very hot, with very hot plates.

Tripes à l'Italienne (*Trippa alla Fiorentina*)

2 lbs. tripe
Ingredients for the *bouillon* as in preceding reci-

pe, with the addition of
some white wine

_____ *Well-flavored Tomato Sauce* _____

1 onion, chopped (about
¾ cup)
1 carrot, chopped (about
¾ cup)
Olive oil
1 or 2 cloves garlic,
crushed

1½ lbs. tomatoes
1 tablespoon flour
Some red wine and season-
ings
A pinch of bicarbonate of
soda (baking soda)
Bouquet garni

Cook the tripe as in *tripes à la lyonnaise*, but for 1 hour only. Let it cool down completely and dry.

Start the tomato sauce as soon as you have set the tripe on to simmer in the *bouillon*. Fry the onion and carrot in a little olive oil, with the garlic. Peel the tomatoes. Alternatively, use a 1-lb.-1-oz. can of Italian tomatoes. Sprinkle the flour onto the onion when it is golden, and add ½ cup of red wine and the tomatoes. You can season it with freshly ground black pepper, a spoonful of sugar according to taste, and some allspice. Don't add any salt at this stage, because the sauce should reduce to a delicious thick state and you don't want it to get too salty in this process. Let the sauce bubble gently on a corner of the stove or in the oven with the tripe.

Whilst the tripe is cooling down, keep the sauce bubbling. Add more red wine if it is too thick, and finally a pinch of bicarbonate of soda, some salt and seasoning. If after the addition of extra sugar and pepper, the sauce still seems slightly insipid add some Italian tomato paste; even bottled tomato ketchup (if you have nothing else on hand) will give it a lift.

Add some fresh basil if you are lucky enough to have some, dried if you haven't; wild marjoram, the Italian oregano, can be found in England and the U.S. quite easily, and that, or the sweet marjoram of the herb gardens, can also be used. Then put in the pieces of tripe, and simmer for an hour.

Serve in well-heated earthenware pots or bowls, with grated Parmesan cheese to sprinkle on top. Good, thick hunks of crusty bread and red wine are most satisfactory accompaniments.

Tripes Frites

Prepare and cook the tripe in a *bouillon*, as in the recipe for *tripes à la lyonnaise*.

Whilst it is cooking, make a light frying batter, in which you add the beaten white of an egg at the end.

Decide on which spicy, piquant sauce you intend to serve with the tripe and make it. The tomato sauce (page 60) is a good one; a piquant sauce such as *sauce diable* (page 49), or a *sauce Robert* (page 57), do very well too. If you are pressed for time, broil some halves of tomato, sprinkled with chopped garlic and salt and melted butter, and serve them round the tripe fritters with lemon quarters and a dressing of chopped parsley.

When the tripe is cooked, drain it well and dry it. Cut it into squares, and dip them in the batter, to which you have just previously added the beaten white of egg. Fry in deep smoking oil.

Tripe à l'Espagnole

3 lbs. tripe
3½ cups each of water and dry white wine
2 large onions stuck with cloves

3 medium carrots, quartered
2 stalks celery
Salt, pepper, spices

———— For the Sauce ————

Olive oil
1–2 cups of tomato sauce as described on page 60, but made with dry white wine, not red wine

¼ teaspoon ground mace
An extra clove of garlic
¼ lb. black olives
Lemon juice
Parsley

Prepare and cook the tripe in the *bouillon* ingredients, along the lines for *tripes à la lyonnaise*, for at least 2 hours.

Drain and dry it well, cut it into small squares. Heat the olive oil in a large heavy frying pan and put in the pieces of tripe. Fry them for 10 minutes, then add the tomato sauce, the mace, and some parsley, rather than the basil or marjoram mentioned for *tripes à la lyonnaise*. Correct the seasoning, transfer everything to an oven dish that can be sent to table, and simmer in a low oven for ½ hour. Ten minutes before the end add the black olives and lemon juice to taste. Serve sprinkled with more parsley, and plenty of bread in crusty slices.

NOTE: The prolonged cooking of the tripe, as in the recipes on pages 292–5, can be quite well done in advance of the final preparation of the dishes.

Tripe can, of course, be cooked in a *blanquette* or other bland, creamy sauce; the flavor is delicate, but the only word to describe the texture of tripe under these circumstances is slithy.

————◆————

THE ORGANS OR OFFAL OR VARIETY MEATS
(*Abats*)

Organs, offal in other words, or variety meats if you live in the United States, can be a point of prejudice. Before the war I remember hearing "*Ai* never eat Offal" spoken with emphasis and pride, a brave flicker of light in a crude waste of offal-gobblers, yet another pea felt through twenty mattresses. War shortages taught better sense. Nutritive values were proclaimed and prejudices fell, at least as far as kidneys, liver, and hearts went. Lungs and spleen make no grand public appearance in our country or in America, any more than they do in France. Unknowingly we buy them in faggots, sausages, and pâtés. Knowingly we may buy them to feed our cats and dogs.

But I suggest that next time you buy some pig's pluck, you prepare it for the family in the various French ways I've listed at the end of this section. But first—

THE KIDNEYS

Along with all the other parts of the pig, you can buy kidneys at the *charcuterie*. They are usually sold raw—and very fresh, which is how they should be. If you can, order them in advance, with some surrounding leaf lard. To my mind, the most delicious way to cook kidneys is to pop them into a moderately hot oven, encased in leaf lard, and roast them for an hour. This applies to lambs' and calves' kidneys as well. And you will have a basin of beautiful fat, superb for pastry-making. The next most simple way is to grill them.

Rognons Brochette Grillés

Skin the kidneys; then slit them in two so that they are not completely separated into two halves but can be laid out flat. Remove the small hard white part. If you have some very fine skewers, you could skewer them crosswise in the French style, otherwise use two skewers for each kidney side by side across the two halves.

Brush the cut side with melted butter, and season with salt, freshly ground black pepper, and perhaps some ground sage— be discreet about this. Set the kidneys, cut-side up, of course, under the grill for several minutes at a moderate heat. Then turn them over, brush with melted butter, and grill the outside.

The usual garnish is butter, Pounded with chopped parsley and some lemon juice. In other words, *à la maître d'hôtel*.

— Variations —

1 · When you have brushed the kidneys with melted butter, sprinkle them with bread crumbs.
2 · Serve with *beurre Colbert*, butter, pounded with tarragon, salt, and pepper.
3 · *Beurre de ciboulette*, butter, pounded with chopped chives, salt, and pepper.

4 · *Beurre de moutarde,* butter, blended with mustard (French).
5 · *Beurre d'échalote,* shallots, chopped, then blanched for 3 minutes in boiling water and pounded to a mash. Add butter.

———• Serve with •———

1 · A nice arrangement of bacon, boiled or mashed potatoes, and watercress (*à l'anglaise*), with the addition of one of the butters suggested above, served in little pats, one on each half of each kidney.
2 · On a bed of *risotto.*
3 · Encircled by crisp fried potatoes, whether as straws, or crisps, or fluted crisps. Pats of butter, and a sprinkling of chopped parsley or tarragon or sage, as appropriate.

Here is another simple but delicious way of cooking kidneys:

Kidney Kebabs (*Rognons en Brochette*)

Skin the kidneys, cut them into suitable-sized pieces of a uniform thickness. Alternate them on the skewers with squares of streaky bacon and small mushroom caps. Brush with melted butter, roll them in bread crumbs, and grill. Turn them every few minutes, so that they are cooked all round.

Serve them on a bed of mashed potatoes, laid side by side, with the juices from the grill pan poured over them. Sprinkle them with chopped chives, or parsley, or sage.

This recipe can be varied in all kinds of ways. The main thing is to alternate lean, dry ingredients with fat or juicy ones. I learned this at open-air lunch parties, organized, *en brochette,* by an Anglo-French friend years before the barbecue became fashionable. The day before, he would go down to the butcher's shop and return with a load of kidneys, liver, sowbelly, heart, and smoked bacon, conveniently cut up into rough cubes. Then

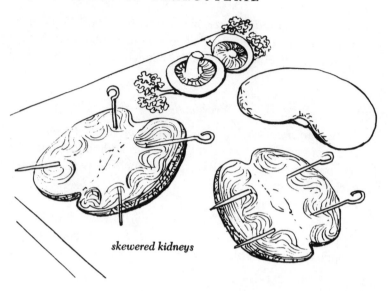

skewered kidneys

he prepared a fearsome marinade in his cave-house kitchen—
oil, red wine, herbs, garlic, spices, and raw onion—and soaked
the meat in it overnight. Next day he left his women guests, soon
oil to the elbow, to string the meat onto long thin, almost bodkin-
thin, fencing foils, which he'd picked up in a Paris flea market.
Tomato chunk, lean meat, onion, fat meat, lean meat, mushroom
cap, bacon, tomato chunk . . . while he built his brick fireplace
and got the charcoal to the right temperature. Food never tasted
so delicious—or was judgment seduced by the strong full wine
of Mesland, the cave-encircled courtyard, and the golden, har-
monious view of Touraine?

Rognons de Porc Sautés

Skin the kidneys, remove the hard white core, and slice thinly.
Melt some butter to a froth in a heavy frying pan, add the kidney
slices, and sprinkle with salt and freshly ground black pepper.
Cook quickly on both sides. Serve with lemon quarters.

Rognons de Porc Sautés en Pilaff

Soften a medium onion, chopped (about ¾ cup), in 6 tablespoons (¾ stick) of butter until it is golden. Add ½ lb. of rice and stir it in the melted butter until it is transparent. Pour in 2½ cups of hot water and boil until the rice is cooked. Meanwhile blanch and fry 2 oz. of almonds. Cook 4 pig's kidneys as in the preceding recipe. Drain the rice, arrange on a serving dish in a ring, put the kidneys in the center, and garnish with the fried almonds. Make a little sauce by swilling ½ cup of good stock round the kidney pan and quickly reducing it; then pour over the kidneys and serve.

Rognons Sautés aux Champignons

You need ¼ lb. mushrooms (sliced) to each kidney for this recipe. And for 4 kidneys, ¾ cup fortified wine (sherry, Marsala, Madeira, sweet vermouth), ¾ cup good meat stock, and about ½ cup sour cream. Cook the sliced mushrooms and sliced kidneys in two separate pans, in butter as for the preceding *rognons sautés*. Put onto the serving dish and keep hot while you make the sauce. Raise the heat under the kidney pan and pour in the wine and stock. Bubble fiercely until you have a rich, well-flavored liquid. Stir in the sour cream, taste, correct seasoning, and pour over the kidneys and mushrooms. Serve with triangles of toast or baked bread slices.

Rognons de Porc Sautés (*a second method*)

This is a good way to cook kidneys, if they have a "gout très prononcé d'urine si désagréable," as one book firmly puts it.

Skin the kidneys, remove the hard white center bit, and slit in two. Put some lard into a heavy frying pan and sauté the pieces of kidney on each side; a minute a side is enough. Remove the kidneys, drain them well. Throw away the fat and juice from the pan, wash it out and put it back on the stove with some butter in it. When the butter foams, put the kidneys in and fry till they are done.

If at the same time you fry some *croûtons* of bread in butter, cut to the same size as the pieces of kidney, and serve the kidneys on top, sprinkled with salt, pepper, parsley, and *chopped* garlic (not crushed) which has been simmered for a moment or two in the pan juices, you will have *rognons sautés à l'ail*. A deliciously hearty dish.

Rognons au Vin Blanc

Another homely and excellent recipe from the same source (*La Charcuterie à la Campagne*, by Henriette Babet-Charton). Prepare the kidneys as in the previous recipe, then instead of frying them in lard, put them into a pan of boiling water for 3 minutes, removed from the heat immediately the kidneys go in. Drain and dry them. Melt some butter in a frying pan, add the kidneys when it is frothing. As soon as they begin to turn golden, sprinkle them with a little flour and continue to cook until they are a yellowish-brown. Add enough white wine to make a little sauce, salt and pepper. Let it bubble away for a few minutes, and turn it all into a serving dish; keep warm in a low oven whilst you make some triangular *croûtons*, enough to go round the edge of the kidneys in the dish.

Rognons de Porc en Casserole

To each kidney, you will need ⅛ lb. of bacon, 4 tiny onions, ¼ lb. small new potatoes, nearly cooked, ½ small clove of garlic, ¼ cup of good stock.

Use a casserole that will go on top of the stove as well as in the oven. Enameled cast iron is best. Otherwise use a frying pan for the preparatory cooking, then transfer the ingredients to an earthenware or Pyrex dish.

Put some butter into the casserole, fry the bacon (diced) and the onions (whole). When they are golden, the bacon transparent, remove and keep on one side whilst you sauté the kidneys, skinned but whole, on both sides. When they have changed color, put the onions and bacon back into the pot, and surround the kidneys with the small new potatoes. Add a little more butter, salt, pepper, and garlic. Put the pot into the oven, *without covering it*, at a medium heat, and leave to finish cooking—about 25 minutes. Five minutes before the end pour in the stock, which should be enough to moisten the ingredients rather than drown them. Serve in the cooking dish.

Rognons de Porc à la Liégeoise

This is a delicious recipe if you have some fresh juniper berries. The number you require depends on the number of kidneys you are using. Follow the preceding recipe except that you omit the vegetables and bacon. Five minutes before the kidneys have finished cooking in the oven, pour on a little stock, add the juniper berries (crushed—about 2 or 3 per kidney), and a jigger (1½ oz.) of gin, which has been warmed and set alight.

Rognons de Porc Clémentine

Follow the preceding recipe, omitting the vegetables and bacon. Five minutes before the end add ½ lb. of small mushroom caps (per 2 kidneys), which have been sautéed in butter for 5 minutes first, pour on ½ cup of port (or other fortified wine like Marsala, Madeira, or sherry) and let this bubble down to a good sauce. Season with a teaspoon of French mustard, and put the casserole back in the oven for 5 minutes.

Omelette aux Rognons

Grind or chop finely a pig's kidney into a small saucepan. Pour on enough boiling water to cover. Leave for 2 minutes. Strain and sauté the kidney in hot, frothing butter until it is cooked. Beat 2 eggs lightly in a basin, tip in the cooked kidney, and season. Run a small knob of butter round a heated 8-inch omelette pan until it is coated. Pour in the mixture and draw the cooked part up, away from the heat, tilting the pan slightly. Use a palette knife or a small fish-filleting knife to do this, and let the runny part flow down. Don't overcook—omelettes are best when they are firm outside and almost liquid in the center. Fold in half, slide onto a very hot plate, top with a knob of butter and a little chopped parsley, and rush to the table.

This is enough for one person. If you have a number to feed, it is advisable to make one large omelette in a huge pan rather than a lot of small ones.

Pithiviers aux Rognons

This is an old, exotic version of the un-kidneyed Pithiviers cakes that are sold in many northern French *pâtisseries*. Nobody will be able to guess what gives the delicious almond filling its interesting, nutty texture. Serve it warm, with light cream, as a pudding in the traditional French Sunday-lunch way. This recipe is slightly adapted from Carême's (Part VIII of *French Cookery*, the translation by William Hall, published in 1836). You can, of course, leave out the kidney—but don't.

The rose shape is traditional to the *gâteau de Pithiviers feuilleté*—Pithiviers is a small town in the Loiret, south of Paris, where the cake was, by tradition, first made. You can make a good stop at the small modern restaurant Au Peché Mignon on the outskirts of the town; start with the other great speciality, lark pâté, and drink Quincy, a beautiful Loire wine.

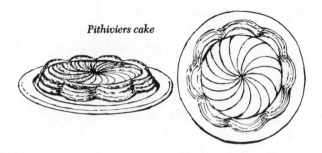

Pithiviers cake

Buy or make 1 lb. puff
pastry

———•— *Filling* —•———

1 pig's kidney, baked for
10 minutes in a hot oven,
then ground

¼ lb. ground almonds
(about ¾ cup)

6 tablespoons (¾ stick)
softened butter

⅜ cup granulated sugar

1 oz. crushed macaroons or
ratafias (optional)

The finely grated rind of
1 lemon

2 egg yolks

4 tablespoons heavy cream

Egg glaze—1 egg beaten
with 2 tablespoons water

Confectioners' sugar for
final glaze

Mix all the ingredients together for the filling. An electric
blender is the best solution. It should result in a smooth yellow
cream with little flecks of kidney.

Line a 9-inch-diameter pie plate (shallow, like a dinner
plate with an inch rim) with half the puff pastry. Put on the
filling, but keep the raised edge clear. If you have too much, keep
it to make small tarts with the pastry trimmings. Brush the pastry
edge with the beaten egg, and lay on a lid of pastry.

Now the fun begins. Make eight small nicks at regular intervals round the edge, then press up the pastry in and up on either
side of each nick to form eight petals. Pierce a small hole in the
center. Brush the lid with the egg glaze and score it, with a sharp,

pointed knife, with curvy lines—be careful not to go through to the filling—for a flower effect. The illustration will give you a good idea of how this is usually done, the Pithiviers trademark so to say.

Put into a hot oven (430°F.) for 10 minutes to puff up the pastry well. But watch it, and lower the heat to 350°F., so that it can cook steadily for another ½ hour. Lay a sheet of greaseproof paper on top if it shows signs of catching too much. You will observe that the pastry parts along the scored lines now appear white against the rich golden-brown of the rest of the lid. Take it out of the oven, turn the oven up to 450°F., and sprinkle the Pithiviers evenly with sifted confectioners' sugar before putting it back to glaze. Once again, watch it—charring now would be a tragedy—and remove the moment it is shiny and gold.

------◆------

THE LIVER

Pig's liver can be bought at the *charcuterie,* but makes its usual appearance in *pâté de foie* (page 89). It must be confessed that pig's liver is neither so delicate in flavor nor so tender as the fine calf's liver to be bought at a high price in France (English or American calf's liver cannot be compared with it— I imagine this to be the method of rearing or a more lax definition of the word "calf"). Nonetheless, pig's liver is nutritious and inexpensive, and can be turned into dishes that are well worth eating, apart from the delicious pâtés.

Foie de Porc en Brochette

Slice the liver and divide the slices into uniform-sized pieces. An overnight soak in a well-seasoned marinade (herbs, spices, as well as oil and some red wine) is an improvement but not essential. Cut some fat pork into the same number of pieces, and string them alternately with the liver onto skewers. Mushrooms, tomatoes, onions can be used as well. Very fat bacon is also suitable, the kind we buy for a few coppers with hardly any lean at all. Brush with melted butter, roll in bread crumbs, and grill gently until crisp and brown. Turn the skewers from time to time. Serve on a bed of mashed potatoes, surround with watercress, or mushrooms, tomatoes, and glazed onions.

Foie de Porc à l'Anglaise

In other words liver and bacon.

Slice the liver thinly, turn it over in seasoned flour.

Prepare the bacon, as many slices as of liver, and fry it in butter, arranging it nicely in an oven dish. Have some scrubbed, unpeeled potatoes boiling at the same time, so that they will be cooked when the liver is finished. Pour off the bacon fat.

Keep the bacon hot in a low oven, and fry the liver very quickly in a fresh lot of butter. Two minutes a side should be ample, unless your slices are rather thick. Time this carefully— the liver should only just be cooked to a point of juicy succulence. Nothing is worse than leathery liver. Remove to the serving dish which already contains the bacon.

Add the bacon fat to the liver fat and juices, add some lemon juice, and pour over the dish. Sprinkle with chopped parsley.

Drain the potatoes, cut them to a convenient size, take off the skins, and finish them with butter and parsley.

A simple dish, but very much better for taking care with its preparation.

Foie de Porc au Beurre Bercy

Sauté slices of pig's liver and serve *beurre bercy*.

Put 2 tablespoons of chopped onion into a small pan with ½ cup of white wine. Bring to the boil, and leave it to bubble away until it's reduced to half the original quantity. Let the mixture cool, then mix it up with ⅜ lb. (1½ sticks, 12 tablespoons) of butter. Add chopped parsley and lemon juice to taste. Ideally you should also add ½ to ⅝ lb. of cooked beef marrow. You can serve it chilled, in pats; or else make a sauce, by adding the onion and wine mixture to 1 cup of *velouté* sauce (page 61). Simmer it for 5 minutes and just before serving stir in 6 tablespoons (¾ stick) of butter, cut into pieces, and some chopped parsley.

Foie de Porc à l'Espagnole

Spicy combinations of onion and tomato go well with liver. For *foie de porc à l'espagnole,* serve the fried liver on a bed of tomatoes cooked to a pulp and flavored with a little tarragon (sauté chopped onion in butter till golden and transparent, add a crushed clove of onion and ½ lb. of peeled tomatoes cut in quarters. Cover closely and let it bubble down to a good flavory mass, season with salt, pepper, and the tarragon). Garnish with onion rings, soaked in milk for an hour, tossed in seasoned flour, and fried in deep oil. Scatter some chopped parsley on top.

Foie de Porc à la Lyonnaise

Onions alone are a delicious accompaniment. Cover the slices of fried liver with a scatter of onion rings fried gently in butter (not overdone to a burnt frizzle). Add 4 tablespoons wine vinegar or lemon juice to the pan juices, and 1 cup good stock. Bubble it down to a small amount of good sauce, and pour it over the liver and onions. Chopped parsley is the usual finish, but try chopped sage and a dash or two of cayenne pepper.

Foie de Porc Braisé

Buy a large piece of pig's liver, say 2 lbs., and ½ lb. of very fat bacon. Cut the bacon into strips and lard the liver, using a larding needle. More messily, if you don't possess a larding needle, make incisions in the liver with a sharp, pointed knife and push short strips of the bacon in.

Season the liver with salt, black pepper, and parsley, wrap it up in a piece of caul (softened in tepid water), and lay it on some strips of pig's skin (*couenne*) or the leftover pieces of fat bacon.

Pour over it a jigger (1½ oz.) of brandy, surround with 3 carrots, cut into rounds, 3 small onions stuck with 2 cloves each, a *bouquet garni* (parsley, thyme, bay leaf), a large clove of garlic, crushed, and some black peppercorns.

Add enough white wine, or white wine and stock, to come just below the top of the liver. Put the lid on the dish, jamming it tight with aluminum foil. Simmer it for an hour.

To make the sauce, drain the liquid, skim off the fat, and reduce it by boiling hard.

The two essentials in this recipe are the preliminary larding, and the brandy and white wine.

If you substitute very small onions, the kind sold for pickling, and omit the cloves, you can serve the liver surrounded by carrots and onions, with the sauce poured over and a sprinkling of parsley, as *foie de porc à la bourgeoise*.

Foie de Porc Rôti aux Truffes

This is a magnificent recipe, accompanied by a magnificent sauce, *sauce Périgueux;* Périgueux is the capital of the Dordogne, the most important truffle area, and any dish described as *Périgueux* means that it's been prepared with truffles.

1 large piece of pig's liver, 2–3 lbs.
4–5 oz. truffles
¼ lb. very fat pork
1 cup olive oil
½ cup Madeira
Salt, pepper, spices

1 large piece of caul, enough to wrap easily round the liver
A little good brown jelly from roast meat or poultry to glaze at the end

First prepare the liver. Lard it with small strips of the fat pork, make small incisions with the point of a sharp knife and push in tiny pieces of truffle so that they are well distributed. Leave the liver for 24 hours in a marinade of the oil, wine, and seasonings.

When you are ready to cook, assemble two sheets of grease-proof paper, plenty of aluminum foil, and a shallow oven dish or baking sheet with raised edges, in case the juices from the meat leak out.

Oil the greaseproof paper on one side only, and put one piece, unoiled-side down, on top of the other piece, oiled-side up. Wrap the liver in the caul (run under a warm tap for a moment to make it pliable), and lay it, with the juices from the marinade, on greaseproof paper. Wrap the liver up, lay it on a sheet of aluminum foil, and crinkle the edges together to make a loose but firmly sealed parcel. Lay this in the oven dish or baking sheet and put in a medium oven for 1½ hours.

Just before taking the meat out of the oven, melt down a little jelly from a roast. This you will pour over the caul-wrapped liver, when the greaseproof paper and foil have been removed, and return it to the oven for a moment or two to glaze, whilst you finish off the *sauce Périgueux*.

Sauce Périgueux (page 54), might just as well be made from a GOOD *sauce Espagnole,* since the truffles cost so much, rather than the remains of the gravy from a roast or stew. Do the hard work the previous day, and add the Madeira and truffles just before the liver is ready to serve. *Remember that the sauce must not boil* after the truffles and Madeira have been added.

HEART, LUNGS, AND SPLEEN

The heart, lungs, and spleen do not make an appearance in the *charcutier*'s shop, any more than they do (except for the heart sometimes) in an English or American butcher's. But they aren't wasted, disappearing discreetly but nutritiously into pâtés, *gay-*

ettes, sausages, and faggots according to nationality. Here is a recipe for all three of them together.

Fressure de Porc à l'Anglaise

Pig's heart, lungs, spleen
Plain flour
Salt and pepper
Clarified butter or butter-
    and-oil mixture

½ cup Madeira, Marsala,
    or equivalent
½ cup beef stock
A dash of Worcestershire
    sauce or lemon juice
Parsley

Set a pan of water, salted, on to boil. Put the lungs and spleen in when it is bubbling. The lungs will float, as they are full of air, so they must be held down. The other alternative is to beat the air out of them first. Keep the water bubbling away for 15 minutes. Cut the heart into thin slices, then the lungs and spleen when they have finished blanching. Dredge the slices with flour, salt, and pepper.

Melt the clarified butter in a large, heavy frying pan, and brown the meat gently. It should be an appetizing golden color, not frizzled.

Arrange the pieces on an ovenproof dish attractively—remember that you have a certain amount of prejudice to overcome. Keep warm in a low oven whilst you make the sauce.

Stir 2 tablespoons of flour into the pan juices, to make a medium-brown *roux.* Next moisten with the wine and beef stock. Add more stock if you require a runnier sauce. Finally flavor with salt and pepper, if necessary, Worcestershire sauce or a dash of lemon juice, pour it over the meat, and sprinkle with chopped parsley. It is absolutely essential to serve this with crisply fried, golden-brown *croûtons.* Cut the bread into triangles, fry them in butter-and-oil mixture; then dip one corner in sauce, then in more chopped parsley and stick the opposite corner into the dish.

Coeur de Porc à l'Orange

The heart can be cooked to provide a most delicious dish—to my mind, greatly preferable to the *fressure à l'anglaise*. One heart per person is ample—and four would do for five people.

4 pig's hearts
½ lb. onions, chopped
  (about 1¾ cups)
1 or 2 slices bacon
4–6 tablespoons butter-and-
  oil mixture
2 tablespoons flour
2–2½ cups stock

¾ cup wine, red or white
1 clove garlic
Salt and pepper
2–4 tablespoons marma-
  lade
1 orange, juice and peel
3 tablespoons orange li-
  queur

Cut the surplus fat off the hearts, brown them with chopped onion and bacon slices in a large heavy frying pan, in the butter-and-oil. Remove the meat and vegetables to the casserole, stir enough flour into the pan juices to make a brown *roux*, and add stock and wine enough to make a sauce. Add the garlic, salt and pepper to taste, and the marmalade (the bitter chunky kind). Pour this into the casserole, and simmer gently until the hearts are done—about 1½ hours.

Remove the hearts, slice them thinly, and arrange in a shallow ovenproof dish. Skim fat off the sauce and taste it. If it is a bit tasteless, boil it down hard until it improves. Flavor finally with orange juice, orange peel, and liqueur. Barely cover the hearts with this sauce, putting the rest into a sauceboat to pass separately. Warm through in the oven and sprinkle with chopped parsley.

Serve with boiled potatoes, and an orange and tomato salad.

Another way to finish the hearts is to spread a layer of bread crumbs, ¼ inch thick, on top of the hearts and sauce and put the dish into a hot oven for the bread crumbs to brown. You could dot them with tiny bits of butter, but don't make them too fatty.

Coeur et Rognons en Brochette

In other words, heart and kidney kebabs. Amounts depend on the number of people who are eating—I allow ⅜ lb. of meat per head. So for four people you would need ½ lb. of hearts, ½ lb. of kidneys, and ½ lb. of very fat sowbelly, fresh salted. Cut them all up into cubes.

Marinade them overnight in a spicy and herby mixture of 1 cup of oil, ½ cup of red wine or wine vinegar, 2 medium onions, cut up roughly, 2 sprigs of thyme, 2 bay leaves, plenty of ground pepper, salt, 3 cloves of garlic, crushed, a teaspoon of *quatre-épices* or of any mixture of spices that you like. You can of course add orange peel, lemon peel, and juice—anything that imagination and experience suggests. Give everything a good stir up before you go to bed, and again first thing in the morning. Incidentally, marinade is the poor man's refrigerator—you can keep meat in it for 4 or 5 days in cold weather. Anything that can't really go into the brine tub can soak in a marinade. Prepare the kebabs by stringing the meat onto the skewers—fat pork, kidney, heart, fat pork, kidney, heart, fat pork . . . Grill gently, turning them over from time to time and basting with the marinade. This gives some good flavory juice in the grill pan.

Serve the kebabs, sprinkled with parsley, on a bed of rice or mashed potato, with the juices poured over them. A cool green salad is all that's required by way of a second vegetable.

THE LIGHTS (LUNGS)

Lights have no great nutritional value, whether for humans, cats, or dogs. They can be delicious, however, which is another thing. The trouble is that most people cheerfully beat out some veal or steak but balk at beating the air out of lungs. I suspect that this is the main reason why they are not usually displayed for sale in France or England or the United States, rather than their lack of food value. But take courage. The way to cook them is to stew them—here is the basic method, with variations:

Civet de Mou de Porc

Beat the lungs to expel the air—an all-wooden rolling pin is ideal for this. Cut them into small pieces, discarding the larger tubes and windpipe. Season with salt and pepper.

Set a heavy frying pan on a medium heat, with clarified butter, butter-and-oil, or lard in it. It is important to keep flavors clear when frying, particularly in the preparation of slightly off-beat food, so never use a muddle-up of weeks of dripping. This dish would be ruined if the preliminary cooking were done in a tired combination of mutton and beef fat—in fact, I can think of no dish that would be improved by it, and few that could stand it. If you have no clarified butter to hand, the addition of oil to ordinary butter will prevent it from browning rapidly. Pure fat from cooking bacon would, of course, do instead of lard.

Brown the pieces of lung evenly, then add 4 tablespoons of flour.

Let it color to a coffee shade before adding stock (chicken-cube stock, or veal stock) and red wine in the proportion of 2 to 1. Stir until everything bubbles away gently, with the meat bathed in a smooth sauce. Turn into a casserole with a well-fitting lid. This is the time to add embellishments—a clove or two of garlic, crushed; celery stalks, cut into two lengthways; leeks, cut into two lengthways; a large onion, quartered; carrots, quartered; a *bouquet garni*, tied together. The point being that all these things, apart from the garlic, will have eventually to be removed, so keep them large.

Cover closely and put into a gentle, simmering oven for 1½ hours.

Take out the vegetables and *bouquet*, put the meat into another oven-worthy serving dish. Add finely grated lemon peel to the sauce, and some lemon juice to taste, then pour enough over the pieces of meat to keep them moist, without drowning them. Lid on (or aluminum foil), and into the oven for another 30 minutes' simmering.

Serve with a sprinkling of chopped parsley on top and an accompanying dish of plainly boiled *pasta*—spaghetti, noodles, bows, shells, what you will. Devotees always of crispness, we like triangles of toast or fried bread; in early summer, green beans just cooked until they still retain a hint of crispness (*al dente*) and not a second longer.

Mou à la Bourgeoise

When the meat is transferred to the second casserole for its final cooking, add tiny white (pickling) onions cooked in a small amount of red wine and 2 tablespoons of brown sugar and 2 tablespoons of butter (shake them often to make sure they don't catch, and don't use a small pan—one layer of onions is the most satisfactory), glazed carrots (cut in rings, cooked in a tight-lidded pan with 2 tablespoons each of water and butter and granulated sugar), and sautéed cubes of bacon.

Mou à la Bonne Femme

Add mushroooms instead of the carrots in *mou à la bourgeoise*, and small new potatoes.

Mou à la Provençale

Essentially garlic in the first instance, when you fry the meat. Then no flour but white wine—boil it hard to reduce to a good flavor. Then add chicken stock and tomato sauce or tomatoes (if fresh, peeled and quartered). Half a pepper is a good addition—cut into strips, seeds removed. When this is all bubbling away, pour some of the liquid onto 4 to 6 tablespoons of flour in a bowl. Stir so that there are no lumps, and return to the pan. Cook in a covered casserole for 1½ hours, then transfer the pieces of meat to a second casserole, arrange black olives around them (2–4 oz., according to taste and the amount of lung), and some of the sauce, and simmer for ½ hour.

Initially it is best to fry the meat in olive oil. If you haven't got any, soak the black olives in some plain vegetable oil for a few days. I normally keep black olives in a jar of this oil in the store cupboard, and use it for dishes *à la provençale.*

Mou en Blanquette

Cook as in the basic recipe, but use white wine instead of red, and add mushrooms, leeks, and onions only. Add an extra chicken-bouillon cube. Of course if you have some good chicken stock, this is the ideal. After 1½ hours remove the meat to the second casserole and keep it warm whilst the liquid reduces by boiling hard. Keep tasting.

For 2½ cups sauce, mix 2 egg yolks and ½ cup of cream to-gether in a bowl. Just before you are ready to serve, pour the sauce onto the yolks and cream, stirring briskly. Return this to the pan and cook gently over a very low heat until it is thick and bland. *It absolutely must not boil.* If you feel nervous about this, don't return the sauce to the pan, but set the bowl over a pan of simmering water and stir it with attention. This should

spleen

certainly be safe from curdling. For the second process allow
yourself 10 minutes, and clear the kitchen. Finally add some
unsalted butter, lemon juice to taste, and chopped parsley. Pour
this over the meat and serve.

Wienerbeuscherl

Austrian *Wienerbeuscherl* is a variation of these recipes, using
the heart as well as the lungs. Do not fry them to begin with, but
cook for as long as necessary in the *court-bouillon*. Melt some
butter in a medium-sized saucepan, and cook 2–3 tablespoonfuls
of flour in it until you have a golden *roux*. Leave this to one side
whilst you cut the meat into small strips. Make a lightly thickened
sauce by returning the *roux* to the fire and pouring on some of
the strained *bouillon* in which the lung and heart cooked. When
this is ready, add the chopped meat, warm it through and give
a final favoring of lemon peel, finely grated, and some lemon
juice. The sauce should taste pleasantly sharp. Let it simmer for
5 minutes very gently. Serve it in a sturdy dish, and accompany
with *pasta* or potato dumplings.

THE SPLEEN

The spleen (*rate*) is a long flat oval of dark reddish-brown
meat, with a line of white fat running from end to end. It usually
disappears—in England and the United States, as in France—
with the rest of the pluck into faggots, sausages, and pâtés. In
the *charcuterie*, however, you do see small succulent rolls of an
appetizing brown on occasion; these are the spleen, cut in half,
rolled up round the line of fat, speared with a toothpick and
cooked in with the *rillons* (page 333), which provide necessary
extra fat. They are eaten cold, with plenty of French mustard,
and bread.

rolled spleen

Cut 1 lb. fat sowbelly into 2-inch cubes. Remove the skin and keep it to enrich a beef stew. Cut two spleens in half, roll up each half with the line of fat turned inwards, and spear them through with a toothpick or sharpened matchstick. Set a heavy pan to heat with a ladle of water. Put in the cubes of sowbelly and the spleen rolls. Cover and set in a slow oven for an hour. Remove the spleen rolls. Leave off the lid and give the pork *rillons* another hour to brown all over.

Country people in Wiltshire make a good sage-and-onion stuffing, spread the spleen thickly with it, and sew it up. Wrapped in a large piece of caul softened to pliability in tepid water and tied with string it is then roasted in a medium oven for an hour.

THE TESTICLES

Unless you breed and rear your own pigs, the testicles are a delicacy unlikely to come your way—whether in England, the U.S., or France. Most male pigs are castrated soon after they are born, so even the most cooperative butcher will not be able to help you. I have recently bought and cooked calf's testicles from a butcher in the covered market at Tours. He maintained that the testicles of horses and calves were much the best, and showed me how to cut the *rognons blancs*, which seems to be the polite name in our part of France. He had scalded them and removed the skin, so that they looked like a row of pinkish white shelled

eggs that had been nicely boiled to the mollet stage. The correct
way to cut them is to slice first from right to left, but not all the
way through, then from left to right, so that the *rognon* opens
out like a triptych. Then you season it and simmer it in butter
for about 15 minutes. Quite a lot of juice comes out, so then
the heat must be raised to evaporate and concentrate the juices.
At this stage a good chopping of parsley and garlic is added, and
finally some cream if you want to extend the sauce a little. With
our cream, you need to add a squeeze of lemon juice, or a proportion of soured cream, to give the sauce a slight tang. Serve the
rognons blancs with toast or triangles of fried bread, something
crisp to set off their tender firmness.

Here is a summary of some recipes from *Larousse Gastronomique* that Prosper Montaigne gave for sheep's testicles—they
would be as suitable for pig's as the recipe above from Tours
market:

Animelles de Porc Frites

Prepare and slice.

Marinade for at least an hour, or until you are ready to start
cooking, in a small amount of oil, vinegar, spices, and herbs. Dry
them well, then sprinkle with seasoned flour or dip in batter and
fry in foaming butter.

Serve them with fried mushrooms (*aux champignons*) or
fried parsley. I can never bring myself to fry parsley—to me the
idea has bituminous, mummified overtones, ever since I read that
Richard Wilson compared Gainsborough's trees to fried parsley.
But I pass on the suggestion.

Animelles de Porc à la Crème

Prepare and slice, but don't marinade. Fry in butter until they are
cooked.

At the same time have 1 cup of unsalted *béchamel* sauce

(butter, flour, and milk) reducing. If you have cream to spare, enrich the sauce with this and 2 tablespoons of butter just before adding the fried *animelles*. Season with salt.

After this point do not let the sauce boil again or you risk curdling. Keep it just under the simmer for about 10 minutes. If you feel nervous about this, do it in a double boiler or a bowl over a pan of barely simmering water. Don't take any risks.

If you want to stretch the quantity to a more substantial dish, serve the creamed *animelles* in a prebaked puff-pastry case or in small *vol-au-vent* cases.

Instead of frying the slices of *animelle*, simmer them in a *court-bouillon* of a light kind—white wine, for instance, not red. Then drain them and add to the cream sauce I've just described, or serve them with a lemon-juice–and–oil vinaigrette.

THE FAT OF THE PIG

PORK FAT

From early times, one of the pig's most valuable assets was the high proportion of fat his carcass provided. Apart from being important to the human body's welfare, fat makes a good preservative of lean meat, particularly neutral-tasting pork fat. Even nowadays, with refrigeration, many farmers' wives in France like to preserve pork, goose, turkey, rabbit, and duck in lard. These *confits*, as they are called, may be used gradually. One has only to melt the huge crock of meat and lard very gently, take out enough pieces for the occasion, then return the crock to a cool larder for the fat to solidify again. This can be repeated a time or two, so long as the remaining pieces of meat do not come in contact with the air but stay covered by the lard. Goose is preserved in its own fat, eked out with lard; joints of it go into the famous *cassoulet* of Languedoc (page 168), and the fat imparts a delicious flavor to potatoes and bread fried in it.

But the *confits* are really farmhouse preparations, for the protracted convenience of a single, often isolated, family. In the *charcuteries*, the fatness of the pig is delectably presented in three other ways. Firstly, in great white earthenware pots of whipped and whirled lard; secondly, in large and small bowls and mugs of *rillettes*, a kind of potted pork; and thirdly, in golden-brown cubes called *rillons*, sowbelly cut up and cooked in its own fat until crisp outside and moist within.

If, as often happens in small towns and villages, the *charcutier* is also the butcher, you will see how beautifully he prepares joints of beef for roasting. By English standards, or lack of standards, they are hardly recognizable, these elegantly tied, sausage-shaped pieces of beef, with wide strips or bards of pork fat along the sides to keep the meat basted while it roasts.* For a dinner party, you may find that the joint you ordered has been further embellished by flowers or geometric shapes cut in pork fat, at once decorative and practical.

Should you wish to lard your own fillet steak, or hare saddle, or pigeon, you can always buy small chunks of pork fat for the purpose (page 325). I find larding one of the most satisfactory of the quieter kitchen occupations. It is a soothing and unhurried performance; and I like being reminded, too, of Perrault's Princess, in *Riquet à la Houppe,* who saw the ground open before her and a number of roasting cooks emerge, who promptly set to work with their larding needles on joints of meat, set on a trestle table beneath the high trees of the wood. Only a French fairy story would pay such nice attention to cooking!

Rillettes and *rillons,* the former often sold in brown-glazed stoneware mugs of various sizes, are on sale throughout France, but I look in vain, even in Tours itself, for a *quiche Tourangelle.* I always end up buying the *rillettes* and *rillons,* and making one myself (page 337). In England, of course, you have to make everything yourself—unless you are in easy distance of Soho.† It's worth doing this in large quantity. *Rillettes* and potted *rillons* can be kept for months, so you have a ready-to-hand hors d'oeuvre, or the basic materials for a *quiche Tourangelle,* which most people would find adequate as a main dish.

In France, don't make the mistake of asking for *lard* if you want lard. *Lard* is the French for bacon, and very expensive it is

---

* American butchers, I am told, are somewhat better about preparing joints for roasting than our English butchers are.

† In the United States, the same is true—unless you live in New York or some other large city, you will have to make most things yourself.

storage and preserving jars

too. Where we might use it in pâtés or *daubes*, the French house-wife would use thin strips of pork fat, or salt pork, or a slice of fresh sowbelly. This is worth following, the result is blander and less aggressive. If you intend to make your own fat pork dishes, it is worth searching for stoneware pots (*pots de grès*) in which to preserve them. Not earthenware. Its coarser clay and glaze need firing at a low temperature, which means that the glaze chips easily, and the body is frequently porous and easily cracked, making sterilization impossible. Wide-mouthed French preserving jars (*bocal*, pl. *bocaux*) are excellent (Mason jars are quite all right though the narrower openings are not so convenient). French *bazaars* are the best places to get suitable preserving con-tainers—they cost very little, and there are many attractive shapes to choose from. A *bazaar* is not a few stalls and a bran tub opened by the squire's wife, but a most useful emporium where you may buy a wide range of things from hair clips to saucepans, toys, and household china both useful (storage jars, casseroles) and frivolous (wild duck plaques, of a garishness only the French could achieve).

The different sorts of pork fat are:

La panne (leaf lard; also flair, flare, flay fat, etc.), a sheet or layer of fat forming an interior covering to the loin and enveloping the kidneys. Best taken from bacon-type pigs, and used for the best lard, *boudins blancs* (page 147), and fine pâtés.

Lard de poitrine—the fat sowbelly, which includes the hard fat lying under the skin, the lean meat, and the softer fat. When cured and smoked, this gives smoked streaky bacon. In France this self-basting cut is used for *rillons, rillettes* (pages 333 to 337), and *petit salé* (salt sowbelly, page 181) by the *charcutier*, and as an enriching ingredient in beef stews by the housewife.

Gras dur (fat back, speck), the hard layer of fat under the skin (*couenne*), can be salted for keeping, melted for good-quality lard, or used fresh in sausages, stuffings, pâtés, and for larding. Expertly cut slices of this hard fat are tied neatly round lean joints of beef for roasting, or poultry, or game, to keep them moist.

Gras mou or *fondant* includes the poorer-quality fat immediately touching the lean pork, and all the scrapings (*les ratis*) of fat which surround the intestines and the mesentery (mud-

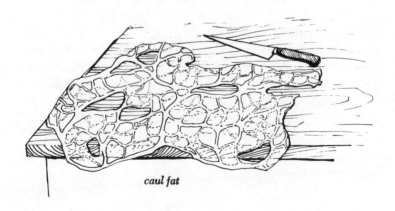

caul fat

geon, gut fat, crow, or frill, page 289) which holds the intestines in place. This fat provides an inferior lard, which should not be mixed in with the fine lard coming from the leaf lard and hard fat back.

Crêpine (caul; also veil, kell) is a veil of fat surrounding the stomach. Made pliable in tepid water, it is wrapped round lean meat for roasting, or pâtés, faggots, and *gayettes*, to provide a permanent basting layer.

Grillons, or *grattons* (cracklings, sketchings, scribblings, graves, greaves), are solid scraps remaining after the fat parts have been melted down for lard and the liquid poured off. They can be potted and eaten like *rillettes* (page 334), or, in the case of the mesentery, eaten immediately as an hors d'oeuvre.

LARDING

Larding is the introduction of small strips of pork fat known as lardoons (*lardons*) into very lean meat such as fillet steak, pigeons, saddle of hare, which might otherwise be too dry when cooked. For this pleasant little job you need, like the roasting cooks in Perrault's *Riquet à la Houppe,* a larding needle (*lardoire*), which is shaped like a very elongated, sharp-pointed cornet (page 19).

You can cut bacon fat into strips (*lardonner*), but the ideal is a nice slab of hard fat back, cut from under the skin of the loin. Chill it if possible, then cut into slices downward and then across—see the illustration. Push each little *lardon* into the open end of the needle.

As one nineteenth-century cookery book says, seat yourself comfortably, lay a clean linen cloth on your left knee, then put the joint to be larded on top of the cloth. Take a stitch in the joint from right to left and pull the needle through, whilst releasing the *lardon*. It should project neatly at each end, like the second illustration on the next page.

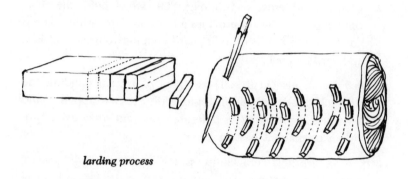

larding process

This operation is great fun to do, and most soothing. It adds to the tenderness and flavor of the meat, and looks sensational. What more could one ask?

* * *

LARD
(*Saindoux*)

When the pig has been split in two, after the insides have all been removed, a sheet of fat can be seen lying on the inside of the ribs. It's easy to rip off, and from it and the hard fat underneath the skin the best lard is made. At the bacon factory, other fat parts are included in the final lard; the mesentery is one of them. But if you have a good fat bacon pig, keep this leaf lard (*panne*) apart from the rest. For one thing it melts at a different rate, and if it catches, it is spoilt. Of course you can, if you wish, amalgamate the two kinds of lard once they have been melted and are off the fire but not set.

If you want to have a bladder of lard to hang up in the larder, you will have to soak the cleaned bladder in water until it is soft. Don't pour in the lard (best quality only) before it is half-set. Tie the bladder up so that there is no air space between the lard and the string, and leave it to cool off completely in cold water. Keep it hung up in a cool, dry place.

Preparation of Lard

NOTE: Do not add salt (it merely falls to the bottom of the melting pot) or herbs and spices (you may wish to use the lard for recipes where such flavors would be inappropriate).

Panne, or leaf lard in English. Remove fibers and any blood-stained part of the fat. Cut it into suitable sizes for passing through a grinder—an electric one saves a lot of time and strength—then soak it for 5 hours in cold water: ½ cup water to 1 lb. fat.

You can omit the soaking, and put the ground fat into a heavy pan (cast iron, or enameled cast iron) with about ¼ inch of water in the bottom to stop the fat sticking.

If you've soaked the fat, you will need hardly any water in the pan. Just a little to start it off.

Now set the pan on a very low, steady heat. Do not hurry this part of the process or you will end up with a grimy-looking grease instead of beautifully snowy lard.

Pour off the fat as it melts to a milky liquid, through a strainer straight into sterilized glass jars. Even stoneware pots are too porous for the long-term storage of lard, and I do not suppose that most households have suitable metal containers, such as *charcuterie* handbooks recommend. In any event fill the jars right to the brim; the fat contracts as it hardens. Do not cover for 48 hours, then use jam-pot covers, with a final cover of aluminum foil tied on tightly with fine string.

Lard gras dur. It is easy to see in a piece of loin or sowbelly how the fat between the skin and the first bit of lean meat divides into two layers quite noticeably. The outer layer is easily pulled off, and makes excellent lard.

Skin it, and grind it as for the *panne* above. Then leave it to soak for 5 hours in cold water: if you have a pound of fat, soak it in ½ cup of water.

You will find that this melts much more slowly than the

panne fat. Whatever you do, don't hurry it along. If you doubt the thickness of your pot, use an asbestos mat to be absolutely sure. The little hard bits, the *grillons* as they are called, may take on a light-brown color, but this is all right. Just keep pouring off the liquid lard through a strainer, into jars, or into a large bowl if you intend to use it fairly soon. It can be mixed with melted lard from the *panne*, or leaf, at this stage. *Charcutiers* whip the fat electrically as it cools. If you have an electric beater you could do the same. It makes a very light and delicate substance.

Soft fat, and scraps of fatty meat, the mesentery, can all be used to extract fat for quick consumption. Cut it into rough pieces, skin and all, except for the mesentery, which should be cut into 6-inch lengths. Soak the pieces for 5 hours in cold water as in the above recipe), and use the same method of cooking. With the golden-brown pieces left in the strainer you can make:

GRATTONS, OR GRILLONS

The simplest way is to salt and pepper these bits, and eat them hot with mashed potatoes, or cold on bread as an hors d'oeuvre. You can keep them too, by packing them closely into sterilized stoneware pots or glass jars, and covering them with ½ inch of melted lard. If you're not going to eat the frilly mesentery separately (see page 289), chop the pieces to a uniform size with the other *grillons*. A moment or two in an electric blender produces quite a satisfactory result, somewhere between a laboriously acquired chop and an unsatisfactory mush of grinding.

—— Variations ——

Leave the remains to cool down properly. Chop them small (or whirl them in an electric blender, dropping them through the hole in the lid onto the fast-spinning blades—but don't overdo it to a purée), and season with salt, freshly ground black pepper, *quatre-épices* or other spices, some chopped scallions and crushed garlic and thyme. Put ½ cup of white wine in a heavy pan or casserole, add the meat mixture and let it simmer gently but steadily for an hour and a half. Be sure it doesn't catch. The best way to do this is to stir it often with a wooden spoon, and put the pan on an asbestos mat if you are using gas.

Unless you have had a marathon lard-making, there will not be enough *grillons* to keep. But you can always pot it in sterilized jars, and cover it hermetically with ½ inch of melted lard.

Grillons Fines

These are really a sort of *rillettes* (page 334) because you don't just make them from remains as in the two recipes above but from fresh meat. But as they are known as *grillons,* I give the recipe here.

You need equal quantities of lean pork and the hard fat beneath the skin. Chop them roughly and leave them overnight in a mixture of salt, pepper, and *quatre-épices* (or your own mixture of spices). The proportion of salt should be 2 oz. to 3 lbs. of meat and fat together, with pepper and spices according to your own tastes but about one eighth of the amount of salt.

Next day put ½ cup of dry white wine in the cooking pot— proportionately more if you have over 3 lbs. of meat. Add the meat, after washing it in a colander under the tap, and leave to cook very slowly for 3 hours, giving it an occasional stir with a wooden spoon to make sure it isn't sticking. About an hour before the end of the cooking time, correct the seasoning. Add more spices, and some chopped mild onion or scallions and garlic.

When they are cooked, strain off the fat, pack the *grillons* into sterilized stoneware pots or glass jars. When they are cold, melt the fat again which you strained off and cover the *grillons* to about ½ inch deep, at least, better ¾ inch. When the fat has hardened, cover with a close layer of aluminum foil and keep in a cool, dry place. This way they will last for months.

Grattons, or Gratterons

Larousse Gastronomique gives this recipe for *grattons,* or *gratterons,* from the Île de la Réunion. It is a huge success with children and anyone who likes crackling.

Ask the butcher for a sheet of pig's skin with about ¾ inch of fat attached—in other words, the skin and layer of hard fat I was talking about, that can be separated quite easily. Ask him not to score it for crackling. Stress this: most butchers do it quite automatically.

Cut the skin and fat into 3-inch squares, and score the fat side only into smallish diamonds.

Now set a heavy pan on a gentle heat, and melt 4 tablespoons of lard. Add the pork, fat-side downward, and transfer to a gentle oven for about 4 hours. The skin will look quite transparent. Now turn the heat up and leave the skin for another ½ hour, watching that it doesn't burn. The idea is that it should swell into golden, crisp bubbles—a crackling *de luxe.*

When they are done put them in a dish, well drained of fat, sprinkle with salt, and serve.

As this dish can quite well be cooked on top of the oven—remembering not to cover the pan at any stage of the cooking whether you do it in the oven, or on top—I often serve it as an accompaniment to a piece of roast pork.

PRESERVED PORK, GOOSE, TURKEY, DUCK, AND RABBIT
(*Confits de Porc, d'Oie, de Dinde, de Canard, et de Lapin*)

Nowadays *confits d'oie* are particularly associated with the southwest of France, but the goose is traditionally under the protection of St. Martin of Tours (315?–?399), that most untypical Roman soldier who halved his cloak with a beggar one freezing night, and who was loved and commemorated in churches all over Europe from his lifetime onwards (even in far-off Galloway,

St. Ninian built a church dedicated to him in about A.D. 400).

Back in not-so-far-off England after a good vintage in our small Loire village, I like to make *confits d'oie et porc* for the winter ahead, soon after his feast day on November 11 in the golden days of St. Martin's Summer. Even in the time of St. Martin and St. Ninian, Gaul had long been celebrated for its hams. Did these great ascetics occasionally profit by Touraine's tradition of *charcuterie*? I hope so; and I am sure that later pilgrims did, who stopped at Tours on their way to St. James at Compostella. Without doubt they ate *confits* and drank Loire wines on freezing nights, *in memoriam Sancti Martini*, as a shield against the weather outside.

BASIC METHOD FOR ALL CONFITS

Use boned pork from the loin end. Cut it into large pieces and tie them with "heavy-duty" white thread so that they will not lose their shape in cooking.

Joint the birds and rabbit. Do not bone.

Leave the meat to salt for 24 hours, in the proportions of 2 lbs. meat (boned pork, unboned birds and rabbit) to a mixture of 3 tablespoons salt, a good pinch of saltpeter, ½ teaspoon of thyme and ½ bay leaf, and ¼ teaspoon of freshly ground black pepper. Rub the salt mixture into the meat, then leave it. Meanwhile assemble your pots: stoneware (*not earthenware*, it's too porous) or porcelain or wide-mouthed glass preserving jars. Wash them with boiling soda water to make sure they are absolutely clean, then sterilize them when the meat is nearly cooked and ready to be potted. Also prepare some wooden sticks by boiling. You need to lay two crosswise in each pot, so that the fat is able to encircle the meat completely.

Although one can in theory use large jars, and remove the preserved meat over a period of time at intervals, I have never pushed this too far. I use lidded stoneware storage jars of the kind sold widely in household *bazaars* in France, of a size to hold about six or seven pieces of meat, or even less (page 323).

Set a heavy cast-iron pan or large casserole on a gentle heat and melt in it half the amount of best lard (see page 324) that you have of meat. If you are lucky enough to be making *confits d'oie*, use the fat from the goose, and make it up to half the weight of meat with lard if necessary.

When the fat is hot, add the pieces of meat and cook them gently for between 1¼ and 2 hours. The way to judge when they are cooked, is to pierce them with a knitting needle. If no liquid comes out, they are cooked; try the pieces at 1¼ hours, then at 15-minute intervals, because you do not want to overcook them. They will look pinkish because of the saltpeter, so don't be put off by that.

Put some strained fat into the jars you intend to use, up to the top of the cross of sticks. Then pack in the pieces of meat, leaving 2 inches at the top of the jar. Pour over the strained fat right up to the brim, remembering that it will contract as it cools.

When the contents are quite cold, cover the jars with aluminum foil, pressing it right down onto the lard. Untouched the meat will keep for 6 months to a year.

To remove some meat from the jar, stand it at the side of the stove when it is warm, until the lard melts enough for you to spear the pieces. Put the jar back into the cool, and cover with a fresh piece of aluminum foil when the lard has hardened again. Make absolutely sure that all the remaining pieces are still well covered with a thick layer of lard.

As the meat is cooked, you can eat it cold with a salad and new potatoes or a potato salad. More frequently it is eaten hot (having been heated in a frying pan with some of its own fat), and accompanied by mashed potatoes. Odd pieces find their way into *cassoulet* (particularly goose *confits*) and *potée*, which is halfway between soup and stew (pages 168 to 174).

You can insert pieces of garlic into the pork, rabbit, and goose before cooking them; and eventually serve them hot with a sprinkling of finely chopped garlic and parsley.

See also *cou d'oie* or *de dinde* (page 124).

SOWBELLY
(*Poitrine de Porc*)

In France, sowbelly is either salted and smoked for bacon, salted and boiled to be eaten cold (*petit salé,* page 181); or else cooked slowly in lard and turned into *rillettes* and *rillons.* Both can be preserved for a long time under a deep layer of lard, but, in the *charcuterie, rillons* are usually sold soon after they are made, and *rillettes* as well. The difference between them is one of size (*rillons* being solid cubes of golden-brown, and *rillettes* being a solid mass of pounded and succulent fibers); they can quite well be cooked together in the same pan.

BASIC METHOD

1 lb. sowbelly, cut into 2-inch cubes

1½ lbs. sowbelly, cut into small strips about 1 inch long and ¼ inch wide (you can use shoulder of pork instead)

1 lb. leaf lard, cut into smallish pieces (use the hard fat from under the skin if you can't get leaf fat)

Salt, pepper, spices, thyme, bay leaf

Using a heavy pan, put in the pork pieces and ¼ cup of water, so that the meat doesn't stick. Cook over a gentle heat, or in a low oven, covered, for 4 hours.

Separate the cubes of pork (the *rillons*) from the rest, and leave them to brown in a hotter oven, uncovered, or in an open pan on top of the stove.

Whilst they are finishing off, deal with the *rillettes.*

Put a large strainer over a strong earthenware bowl and pour the meat and fat from the cooking pot into it. Press the meat gently, so that as much fat as possible falls through the mesh of the sieve, and transfer it to a mortar so that it can be pounded. Finally put it back in the sieve, and tear it apart with two forks into an even mass of fibers.

I cannot pretend that this is quick or easy, but the success of *rillettes* depends on it. You can eliminate the pounding by dropping the meat onto the fast-whirling blades of an electric blender. This demands judgment, because you must not reduce the meat to a porridge-like slush.

But whaever you do, don't put rillettes through the grinder, either before or after cooking.

Now season with salt, pepper, *quatre-épices* or other spices, a little garlic and thyme. Flavor is needed. Return to the pan and give the *rillettes* a quarter of an hour more on a gentle heat, so that the seasonings are well distributed. Pack lightly into sterilized stoneware (or glass or porcelain) pots, and cover with the fat from the cooking melted to a pouring consistency. Be careful not to include the meaty juices when you take the fat out of the bowl. A depth of ½ inch of lard will preserve the *rillettes* beneath for 6 months to a year.

Next day, cover the lard with a close covering of aluminum foil, and another piece of it over the top of each pot, tied on with string. If you intend to keep the *rillettes* for a day or two only, no lard covering is required.

During all this, keep an eye on the *rillons;* put them to drain when they are an appetizing brown all over. Eat them cold, like *rillettes,* as an hors d'oeuvre.

Alternatively, you can pot *rillons* like *confits.* In that case they are best heated through in an open pan when you come to eat them, in a little of their preserving fat, and served with mashed potatoes and a tart apple purée or baked apple rings.

Rillettes de Paris

1 lb. sowbelly
2 tablespoons good lard
1 tablespoon salt

Pepper and spices according to taste

The point of this recipe is the very prolonged, gentle cooking of the pork, so that it is in the most melting condition possible by the time you have finished—and not "dry and sandy."

Cut the meat into pieces about 1 inch or 1½ inches long. Put them on to cook with the lard in a heavy pan on a very low flame indeed. Keep stirring so that the meat colors evenly to a pale gold.

Pour off the fat, and leave the meat to go on cooking for a further 5 hours on the lowest possible heat. From time to time pour on a little water to prevent the meat sticking.

Let the meat get quite cold. Then drop it onto the blades of an electric blender, if you have one. Otherwise you are condemned to chopping and pounding. The final result is a smooth, "unctuous" pâté, which you season with salt, pepper, and spices, and add according to your own discretion as much of the drained-off fat as you like. "Too high flame will fry the pieces of meat and harden them," so this is the point to watch.

Rillettes d'Angers

1 lb. fresh pork
2 lbs. boned goose
½ lb. of best lard

2 tablespoons salt,
pepper, and spices to
taste

Follow the BASIC METHOD.

Rillettes du Mans

1 lb. fresh pork shoulder
1½ lbs. fat back, skinned
1 lb. chicken or rabbit,
boned when weighed

2 tablespoons salt, pepper,
cloves, bay, thyme

Follow the BASIC METHOD, but include the bay leaf and thyme from the start of the cooking, and the cloves too.

Rillettes de Lapin

2 lbs. young rabbit
¾ lb. sowbelly, not too
lean

¼ lb. fat back, skinned
Pepper, spices, and salt as
required

Follow the BASIC METHOD. The meat is cooked when the rabbit falls from the bones easily—about 4 hours.

You can use salt pork for this recipe—if you do, you probably won't need to add extra salt at the seasoning stage.

Rillettes d'Oie, de Dinde, or de Canard

2 lbs. of goose, turkey, or
duck, jointed, not boned

2 lbs. of leaf lard (*panne*)
Salt and paprika

Grind the leaf lard, put it in the cooking pot to melt slowly. When it runs, add the meat and ⅜ cup water. Cook for 6 to 8 hours, so that the meat simmers in the fat and juices rather than fries. The bones should fall out. Drain off the fat, and pound the meat (or use the electric blender, see BASIC METHOD) until it is smooth. Season with salt and paprika, and add a proportion of the drained-off fat to taste. Hot it through gently for 15 minutes and pot.

Rillettes d'Oie, or de Canard

Same ingredients as for the preceding recipe, except that you have to bone the goose or duck before weighing, and have an equal quantity of leaf fat.

Set the fat to melt, then pour off the liquid and add the goose or duck to the *grillons* left behind. Put in ½ cup of water to every 2 lbs. of poultry.

NOTE: For economy's sake, pork is often substituted for part of the poultry.

Keep this cooking at a simmer for 5 to 6 hours. Reduce

by pounding and chopping, or by means of the electric blender, to a smooth mass. Season with salt and paprika, add as much of the drained-off fat as you think the mixture requires. Heat through for 10 minutes; pot, and keep in the cool, in the usual way for *rillettes*.

NOTE: Poultry and rabbit *rillettes* can afford to be very smooth indeed—the texture almost of English potted meat. But I find that most people prefer pork *rillettes* to be a lighter, thready texture. All *rillettes* should be well-seasoned, and served with salt, butter, and hunks of crusty bread or toast.

Quiche Tourangelle

—— Short-Crust Pastry ——
(to line a shallow 8-inch-diameter flan ring—tourtière)

2¼ cups plain flour, sifted with 2 tablespoons sugar and a good confectioners' pinch of salt
10 tablespoons (1¼ sticks)

butter and lard, rubbed into the flour, etc.
Enough very cold water to mix to a dough

Line the tin, brush with white of egg, to keep the pastry crisp.

—— Filling ——

¼ to ⅜ lb. of *rillettes* (pork), spread about ¼ inch thick
⅜ lb. *rillons*, no bones, cut into small dice, and laid on the *rillettes*
½ cup boiling milk, poured

onto 2 beaten eggs, and whisked together
A good ¼ cup heavy cream added to the milk and eggs, with a seasoning of salt, pepper, and parsley

Pour this custard onto the *rillons* etc., and bake for 40 minutes in a gentle oven (350°F.).

Serve warm, not hot from the oven, or cold.

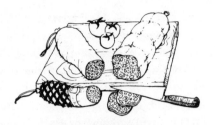

 # BLOOD AND
BLACK PUDDINGS,
OR BOUDINS NOIRS

Black puddings are the easiest things to recognize in the *charcuterie*. They may hang in a long string of black sausage shapes, contrasting with the creamy whiteness of *boudins blancs* (page 147), and the mottled brownish-pink of the usual *saucissons* (page 134); or they may lie on a basketwork tray in a smooth unbroken spiral or coil, eggplant-black and gleaming. In either case they are about the cheapest thing you can buy there, and not the least delicious, whether fried or grilled, and served with a purée of apples or potatoes, or used to stuff a roasting chicken.

If you are accustomed to English—or American—black puddings, you will find the French ones a lot lighter in texture. This is because the blood is mixed with pork fat, onions, and cream, rather than barley, flour, and oatmeal. They are spiced, too, with considerably more finesse.

The rub comes when you get home and want to make French-style black puddings yourself. Unless you know somebody who is killing a pig, it means a trip to the slaughterhouse, or a particularly understanding butcher.

One friend of ours, a Vendômois farmer's daughter, always tried to persuade the visiting *charcutier* to cook some of the blood for her very gently over the fire, mixed with a little fat and cream; a *sanguette* she calls it. I suppose her success was the measure of her beauty. On pig-killing day few people have time to stand and stir a small pan over a low fire. The moment blood boils, it curdles, so great care has to be taken. But apart from treats for small girls, the blood would be put aside until the intestines had been cleaned, scraped, and cleaned again in the river. The mixture would be varied according to the resources of the farm—a tree of *Reinette* apples, a good row of spinach, or a nearby chestnut wood, certainly cream, onions, spices, and a locally produced *eau-de-vie.*

If you don't want to risk filling skins—though this is not really difficult—any black pudding mixture can be baked slowly in shallow, greased dishes. When you want to use it, cut in slices and fry.

BASIC METHOD

You will need a funnel, in plastic so that the edge won't pierce the intestines; and either a ham boiler, a fish boiler, a chip ("French-fry") basket or metal salad shaker, so that the *boudins noirs* can be lowered into hot water with the minimum chance of them bursting.

Intestines or skins, in suitable lengths, knotted at one end, and lying in a bowl of water
3⅛ quarts blood
3 lbs. onions, chopped (about 10½ cups)
3 lbs. pork fat, leaf lard for preference
3 cups heavy cream (you can use evaporated milk)

1½ cups bread crumbs
6 tablespoons coarse salt
1 teaspoon *quatre-épices* or other spices
1 teaspoon of sugar (brown, preferably)
Chopped parsley, or chives, or sage—to taste
A scant ¼ cup rum (optional)

Put the bread crumbs to soak in the cream.
Add the seasonings to the blood.
Cut the fat into small dice, and try out about ½ lb. in a

heavy frying pan. When the lard runs out, add the chopped onions and cook them slowly without allowing them to catch. They should melt rather than fry.

When they are ready mix in the rest of the fat, which has been diced, and the cream and the bread-crumb mixture. Stir it well together and pour in the blood, still stirring.

Take the first length of intestine and fit the unknotted end over the edge of the funnel, being careful not to split it. Then ladle your mixture into the funnel, which should be held firmly in the left hand so that the skin does not slip off. Don't fill the skins too full, as the mixture swells in the cooking; and let the *boudin* fall into a coil on your strainer tray or into your wire

making black puddings

"French-fry" basket. The next coil can go on top, if there is room. Leave enough skin at the end to be knotted.

Bring the cooking pan, half filled with water, to the boil. Remove it from the heat, and lay in the tray of *boudins*. Be absolutely sure that the water is off the boil when you do this, otherwise your labors will be lost in a blood-and-water mush.

Return the pan to a low heat for about 20 minutes, keeping the water at a bare shudder. After 15 minutes, prick the *boudins* very gently with a needle. If a brown liquid comes out, they are cooked; if blood comes out, they aren't, so try again in 5 minutes. They will be nicest if they are caught as soon as they are firm and before they are overcooked. If they float to the surface whilst cooking, prick with the needle.

Remove the pan to the drainboard, and transfer the strainer tray or basket *carefully* (they can burst quite easily when they are hot) into a bowl of cold water. Leave it for 1 minute. Transfer the load to a flat surface, where the coils can be laid out separately to be brushed with some melted lard to form a glaze and to finish cooling.

To serve the *boudins*, cut them into lengths, prick them all over as you would a sausage, and fry or grill them. Dish up on a bed of lightly sweetened apple purée, or mashed potatoes with fried apple rings. Spinach is an ideal accompaniment too, either outside the skin, creamed, or inside with the mixture:

Boudin de Poitou (aux Épinards)

3⅛ quarts blood

2½ lbs. spinach, or spinach and the white part of salad endive (curly leaved), mixed

¾ lb. leaf fat or good-quality lard

½ cup of hard liquor, vodka or gin would be better than a fine cognac, in this instance

¼ cup of Orange Flower Water (obtainable at drugstore)

Quatre-épices and crushed thyme to season, and salt

You can use more or less spinach according to taste. Frozen spinach will do—allow 1½ lbs. With fresh spinach and endive, wash it well, then cook it covered in a large pan, in which you have first melted some of the leaf fat or lard. Add no more water, enough will cling to the washed leaves. Drain it well when it has cooked down, chop or sieve or whirl in an electric blender to a purée. Cook frozen spinach according to directions.

Melt the lard and cook the spinach purée gently in it for 10 minutes. Mix into the rest of the ingredients, season it well with salt and spices, and fill the skins according to the BASIC METHOD.

Boudin de Poitou (aux Épinards)

A very delicate, digestible recipe, adapted from *La Charcuterie à la Campagne,* by Henriette Babet-Charton.

2½ quarts blood
3 lb. cups heavy cream
2½ cups milk
1½ lbs. spinach, or spinach and wine endive combined
3 medium eggs
1½ oz. semolina

1 oz. Boudoir biscuits or other suitable biscuits
1 large onion, chopped (about 1 cup)
Extra butter and lard for cooking vegetables, salt, pepper

Make as dry a spinach purée as possible (see preceding recipe). Cook the chopped onion to a melting mass in some lard, and give the spinach purée 10 minutes in some butter and lard.

Cook the semolina and milk to a thickish cream, stirring to prevent lumps. Add the cream, and eggs off the heat.

Crush the biscuits.

Stir everything well and thoroughly togethe ·, season to taste, and finish as described in the BASIC METHOD, page 339.

Boudin de Lyon

3⅛ quarts blood
1½ lbs. leaf lard
1½ lbs. onions, chopped
   (about 5 cups)
1 tablespoon pepper

2 tablespoons *quatre-épices*
½ cup coarse salt
A dash of paprika
Plenty of chopped chives, parsley, and thyme
¼ cup of good brandy

Melt a scant ½ lb. of the fat, and cook the onions to a pulp in it without letting them brown. Meanwhile cut the rest of the fat into strips about the width of a little finger and 5 inches long, if you have plenty of time; otherwise cut them into much shorter pieces, and not quite so thick.

Add herbs, spices, salt, and brandy to the onion pulp, stirring it well together. Take the pan off the fire and add the contents slowly to the blood, turning it well all the time. If you have chopped the leaf lard into small, rather than long chunks, stir that in too. Fill the skins and cook according to the BASIC METHOD.

If, however, you have cut the correct longer strips of fat, you have to introduce them skilfully in between ladles of the mixture so that they lie end to end of the *boudin noir* coil. Finish according to the BASIC METHOD.

Boudin d'Auvergne

3⅛ quarts blood
¾ lb. fat hard fat back
¾ lb. leaf lard
2 lbs. onions, chopped

2½ cups milk
6 tablespoons salt, and pepper and *quatre-épices* to taste

Cut the two sorts of fat into small dice, melt them gently, and add the onions. Cook to a mush. Add to the milk, blood, and seasonings. Finish according to the BASIC METHOD, but cook for ½ hour.

Boudin du Languedoc

This is a meatier affair altogether, including lean pork as well as fat.

3⅛ quarts blood	3 level tablespoons coarse
3 lbs. pork taken from the neck	salt (approximately), and ground pepper,
¾ lb. leaf lard	*quatre-épices*, and a
2 lbs. onions, chopped (about 7 cups)	good pinch of caraway seeds or aniseed

For the neck of pork, you could substitute 2 lbs. of sow-belly and 2½ cups of milk; and plenty of chopped green herbs, if you don't like the characteristic caraway and aniseed flavor.

Cook the neck of pork (or belly) the previous day, simmering it for about an hour and a half in salted water. It should get quite cold before you chop it into small dice.

Follow the BASIC METHOD (page 339), adding the chopped lean meat with the onions and seasonings to the 3⅛ quarts blood, and the milk, if you are following the second alternative.

Boudin aux Pommes

All over northern France, apples are added to *boudins noirs*, in Normandy of course, but also in Brittany and Nancy. Usually it is the firm, yellow, keeping apple that one sees on every garden tree, vying with the quinces in golden pleasure. Returning to France in the following May, I've been handed great baskets of these *Reinettes* by my next-door neighbor, a little more crinkled than they were in October but sweet-smelling and delicious still. Bauchant put them into his tapestry, *La Fruitière*, and going into caves near Montoire where he died one suddenly remembers him by the way they shine out of rocky shadows in unexpected order on their wooden racks.

Orléans *Reinette*—"the best apple grown in Western Europe"

—has been grown in England fairly widely during this century.*
If you don't have a tree of them, substitute good, crisp eating
apples.

3⅛ quarts blood	spoons (½ stick) butter
3 cups cream	3 lbs. onions, chopped
4 lbs. leaf lard	(about 10½ cups)
2½ lbs. apples, and 4 table-	⅔ cup white bread crumbs

You can cook the apples the previous day, in which case
peel, core, and cut them up. Melt 4 tablespoons of butter in a
heavy pan, and stew the apples slowly with the lid on. Add more
butter if necessary—*never stew apples in water.*

Alternatively, you can cook them with the chopped onions
when you intend to make the *boudins noirs*. In this case you
won't need the butter. Melt some of the leaf fat instead, and
cook onions and cut-up apples in that. Keep stirring every so
often to prevent them catching. This is a slow operation which
should take about an hour; don't rush it.

Mix all the other ingredients, adding the apple and onion
last of all. Finish according to the BASIC METHOD.

Boudin à la Crème

An expensive version, not usually to be found on sale in the
charcuterie. Having regard to the price of cream in England
and the U.S., the quantities are small.

1¼ quarts blood	1 lb. onions, chopped
2½ cups cream	(about 3½ cups)
1 medium egg	3 tablespoons salt
⅜ lb. (1½ sticks, 12 table-	*Quatre-épices* and other
spoons) butter	spices

* Edward A. Bunyard: *The Anatomy of Dessert* (2nd edition; London:
Chatto and Windus; 1933).

Melt 4 tablespoons of butter in a heavy pan and gently cook the onion almost to a purée. When this is done, take the pan off the fire and add the rest of the butter. Whilst it is melting combine the cream, egg, spices, salt, and blood, and finally add the onions. Finish according to the BASIC METHOD, but take great care not to fill the skins too tightly, and be very gentle when putting the *boudins* into the cooking water and taking them out.

Boudin aux Marrons

The most satisfactory *boudins noirs* I've ever bought came from a small *charcuterie* on the outskirts of Brive in the Corrèze. Our fingers were sore with picking up a boxful of chestnuts, after a picnic in the hills above Collonges, and we wondered what we were going to do with them all; then we saw the notice *boudins aux marrons*. They were so good that from that time on I've added roughly chopped, cooked chestnuts both to *boudins noirs* and sausage-meat *crépinettes* (page 117), always with great success. Most recipes tell you to purée the chestnuts, but I think that the *boudins* taste better if the chestnuts are chopped into small bits. The one we bought were like that, and they could not have been nicer.

3⅛ quarts blood
3½ lbs. leaf lard
2 lbs. chestnuts
3½ cups cream
2 lbs. onions, chopped
   (about 7 cups)

3 tablespoons coarse salt;
   black pepper and *quatre-épices* to taste

Deal with the chestnuts the day before, unless you have helpers. Slash them on the rounded side, put them in a hot oven for 10 minutes, remove both skins, and simmer in salted water for 20 minutes. Chop them small, but not to a crush.

Follow the BASIC METHOD, adding the chestnuts to the mixture last of all. Fill the skins and cook with great care.

Boudin Noir à l'Ail

In some parts of Périgord, they add a large egg and ½ lb. of chopped garlic to the basic mixture—no alcohol or spices either, to get between you and the garlic. Use half leaf fat, half hard fat from the back.

Boudin de Saint-Quentin

Boudin de Saint-Quentin provides another, almost equally demanding test of family affections. Perhaps that is why one is recommended to eat it at midday, rather than in the evening. Good solid food against the cold winters of Aisne—and of Great Britain too, for that matter.

2½ quarts blood
4 lbs. onions, chopped
(about 14 cups)
3 lbs. leaf lard
½ lb. finest lard
6 tablespoons coarse salt

2 tablespoons black pepper and *quatre-épices*, mixed
¼ teaspoon cayenne
1 tablespoon brown sugar

Mix according to the BASIC METHOD, but cook the *boudins* for a little longer. Serve with a very light purée of potatoes, and apple sauce made with eating apples, stewed in a little butter, and finished with a squeeze of lemon juice.

English Black Pudding

4 quarts blood
4 lbs. leaf lard
¾ lb. pearl barley
¾ lb. fine oatmeal
¾ lb. flour (about 3¼ cups)

½ lb. onions, chopped (about 1¾ cups)
7 tablespoons coarse salt
5 tablespoons black pepper, cayenne, and coriander

Cook the pearl barley in boiling water. Follow the BASIC METHOD, adding the barley at the end. Because of the cereals, this takes 45 minutes of simmering.

I cannot recommend this recipe. It makes too solid a black pudding for pleasant eating. But the comparison with French recipes is interesting.

Gogue

Black-and-white puddings are festive fare in France, for the *Réveillon* meal after Christmas Midnight Mass. In Anjou they make a very large black pudding, using the big intestine of the pig, for Easter as well. The springtime note is the use of chard or beet leaves, which have a nice combination of spinach-like green and seakale-tasting white ribs.

3⅛ quarts blood
5 cups heavy cream
1 cup milk
2½ lbs. beet leaves
3 large eggs
1 large onion, chopped (about 1 cup)

⅔ cup white bread crumbs
¼ lb. best lard
2 tablespoons salt
¼ teaspoon white pepper
A length of the pig's large intestine, cleaned and tied at one end

Melt a little of the lard in a heavy pan, add the washed beet leaves, and put on a well-fitting lid. Make into as dry a purée as you can, preferably in an electric blender as it halves the work.

Soak the bread crumbs in the milk.

Cook the onion in a little more of the lard very slowly until it has melted almost to a purée too. Add the rest of the lard, and when it is in a liquid state, put in the beet leaf purée and mix it all up well. Season, and leave on the heat for 10 minutes. Take off the fire to cool down whilst you mix together thoroughly all the other ingredients, adding the vegetable mash last of all.

It is a good idea to have some help whilst you ladle the filling into the large intestine. It is more convenient to make two or three *boudins*, rather than one.

Poach them in water which barely simmers for ½ hour. Drain them, leave them to dry, and hang them up in a cool, dry place for 4 days. To serve, cut in slices and fry quickly, or grill.

INDEX

· *i* ·

A NOTE ABOUT THE AUTHOR

Jane Grigson is an Englishwoman who was inspired to write this book when she and her family spent a vacation in France in 1961 in the heart of all the world's best areas for food and wines (just north of Touraine and south of Normandy). Fascinated and bewildered by the variety of cooked pork products and sausages in the shops, she found that no comprehensive book existed on *charcuterie* in French or English, so she set about researching the subject, testing, reproducing recipes in her own kitchen, and traveling around France in the summer for new material. The book, which took more than six years to finish, was immediately approved by the British culinary authority on France, Elizabeth David.

Mrs. Grigson, who received a degree in English language and literature from Newnham College, Cambridge, has had published many translations from the Italian. At present, she is writing a series of articles on food for *The Observer*.

A NOTE ON THE TYPE

The text of this book is set in Caledonia, a Linotype face designed by W. A. Dwiggins. This type belongs to the family of printing types called "modern face" by printers—a term used to mark the change in style of type-letters that occurred about 1800. Caledonia borders on the general design of Scotch Modern, but is more freely drawn than that letter.